Emmylou Harris

Angel in Disguise

Emmylou **H**arris

Angel in Disguise

Jim Brown

F O X
M U S I C
B O O K S

The publisher acknowledges the support of the Government of
Canada, Department of Canadian Heritage, Book Publishing
Industry Development.

ISBN 1-894997-03-4

Design by Gordon Robertson.
Typeset by Laura Brady.

Printed and bound in Canada.

Published by Fox Music Books, PO Box 1061,
Kingston, Ontario K7L 4Y5 Canada.

Contents

"To me, life is about searching, and music should reflect that search. That's one of the reasons that music means so much to us. Whether you are listening to Billie Holiday or Loretta Lynn, Hank Williams or Bob Dylan, the best artists are trying to articulate what we all feel inside."
— Emmylou Harris

Stumbling into **G**race

Emmylou Harris was scheduled to play the finale at the inaugural Calgary Blues and Roots Festival, the pet project of Bryan Taylor, her former tour manager and concert promoter. Also booked for the three-day festival were Los Lobos, Buddy Guy, Richard Thompson, Buckwheat Zydeco, Sue Foley, Dan Hicks, Kieran Kane & Kevin Welch, Otis Rush, the Buddy Miller Band, Solomon Burke, and the Jayhawks. Taylor had several reasons for booking Emmylou to perform the final set on that hot weekend in August 2003. "She gave us instant credibility," he told me. "Emmy has gone from being the Sweetheart of Country Music to the Queen of Alt Country in her career, and then on to being a front-line artist on AAA and Americana radio. She is one of the performers who helped launch both radio formats, and both formats are seen as being the home of roots artists." Emmylou Harris offered more than a strong draw, as Bryan made clear. "Choosing her to close the event was strategic. All along I kept telling people that the perfect ending would be hearing Emmy's voice as the sun went down over the mountains. It would be a spiritual and mellow way to send the audience home."

When Emmylou Harris took the stage accompanied only by Buddy Miller, the audience was ready to have their souls rocked in "the bosom of Abraham," as she had sung in *Boulder to Birmingham*, her ode to country rock founder and personal mentor Gram Parsons, lyrics she had written for her album PIECES OF THE SKY almost 30 years ago. Emmylou opened with *Easy From Now On*, *Blackhawk*, *One Of These Days*, and *If I Could Only Win Your Love*, her high lonesome voice ringing out into the gathering night. The audience became quiet, almost reverent, as Emmylou and Buddy launched into *Pancho & Lefty*, *Red Dirt Girl*, *Never Get Out Of Your Love Alive* . . . and then Kate and Anna McGarrigle's *All I Left Behind*. By the time they struck the first chords of *Love Hurts*, there were tears in everybody's eyes. Emmylou's rendition of Steve Earle's *Goodbye* was next, followed by *Orphan Girl*. *Strong Hand*, she told us, had been written in loving memory of June Carter Cash and recorded for her new album, STUMBLE INTO GRACE, her 25th long playing record.

As the night grew darker and cooler, we felt that we had indeed stumbled into a state of grace as Emmylou delivered song after song from her extensive catalog of traditional country, country rock, and alternative country classics — *Voice Of A Stranger*, *Great Divide*, *Sweet Old World*, *Michelangelo*. During *Hickory Wind*, composed by Gram Parsons, Tammy Rogers strolled into view, adding her fiddle to the mix, and when the music died away, Emmylou said farewell. "This is a really nice little festival. I hope it continues." She came back for an encore with Tammy Rogers, Fats Kaplan, Kieran Kane, Bryan Owings, Rick Plant, and Buddy Miller to deliver rousing versions of Gram Parsons' *Wheels*, Paul Kennerly's *Born To Run*, and Rodney Crowell's *Leaving Louisiana In The Broad Daylight*. Bryan Taylor had indeed hired an angel to take his children home.

"Emmylou does those three songs in every show she plays," Bryan told me on the way to the wrap party. "*Born To Run* is a kind of unofficial theme song for her." I was barely aware of him speaking, barely able to reply. Like many of the people at the show, I had been mesmerized by Emmylou Harris's voice. "Everybody I know in the music industry," Bryan continued, "which includes a lot of people, will tell you 'the moment I heard her voice, I became a fan.' I believe that her voice is one of the most unique musical instruments ever created. Along with her integrity — sticking to what is most important artistically at the cost of other concerns, financially or whatever — she just has credibility with me and everybody else I know in the business that most artists don't have. Emmylou did a great version of *Coat Of Many Colors*, a Dolly Parton song. It was Linda and Emmylou recording Dolly's songs that got Dolly going and helped her become independent of the good ole boy system in Nashville."

Among those lightning-struck fans is Linda Ronstadt. Emmylou's harmonies with Gram Parsons on songs like Boudleaux Bryant's *Love Hurts* or their own *In My Hour Of Darkness* brought tears to Linda's eyes the very first time she heard them performing together at a club in Houston in 1973. "I heard Emmy's voice with that Appalachian purity, that conviction, and it knocked me over," Ronstadt recalls. "She and Gram sang *Love Hurts*, and it made me cry, everybody — even their band — was in tears." After that 1973 show, Harris and Ronstadt were introduced and became instant friends. "When I met her," Linda recalls in a recent interview with *Goldmine*, "I thought . . . I would give anything to be able to sing with Emmylou Harris. I wished we could become the Everly Sisters." They would later joke that when they sang with Dolly Parton they were the 'Queenston Trio'.

"She had a singing partner, Gram, and I thought it was a wonderful combination," Linda adds. "I remember telling my boyfriend at that time, who was Albert Brooks, that Emmy could sing higher and lower, and louder and softer, and she could phrase a lot better than I could. She really had country rock nailed. Country rock had been my little niche, but I'd been getting pushed very hard to move it into rock 'n' roll. And I said, 'She just does this so well, I think I'll stop fighting this, because she just does it better than anybody. I made a choice. I decided that loving her music was more important than feeling that I was the 'Queen of Country Rock'. And then I made a decision that she was my singing sister, and that when I got the chance to sing with her, I would do it."

A similar sense of wonder fills Emmylou Harris when she discusses her vocal talent. "I look at my voice and my abilities as a gift. I don't feel that I can even take any credit for it, but it's such a huge presence in my life. It is my life. It's my identity, it's everything. And it's given me a great deal of joy and a sense of purpose — I can't imagine my life without it."

According to Linda, there is much more to Emmylou Harris than her angelic voice. "She gave girl country singers elegance, taste, class, and dignity. I don't mean to demean the girl singers who had been in country music before, but they never appealed to me. I must confess that I wasn't a person who hungered for a Kitty Wells record. With all due respect to Kitty Wells, I was raised as Emmy was; we had a little bit more refined upbringing. To me, those women didn't seem like country singers. They seemed like girls who had gone into the city, hung around the bars, and become very jaded. They seemed hard; their makeup was on too thick. I didn't like it as a role model, and their singing was too twangy, too hard, and too nasal — because of the hardness of their lives and attitudes. Emmy brought more country fresh air, a real rural style, more like the Carter family and Jean Ritchie. And with it, elegance and dignity that came from the more refined upbringing, which doesn't have anything to do with hoity-toity, or rich, or anything like that. It just has to do with having been raised like a lady. In the meantime, she could go into the honky tonks with the best of 'em."

Linda Ronstadt is not the only singer enamored with Emmylou Harris. As Rodney Crowell remarks, "Every woman artist now in this business has in some way been influenced by Emmylou and her dignity of spirit." Singer-songwriter Susanna Clark first heard Emmylou's voice on a tape that Rodney Crowell played for her. "Rodney called us over to his little apartment," she told *Goldmine*, "and he said, 'sit there, Susanna, I'm going to play you something. You have to be still.' All of a sudden there was this piercing, beautiful, angelic voice singing *'Til I Gain Control Again*. … I knew he wrote it, and why he wrote it, but I'd never heard it like that before, ever." Pam Tillis notes that "in high school, if you wanted to be a pop singer you wanted to be Joni Mitchell. But if you wanted to be a country singer you wanted to be Emmylou Harris. There are artists who set the standards that everybody follows. It has to do with taste, and her taste is unerringly good."

That impeccable taste has come to bear on her inspired choice of music to record and perform. Emmylou Harris has always referred to herself a mere "collector of songs," but what amazing songs they are. Her ability to pick songs ideally suited to her sensibility dates back to her earliest demo sessions for A&M Records in New York City in 1967. As she told *Billboard* editor-in-chief Timothy White, "the songs I put down on the demo were Jesse Colin Young's *Get Together*, before it was a hit; Jerry Jeff Walker's *Mr. Bojangles*, before it was a hit; I did Doug Kershaw's *Louisiana Man*, and Dylan's *A Hard Rain's A-Gonna Fall*. I had a pretty interesting repertoire, but it went right over their heads. They just didn't have a clue . . . They gave me a bunch of Claudine Longet records, and told me to come back when I could sing like her." As she has remarked elsewhere concerning her song selection, "I think they find you, somehow. It's been a very serendipitous thing — I've just been in the right place at the right time. I don't waste my time with songs that don't absolutely floor me. I have to be pretty passionate about a song. I think you create a magnetic field, in a sense, that draws the songs that shimmer for you. But I'm always looking."

Emmylou Harris's angelic voice and keen ear, combined with a touch of serendipity, led her to her first recording success singing harmony and co-writing songs with Gram Parsons on his classic solo albums, GP and GRIEVOUS ANGEL. Often attributed as the founder of the country rock movement in the 1970s, Parsons schooled Emmylou in the beauty of traditional country music. "Gram did more for me than anyone," Emmylou comments. "He helped give form to my music. He taught me how to reach inward and not be afraid to pull out my deepest feelings, then write about them. In a very real sense, a performer is naked on stage, that is, if he or she is worth their salt. If an artist doesn't allow the audience to see the essential truth, then it's Las Vegas time. Gram had more than his share of problems, but he also had this grand vision of combining folk, rock, and country music. He was really a prophet, as time has shown. The first time I met him I was insecure. That happens when you go for a long time unappreciated. He showed me the majesty and simplicity of country music. 'You have to learn the whys and heart of the basics,' is the way he put it. ... He did stone country stuff. He was serious about instructing his audiences in country music, but he'd also have a rock & roll medley because he knew that people need to cry, but they also need to dance."

During the 1970s, Emmylou Harris became the queen of country rock, performing as a disciple to the prophet, the keeper of the flame, recording a stunning string of eight gold albums, produced by her husband, Brian Ahern, and setting the standard for live performances with her Hot Band, featuring key players who had backed Elvis Presley. By the early 1980s, she was ready to lead rather than follow, inaugurating the new traditional movement in country music with her back-to-the-roots-of-country bluegrass album, ROSES IN THE SNOW, featuring her disciples, Ricky Skaggs and Rodney Crowell. In 1984 she began to take an active role in the production of her albums, co-writing and co-producing the concept album THE BALLAD OF SALLY ROSE with Paul Kennerly, at a time when Music Row frowned on 'women' producers. With her 'Queenston' Trio partners, Dolly Parton and Linda Ronstadt, she stretched the bounds of country harmonies during the recording sessions for their first TRIO album. By the 1990s, Emmylou was ready to re-invent herself again, recording the album WRECKING BALL, the harbinger of the alternative country movement. Emmylou Harris has a well-earned reputation as a risk-taker, always setting trends rather than following formula. "I like being out there in left field," she once told Nashville reporters. "I've always played that position."

Through the years Emmylou Harris has led by example rather than pronouncement. "Emmy has a real democratic attitude and warmth that makes everybody who's exposed to her like her," Linda Ronstadt notes. "Aside from having that miraculous voice,"

Rolling Stone critic Bud Scoppa asserts, "she has great personal charm made up in proportionate parts of intelligence, honesty and self-effacement." Despite such tributes to her talent and her character, Emmylou Harris remains humble, even reticent, never gossiping about others, never promoting herself. "She's an angel in disguise," as those Flying Burrito Brothers Gram Parsons and Chris Hillman might have put it, so many years ago.

Red **D**irt Girl

Emmylou Harris entered this world on April 2, 1947, the second of two children born at East End Memorial Hospital in Birmingham, Alabama, to career Marine Corp officer Walter "Bucky" Rutland Harris and his wife, Eugenia Murchison Harris. "My mother's family were farmers from southern Alabama near Clanton," she told *Billboard* editor-in-chief Timothy White. "My dad came from Glen Ridge, New Jersey, his father working for Tidewater Oil. My parents eloped during World War II, while he was in officer's training, and he proposed in her parlor, then getting a license the next day and taking a train to where my father was stationed in Texas. It was not easy being a new wife during the war, because in those days there was a stigma to being married to someone you just met who then got shipped overseas. People said you weren't really married."

Being in a military family meant Emmylou moved often, never feeling that any place in particular was home, not even when her father was stationed permanently near Washington, D.C., and she and her brother attended high school in Woodbridge, Virginia. As she told a *New York Times* reporter, "My father was a Marine pilot. He tried civilian life for a while, as a police dispatcher, but I think he really loved flying, and he loved the Marine Corp, and eventually he went back in."

In 1952, Walter Harris's F-4U Corsair was shot down over enemy territory in Korea. He was captured and placed in a POW camp. Eugenia and her two young children endured a lengthy, torturous ordeal that went on for 16 months until he was released at the end of the war in 1953. "He was in Korea," Emmylou explains. "He was a prisoner of war. And we went through *that*. I remember getting the telegram that he was missing in action. For about three months we didn't know whether he was dead or alive. I remember vividly when he came back. Birmingham gave him a hero's parade, and then we went up to Washington, where he got the Legion of Merit. But the important thing to me was that my daddy was home. We moved around different bases in North Carolina, and when I was 10, he was transferred to Quantico, in Virginia." The family settled down in nearby Woodbridge, and Emmylou and her brother's lives stabilized, although she would continue to feel rootless.

Emmylou speaks with passion about her father, recalling the time he spent in the North Korean POW camp. "As a major, the senior officer in the POW camp, my father was tortured," she told White. "But he was an extremely strong person spiritually and compassionate toward his fellow soldiers, feeling that everyone had a personal pain threshold, and his captors didn't find his." By 1956, Major Harris's distinguished career was recognized by a permanent posting at Marine Corp Combat Development Command in Quantico. He passed away in 1993.

Piano lessons provided Emmylou's introduction to music. She played saxophone in the high-school marching band. But her life was surrounded by country music. "I listened to country music when I was growing up," she told Alanna Nash. She would often hear country music via the powerful signal of WWVA in Wheeling, West Virginia. "We made a lot of family trips from wherever we were stationed at the time to my mother's family in Birmingham. We'd always travel at night, and that's when you get WWVA the best." Her brother was "a country music fanatic,' she adds, "and he was long before it was hip for his contemporaries to be into it. He's just a couple of years older than me, so I heard it from him. He owned the record player. I heard a lot of Buck Owens, Kitty Wells, bluegrass, so I sort of absorbed it."

Besides, Emmylou has a genuine country pedigree. "I don't consider any place in the world home, but I do relate strongly to Birmingham and the South," she explains. "It's kinda like being uprooted yet carrying a memory seed with you. All my relatives are real country people in south Alabama. I don't believe you have to be born in the South to be able to sing country — that's not a prerequisite. I didn't actually get turned on to country till late in my life, but obviously it was there inside me. I have always had a special feel for it. One of the first songs I worked up was *Louisiana Man*, off a Buck Owens album. It was also the first song that I ever performed on stage." At her core, Emmylou Harris remains a red dirt girl from the South.

Despite her country roots, Emmylou did not take to the music at first, opting instead for folk. "I used to look down on country at the time because I was heavily into folk protest stuff. But I couldn't help being drawn to some of it — like Hank Williams. Country was always creeping in. I was an Ian & Sylvia addict. They had a lot to do with my musical inspiration. Their music was so original. It had a lot of guts, and a lot of powerful beauty. Their harmonies and their choice of material suggested a country approach to some extent. I seemed to take a really roundabout path to where I am today. There were all kinds of little seeds starting from the beginning, but it was only when I met Gram Parsons, and started working with him, that I really got involved with country. That was the turning point in my musical life." The serendipitous moment when Emmylou would meet Gram Parsons was still years down the road.

Settled in Woodbridge, Emmylou was at first glance a candidate for All-American girl and a natural choice for class valedictorian. She upheld a consistent 4.0 grade-point average. She was a cheerleader. She entered and won several beauty contests. Beneath her Pepsodent smile, however, she was dissatisfied because there wasn't much happening in Woodbridge for a girl who aspired to a more bohemian lifestyle. "It was not an especially interesting place," she recalls. "Twenty-five miles south of Washington, D.C., right on U.S. 1; gas stations, motels, and housing developments. Not much happening. And that's where I grew up. I guess it was then, in my teens, that I got turned on to folk music. I had a real intense adolescence, you know — 'What is the meaning of life in Woodbridge, Virginia?' — I was into Pete Seeger, Woody Guthrie, that sort of thing. It seemed there had to be something beyond U.S. 1 . . ." As she commented elsewhere, "You were either a homecoming queen or a real weirdo."

Somewhat of a middle-class misfit, Emmylou fell out of favor with her cheerleading team and her high-school social set. As she explained to a reporter from *The Soho Weekly News*, "I was too tall for the line. I disrupted the symmetry. So they stuck me in front of the refreshment stand. I didn't have what you'd call an active social life — I'd just listen to music and study all the time. Basically, I thought that high school was the pits." Just how introverted she may have been came out in an interview with a Dutch journalist. "I never *did* anything," she explained. "I studied and I was very intense and I never went out on dates. I was fairly sure something was wrong with me. I mean, I won the history award, the English award, the scholarship award, the essay contest. I was valedictorian. No wonder I never got any dates! I was scared of dating. I never got asked out. I admit it. I went to a straight high school, my experience was limited, and high school was the hub of my life."

"High schools are real hip now, but there was no countercul-ture in Woodbridge, Virginia in 1961," she told *Rolling Stone* dur-ing the promotion of her first Warner Reprise album. "You were either a homecoming queen or a real weirdo. I was a 16-year-old WASP wanting to quit school and become Woody Guthrie."

Before she discovered the folk revivalists, Emmylou was drawn to songs by Edith Piaf and Billie Holliday. "I was into female singers who had kind of a dramatic life associated with them," she later told associate editor of the Country Music Foundation Press, Daniel Cooper. "I don't know whether it was the music, or whether it was my sense of the dramatic. But music was not a big part of my life until I started getting involved in folk music."

"I was attracted to the tragedy of Billie Holiday's life," she confided to Robert Hilburn. "I read her biography at a time when I was asking what life was all about, and I was moved by how strong she was — how she never blamed anyone for what happened to her. She has marvelous phrasing."

She was also attracted to Bob Dylan's early albums, drawn to his intelligent lyrics, as sung by his earliest interpreter, Joan Baez. "Dylan was a really big influence," Emmylou told Hilburn. "I loved hearing Joan Baez or Judy Collins do the old songs, but the new songs — the ones by Dylan or Tom Paxton — just had something extra."

Listening led her to performing. "My cousin got a guitar for Christmas one year," she recalled during an interview with *Musician* magazine, "and I spent the entire day playing it. I guess that was when the folk boom was happening, in '63 or '64." Her grandfather noticed her interest, and for her Christmas present the following year, he gave Emmylou a Kay guitar, which she has kept in her extensive collection of vintage guitars to this day, even though it was so difficult to play that her fingers bled. "I got a guitar for my 15th Christmas," she told Fred Schruers. "It has a neck like a baseball bat, and strings that are about six inches off the neck." With strings that were actually less than "an inch off the fretboard," the little Kay guitar was impossible to bar chord, even for someone with hands as strong as a collegiate wide receiver or a professional wrestler, but playable in the root position as are many first guitars. "I learned to play it," she continued. "I was singing Joan Baez songs, and a few country songs, and I played at a few benefits, but I didn't play a lot till I got to college — the University of North Carolina, at Greensboro. By that time I had a real guitar, a Gibson J-50 that cost me 150 bucks."

Emmylou's first paid performance came in the summer of 1965 while she was visiting her grandparents, at a roots festival in Steele, Alabama. She was rewarded for her singing, not with money but with a handmade ceramic platter heaped high with ripe fruit.

On April 2, 1964, Emmylou celebrated her 17th birthday. Within weeks the Byrds' cover of Dylan's *Mr. Tambourine Man* began its climb toward number one on the *Billboard* charts. Dylan followed this initial folk-rock record with one of his own, *Like A Rolling Stone*, which hit the number two spot that summer. In September, ex-folkie John Sebastian and his new band the Lovin' Spoonful hit into the Top 10 with the first of a string of hits, *Do You Believe In Magic*. The electrified, jingly-jangle sounds of the Byrds, the Lovin' Spoonful, Donovan, Dylan, and the Mamas & the Papas revitalized American music, which had been reeling under the impact of the British Invasion.

Despite being shy, Emmylou began to entertain the idea of a career as an actress and eventually secured a scholarship to study drama at the University of North Carolina at Greensboro. The scholarship was her reward for winning the "Miss Woodbridge" beauty pageant, an event that has left many interviewers scratching their heads over the years. "I wasn't very politically correct as a teenager," she told Steve Hammer in 1997. "I just wanted to be popular. I was like every other teenage girl. It wasn't horrible. We're talking Woodbridge, Virginia — There were seven girls in the contest. I was very interested in going to college and I told them I wasn't interested in going on [as a regional contestant] if I won. And they said they didn't care. I did win, and I did get the money."

By the time that Emmylou arrived on the UNC campus, she had memorized her favorite Baez and Dylan songs, mastered a few numbers by Judy Collins and Ian & Sylvia, and sampled the acoustic blues of artists like Robert Johnson, Sun House, Mance Lipscomb, and Bukka White. "I listened to a lot of folk blues," she recalls. "Robert Johnson and things like that. I liked Tom Rush a lot, because he had a wonderful sense of picking songs." Best of all, the college town sported venues where young musicians could perform. "There was a place called the Red Door down on Tate Street," Emmylou told *Greensboro News & Record* reporter Joya Wesley. "I started going down there. They had music every night and you would get $10 and all the beer you could drink, but I didn't drink beer. I started out singing by myself, and then I met a guy named Mike Williams, who I think might have been at UNC Chapel Hill. Anyway, somehow our paths crossed, and we started a little duo, and did a few gigs."

Emmylou's collaboration with Williams was modeled along the lines of her idols, Ian & Sylvia. Mike played an acoustic 12-string. "That didn't last very long," Emmylou explains. "I eventually went back to singing on my own. I was doing Simon & Garfunkel songs, Buck Owens songs, old folk ballads, and Dylan songs, so it was sort of an eclectic mix."

"I was not happy at UNC," Harris confided to *Chicago Sun Times* music critic Jack Hurst. "I don't know if I would have been happy anywhere. I needed to sow a few wild oats and I did not know how to go about it, and I was just . . . having trouble. I was such a perfect student and perfect teenager all those years that I got fed up with it. I felt there was something going on in life that I didn't know about, and that it was time I learned. I had no interest in going out and partying, so I started playing music, finding that I could support myself as a student."

After three semesters at UNC, the restless Emmylou decided that if she was going to get serious about acting, she needed to attend a more prestigious drama school. She applied for entrance to Boston University and set out to earn her tuition money. However, as she later admitted to Joya Wesley, "I think what Greensboro really did for me was to make me realize that I really didn't want to study drama. That was what I thought I wanted to do, but I realized that the real fire in my belly was for music. I went to Virginia Beach. There was a music scene there, and I also wanted to work and earn money to attend Boston University's drama school. So I worked as a waitress by day, and at night I sang in clubs in Norfolk and Virginia Beach."

Emmylou never did attend drama classes in Boston. She "thought about switching over to something like nursing, just because if I was gonna be in college I didn't want to come out with a degree that said 'you have a degree in nothing.' I had had enough of all this nebulous shit, and also, I suppose, there was the element of being a young woman: 'what do you do?' Everybody else is getting pinned, and getting married, and settling down, and you're looking at all that stuff and saying, 'that's pretty silly.'" By 1978, when she spoke with *Rolling Stone* feature writer

Ben Fong-Torres, Emmylou had reflected sufficiently on her time spent in Greensboro that she was able to distil her experience there in one sentence: "I discovered that I loved music and was a pretty lousy drama student."

Singing at clubs in Virginia Beach that summer and meeting new musicians confirmed her suspicions. "I met these other musicians there," she explained to Bob Allen, "and sometimes I'd stay up all night listening to them sing. I suddenly realized I had more in common with them than with anybody I'd known at school."

A seldom-mentioned romance during the 'Summer of Love' may have been a factor in Emmylou's decision not to attend Boston U. "I thought I was going to get married," she later confided to Cameron Crowe in a syndicated profile. "My first big love blew up in my face, so I just went to New York 'cause there was nothing else to do. I was greener than green. I got a room at the YWCA, started going to the Village, playing basket houses, and just hanging out."

Like other folk artists of the era, she was drawn to Greenwich Village. "In 1967, I guess I was 20," she told *The New York Times*. "I dropped out of school and headed for New York City. I don't think I had any burning desire to make it as a singer, but I wanted to sing, to be out on my own singing. That whole folkie thing was a fantasy of mine, but there was no place to do it — all the clubs had closed down." She didn't hitchhike — her brother drove her and helped her get settled in that room at the YWCA. With no contacts to get her better gigs, she just hung out with her J-50 and took whatever crumbs came her way. She had added songs by Hank Williams and the Beatles to her repertoire by this time, but as she later told Daniel Cooper, "No one seemed interested in the kind of music I was doing. People were looking for psychedelic things like Ultimate Spinach or whatever else was selling."

The Greenwich Village folk scene that she had imagined from subscribing to *Sing Out* magazine and reading liner notes to Vanguard and Columbia albums by Joan Baez, Bob Dylan, Leonard Cohen, and Ian & Sylvia had disappeared. Dylan was recording at Columbia Records' 16th Avenue Studios in Nashville. Cohen had moved to a Nashville suburb and was recording in the same studio. Ian & Sylvia would follow, augmenting their usually sparse records with a full ensemble that they called The Great Speckled Bird, their first step in a transition from folk to country.

Emmylou survived by subbing for no shows at the Bitter End and eventually becoming a fixture at Gerdes Folk City, where she hung out with Jerry Jeff Walker, Paul Siebel, David Bromberg, and Tom Slocum, whom she eventually married. Jerry Jeff would write *Mr. Bojangles*, a country hit for the Nitty Gritty Dirt Band, and a pop smash for Harry Nilsson, before clicking at the Armadillo World Headquarters in Austin as a country-rocker. Bromberg played his way into string band history. Siebel and Slocum have not exactly become household names, although Paul Siebel is revered in certain circles as a songwriter's songwriter, whose songs have been recorded by Bonnie Raitt, Linda Ronstadt, Waylon Jennings, and, of course, Emmylou Harris. Her memories of times spent with Bromberg and Walker credit them with continuing the role her brother had begun. "Besides turning me on to country music," she recalls, "they sort of looked out for me. Even so, I must have had some protective kind of bubble around me. I used to walk home from gigs on dark streets at two in the morning with my guitar and never think anything of it. Looking back, I get scared to death."

Emmylou's first recording session came about as a result of interest from an A&M Records executive. In 1968, she was invited to demo a short set of songs so that the label could assess her potential. A&M had just signed a new group in California, the Flying Burrito Brothers, headed by ex-Byrds Chris Hillman and Gram Parsons. Hillman and Parsons had first collaborated on the Byrds' SWEETHEART OF THE RODEO, the first significant country-rock album, and would soon issue the seminal country-rock album, GUILDED PALACE OF SIN. The New York executives who listened to Emmylou's demo tape did not hear any potential in her voice then. However, two years later in 1970, Emmylou signed a recording contract with Jubilee Records and recorded her first album, GLIDING BIRD.

Jubilee Records had seen better days — days when the label had issued records by African American artists like Della Reese and vocal groups like the Orioles. As Emmylou explained to Daniel Cooper, "I had a manager who got me this recording contract. And I didn't really look into the ramifications of it. I didn't get a lawyer. I just signed it, and went in and made a record in three days, and then sort of decided 'I don't like this,' you know? Cause I didn't feel good about the record. And I couldn't get out of the contract." Years later, when she had become a recording star with Warner, she would sue Roulette Records for not paying royalties when they acquired the rights to GLIDING BIRD and reissued it.

During this time, Emmylou and Tom Slocum were staying with actor Richard Kiley and his family in Montgomery, near Middletown, New York, Tom's hometown. Emmylou recalls that Kiley — a star in his own right with a lead role in *Man of La Mancha*, Dale Wasserman's breakaway Broadway musical hit of the year — "treated me like an equal." Kiley would reach into his theatrical trunk and hand Emmylou the plumed hat that she wore during the photo shoot for the front cover of GLIDING BIRD and the full-length velvet cape that she wore for the shot chosen for the back cover.

"Those were exciting years," Emmylou noted during a 1990 interview with a reporter from the Middletown *Times Herald Record*, "the protests at the college, singing in a saloon on West Main Street, and eating cheesecake at the Colonial diner. I remember sitting there, drinking cups of coffee until late at night — talking, getting excited about creating music; and hoping and praying that one day people would really pay attention to what you were trying to say."

Times Herald Record feature writer Chris Farlekas remembers Emmylou's performance at Ian's Coffeehouse in 1968 in vivid detail. "There had just been an anti-Vietnam War demonstration at Orange County Community College," he recalls. "The coffeehouse was alive with the edge of excitement that comes from being young and caught up in a cause. Harris was the last in a procession of singers, most of whom had more spirit than talent. She was wearing typical hippie garb of the day — a long peasant skirt, white embroidered blouse, and several strings of jewelry. But her singing was anything but stereotypical. Even in an era when excellent folk singers were relatively common in Orange County — Pat Monzillo, Denise Assante, Paul Brower, Timmy Johnson, and Pat Pashall among them — Harris stood out because of her assured stage presence and a voice as clear as Waterford Crystal."

Despite her "assured stage presence," Emmylou was unprepared for her recording studio encounter. She had only the demo session sponsored by A&M under her belt when she went in to record. Ironically, the producer chosen by Jubilee Records for these sessions was none other than Ray Ellis, who had worked with Emmylou's earliest musical hero, Billie Holiday, crafting string arrangements for Holiday's LADY IN SATIN. This time, the artist-producer pairing did not result in the same kind of studio magic that characterized successful folk pop albums of the day, those being recorded by Judy Collins, Joni Mitchell, and Joan Baez. In fact, as she told *Rolling Stone*'s Cameron Crowe, "Everybody involved with the record hated everybody else, and I was in the middle trying to keep the peace. It was a disaster."

Emmylou Harris's experience recording for the small New York folk label was just the sort of fiasco Joni Mitchell later revealed she had avoided when she first hit New York in 1967. "I came in late," Mitchell explained to William Ruhlmann in a 1995 career retrospective. "Basically, clubs were folding, and bands were the new thing, and I wasn't ready for a band. . . . Record companies offered me terrible slave labor deals in the beginning, and I turned them down. I turned down Vanguard. They wanted three albums a year or something. In the folk tradition, they come and stick a mike on the table in front of you, and they collect it in an hour, and that's the album."

Without a producer with a vision, Emmylou did the best that she could. "I went in and did a record in three days," she admitted to Bill DeYoung, "and didn't really have a direction. I didn't really have a style. I don't think I really got all those bits and pieces.

I don't think they were forged into anything definable. The good thing about the record is that it shows that I was very much into songwriting. Half the songs on there, they're not the greatest songs in the world, but I'm not embarrassed by them. I wrote — half the album. And I think the song selection, for the most part, was pretty good. I did a Dylan song, and a Hank Williams song. So, there were some seeds of what was to be."

Tom Slocum contributed the title song. Producer Ellis prevailed over Emmylou, insisting that she record Burt Bacharach and Hal David's *I'll Never Fall In Love Again*. She also tackled Fred Neil's *Everybody's Talking*. The better cuts turned out to be her own *Waltz, Fugue For The Fox, Bobbie's Gone*, and an off-the-wall rendition of Bob Dylan's *I'll Be Your Baby Tonight*. Probably the worst of the lot is her version of *I Saw The Light*. She might have been intrigued by Hank Williams' songs, but she still lacked understanding when it came to interpreting country material. She had not yet met someone who could unlock the mystery that lay sleeping inside Hank's lyrics and melodies, a problem she did not have when it came to interpreting contemporary songwriters like Jerry Jeff Walker, Ian Tyson, and Bob Dylan.

When it was released in the early months of 1970, GLIDING BIRD barely saw the light of day. Some 1300 copies are said to have been sold, many of them by Tom and Emmylou in the Middletown area. Her mother hoarded six copies of the LP, but until its reissue in the 1980s, GLIDING BIRD was a difficult collector's item to locate, all the more difficult because Emmylou discouraged discussion of it for many years, suggesting that she'd like to see someone burn the masters and melt down the remaining copies.

Ditto regarding comments about her first marriage. "It didn't last" was all that most interviewers could get from her. In 1977, during an interview with New York reporter Fred Schruers, Emmylou revealed her logic for not discussing that marriage. "I married in 1969. It lasted about two years. Beyond that it is a subject I just don't talk about. That's a contract, an agreement I have with him." Details of her failed relationship with her record label are equally murky, but apparently when the album stiffed in record stores, she was billed $8,000 for the studio costs. Whether or not she felt obliged to pay this unfair debt is further obscured by the fact that in 1970 the label filed for bankruptcy.

The one detail that emerges with certainty during the months following the issue of GLIDING BIRD is that Emmylou Harris learned that she was pregnant. It was "the worst thing a girl could ever do to her budding career," Emmylou confessed to Cameron Crowe. When their daughter Hallie was born, she found she had even less energy and time to devote to promoting her record or playing gigs. Discouraged, Emmylou and Tom lit out for Nashville, where their already foundering marriage failed.

A single mother in the country music capital of the world, Emmylou scarcely had time to knock on doors on Music Row. She and roommate Darlene Shadden found employment modeling for art classes on the Vanderbilt University campus. She posed "fully clothed," she explains. "I didn't have the nerve to do it nude. I had on this long gown, and I was holding an umbrella, for some reason." Years later, in Nashville for a show at the Municipal Auditorium with her Hot Band, she would link up with Darlene Shadden again. Darlene was performing in a rock act in the lounge of the same hotel where Emmylou was staying, but they didn't spend too much time reminiscing about their down and out days in 1970. Those times had not been all that much fun.

As Emmylou told Alanna Nash, "It sounds more colorful than it actually was. I came here in the early summer of 1970. My daughter, Hallie, was about two months old. My husband and I didn't have very much money, and I had been singing in New York unsuccessfully, doing some local tv, doing a few jobs. The pregnancy kind of hampered that, of course, although I did work right up until my daughter was born. It's actually a lot easier to work before you have the baby than afterwards, so it was very difficult for me to find work singing. And a few times, when cash got really low, I was forced into my only other skill, which is waiting tables."

There had been, however, some blessings in disguise. Becoming a single-mother provided Emmylou with an identity that went beyond her teenage vision of becoming the next Woody Guthrie to encompass new ground, upon which she stood responsible for Hallie's well-being. "Up until then, my life had been a little too nebulous. I had no clear vision at all. The pregnancy, although it wasn't planned, gave something very real and present to relate to," Emmylou told Nash. "Nashville seemed a lot easier than Los Angeles, but circumstances being what they were, it was really impossible for me to give it a chance. Perhaps if I'd stayed, things would have worked out. But I was only here for way less than a year. Maybe six months. I worked one concert at Vanderbilt, at their coffeehouses there, and I did a couple of weeks playing a 'happy hour' thing at the Red Lion Pub, one of those big Motor Inns out there on Murfreesboro Road." Mostly, Emmylou took care of her newborn daughter and worked her butt off waiting tables at the High Hat Lounge, the bar in a Polynesian restaurant that she recalls was at that time located across the street from the downtown Greyhound Bus terminal. Emmylou was soon reduced to purchasing baby food for her infant daughter with food stamps. After no more than six months in Nashville, she left, unheard, unheralded, and unsung.

Walter and Eugenia Harris had purchased a farm in Maryland, not far from Washington. They opened their arms and their hearts and welcomed their daughter and their granddaughter back home. She had family. She had roots. "I really didn't know what to do at that time," Emmylou confessed to Nash. "My parents were really concerned about me, and asked me to come home and just collect my thoughts. My family and I are very close, and I went back there and discovered, much to my dismay, a really nice little musical community in Washington. A lot of bluegrass. — I had a job as a hostess in model homes in a housing development in Columbia, Maryland, during the day, and then I would go in a few nights a week and sing in these few bars where you would get a young crowd, mostly college students. And I sort of got back into music. Being in New York, and going through some hard times, had taken the music out of the music, if you know what I mean. Those years I spent in Washington were very good for me. I was able to get back to the reason I went into music in the first place."

Discovering that there was an active bluegrass scene in nearby Washington provided 23-year-old Emmylou Harris with renewed hope. She soon met songwriters Bill Danoff and John Starling, along with their wives, Taffy Nivert and Fayssoux Starling, which led to her meeting guitarist Gerry Mule and bassist Tom Guidera. The Danoffs had a duo act worked up called "Fat City." A small working group seemed like a good idea, so Harris, Mule, and Guidera began rehearsing and gigging together as a trio. Guidera and Emmylou became an item, beginning a relationship that would continue for several years. Harris, Mule, and Guidera were soon working five and six nights a week. Emmylou continued to perform her eclectic mix of what she called "weird songs," and she persisted with those country songs that so intrigued her, tossing an occasional Hank Williams or Kitty Wells song into her set mix. "I did a few country songs almost tongue in cheek, I'm ashamed to say," Harris admitted to Rhino Records Boxed Set liner notes author Holly George-Warren. "I hadn't really heard it — I couldn't get past the layers and that country music was politically incorrect." Keeping after these country songs, even though she hadn't cracked the cultural code, would soon begin to work in her favor.

1971 would turn out to be a very good year for the Danoffs. Bill and Taffy teamed up with ex-Chad Mitchell Trio singer John Denver to write Denver's debut single *Take Me Home Country Roads*. They also sang backing vocals on the record and were invited to open for Denver when he began to tour. In late June, Denver's *Take Me Home Country Roads* entered *Billboard* magazine's Top 40 — before the summer was over, it hit the top of the charts. John Starling's group, the Seldom Scene, secured a record deal with the Rebel label. With Starling on vocals and guitar, John Duffy on mandolin, Mike Auldridge on dobro, Ben Eldridge on banjo, and Tom Gray on bass, the Seldom Scene's acoustic "new grass" stylings of contemporary material appealed to both traditionalists and innovators. The quintet's first album, ACT ONE, was released the following year.

Bill Danoff and Taffy Nivert were scheduled to play the Philadelphia Folk Festival that summer. Emmylou accompanied the Danoffs. "My first visit to the Philadelphia Folk Festival was one of the most memorable experiences of my life," Harris later told *Philadelphia Daily News* reporter Jonathan Takiff. "I was just a spectator. It was so long ago that my first child was still in diapers. It was the festival of the big storms, with mud everywhere. People were walking around with trash bags on their legs. It was quite a sight."

As Bill and Taffy's guest, Emmylou was introduced to many of the performers and musicians that weekend. Her most vivid memory is catching sets by both Joni Mitchell *and* Bonnie Raitt. "My first exposure to both," she told Takiff. "I was blown away by Bonnie's guitar work. At the time, women weren't supposed to be very good at guitar, and both of them were doing exactly what I wanted to do. In fact, I was so cowed by their accomplishments that I seriously contemplated quitting music altogether." Since that time, Emmylou Harris has worked on her guitar playing, and many people, including Bryan Taylor, who has worked with Harris as a tour manager and promoter, believe that Emmylou has become one of the best rhythm guitar players of all time. "Emmylou doesn't get a lot of credit for it," Taylor notes, "even though she was given that Gibson Lifetime Guitar Award. Emmylou is a monster rhythm guitar player. She is very good. One of the best. Which is another reason all these great musicians play in her band and respect her, because she is not just a pretty face that gets up there with a microphone. She can rock. She can play strong." No doubt, Bonnie Raitt's brilliant slide guitar work was an early inspiration, and Joni Mitchell's unique style, which makes use of a variety of open tunings, was another. At the festival, Emmylou met Flying Burrito Brother, Rick Roberts. "I met her," Roberts recalled during an interview with John Einarson, author of *Desperados: The Roots Of Country Rock*, "but I didn't hear her sing. She was a beautiful woman." Emmylou has not mentioned that meeting.

Soon after, when she was singing in Clydes, Rick Roberts and Kenny Wertz, a fellow Flying Burrito Brother, who were playing at the Cellar Door, one of the large clubs on the strip, wandered into Clydes for a beer. The Flying Burrito Brothers were on the brink of breaking up at the time. Bandleader Chris Hillman had already been invited to join Stephen Stills in a band project Stills called Manassas. After success with the Byrds, Hillman had recorded the initial Burritos Brothers album, GUILDED PALACE OF SIN, and the follow-up, BURRITO DELUXE, with Gram Parsons before kicking Parsons out of the band and replacing him with Rick Roberts. By the fall of 1971, Hillman was fed up with putting out albums that the critics loved but nobody bought. Fed up playing smaller and smaller venues to a smaller and smaller core of fans.

Rick Roberts and Kenny Wertz had no expectations of hearing great music when they ambled into Clydes, so they were surprised when they heard Emmylou Harris sing *It Wasn't God Who Made Honky Tonk Angels*. As Roberts later told John Einarson, "Chris and I had talked about adding a female singer to the group. I went to this club and listened to this woman sing and she knocked my socks off. I called Chris and said, 'Get down here!' He was furious that I had bothered him. He said, 'Yeah, I'll come down there but you are not going to like it.' Chris comes in the door looking around and by the time he got to our table he wasn't even looking at us, he was looking over his shoulder at Emmylou, smiling. We had Emmylou sit in with us for the final three nights at the Cellar Door." There was talk of the Burritos asking Emmylou to join the band, but in the end, Chris Hillman decided he would rather go with the new Stephen Stills band. With two weeks of engagements remaining in their tour, the Burrito Brothers soldiered on.

Former Burrito Brother Gram Parsons had recently returned from Europe, where he and his teenage girlfriend Gretchen Burrell had been hanging out with Keith Richards. After he married Gretchen in New Orleans, he looked up his ex-band mates. Parsons sat in with the band during their two shows in College Park near Baltimore, Maryland, where he and Hillman put their past differences aside and resumed their camaraderie. Parsons, Hillman recalled, was no longer the thin, wasted scarecrow whose behavior had become so erratic that his band mates had earlier given him his walking papers. "We had to fire him from the Burrito Brothers," Hillman explained to Bruce Sylvester. "He wasn't working as a team player. He didn't care about the rest of us. He'd become enamoured of the Stones. He was almost a lap dog to those guys. They were in L.A. recording and the Burritos had a show to do, and I couldn't find Gram. I had to track him down. He was hanging with the Stones in the studio. I went in to get him and he didn't want to do the show. Jagger got into his face about it, and said, 'You have a responsibility to Chris Hillman, and you have a responsibility to an audience and to your band. You have to go to work now. We're busy.' I'll never forget that. Jagger's a very professional guy — look at what he's done with his life."

Still, it wasn't difficult for Hillman to put the bad times behind and respond to his colleague with genuine affection. During the backstage banter at their reunion, Parsons told Hillman that he was looking for a "chick singer" as a singing partner. Hillman had a hunch that Gram and Emmylou might be just right for each other. Chris was aware that Gram had a driving passion for country music, which this 'chick singer' just might be very good at — if someone could reveal the hillbilly mystery of it to her.

As Hillman recalled during an interview with *Goldmine*, "I don't recall her doing any country music except one song. Most of it was Joni Mitchell/Joan Baez/Carolyn Hester stuff. She sat in with the Burritos and was dabbling in country, but I don't think she really knew what it was yet. By then I had already been asked to go into Manassas, so I was just putting in a couple of weeks with the Burritos. I told Gram, 'You ought to look up this girl in Washington. You might have something in common.' I got him to finally call her, and finally he went up to hear her, and there it was."

Luckily, while the two men were talking backstage, they were overheard by Emmylou's babysitter, who knew her phone number. When Parsons reached Emmylou by telephone, his suggestion that she drive up to Maryland to pick him up was countered by a suggestion that if he wanted to hear her sing, he could ride a train. When Gram and Gretchen walked into Clydes, Emmylou and her trio partners were playing to a nearly empty room, inhabited only by three or four disinterested patrons and the bar staff. Between sets Parsons and Harris rehearsed a few tunes in the basement. He joined her for her second set.

"Chris Hillman was so enthusiastic when he told me about Emmylou, that I just had to go to see her," Parsons told musicologist Peter Frame. "I was knocked out by her singing. I wanted to see just how good she was, how well she picked up country phrasing and feeling, so after her set I introduced myself and we sang *That's All It Took*, one of the hardest country duets I know. Emmy sang it like she was falling off a log."

Afterwards, Gram and Emmylou retired to Walter Egan's home, where they sat up long into the night swapping songs and singing with Egan, co-author of *Hearts on Fire*, who played in a local bluegrass group called Sagebrush at that time. At the conclusion of this living room session, she recalls, "I drove him and his wife back to Baltimore, and we exchanged addresses and phone numbers." Emmylou and Gram would soon collaborate in creating two of the most influential and beautiful albums in the history of rock and country music.

The Fallen **A**ngel

Gram Parsons' headlong flight toward his inevitable date with destiny in the Mojave Desert, which brought the fame that eluded him during his brief 26-year lifetime, also produced some of the best rough-and-ready music recorded during the 20th century. Through the efforts of his most successful disciple, Emmylou Harris, and many others, his music has not been forgotten. In fact, in recent years he has become widely regarded as the "godfather of 'country rock'," a term that he despised because it was so loosely applied to so many southern California artists and groups. In a letter that he wrote to a friend in 1972, he is quoted by biographer Pamela Des Barres as writing, "I keep my love for variations, even tho I've some sort of 'rep' for starting what has turned out t'be pretty much of a 'country-rock' (ugh!) plastic dry fuck . . . ." Parsons preferred his own term, "Cosmic American Music."

Ingram ('Gram') Cecil Connors III was born on November 5, 1946 in Winter Haven, Florida, the son of Florida citrus heiress Avis Snively Connors and Tennessee-born Cecil 'Coon Dog' Connors — the same day that John Fitzgerald Kennedy was elected for the first time to the House of Representatives. He spent his formative years growing up in Waycross, Georgia in a typical Southern mansion, complete with the obligatory white pillars out front and the vestige of a black servants entrance out back. Gram and his younger sister Avis were chauffeured to their grade school classes.

The Snively family controlled most of the citrus groves in central Florida and the bulk of fresh fruit exported from the state. The Snively family history was not without the odd twist or two that led Emmylou Harris to compare it to the story of the Snopes family chronicled in William Faulkner's novels, or as Chris Hillman once put it, the script of one of Tennessee Williams' plays. As Waycross native and Rolling Stones biographer Stanley Booth explains, "Waycross Georgia is a place with a strong vein of Manichean madness. It is populated by people who know the flesh is evil. It's important to know that, to understand the deep South and its peculiar dynamic, in order to get a handle on Gram Parsons and his music."

Coon Dog Connors was a combat pilot in WWII, flying more than 50 missions over enemy territory before settling down in 1945 with his new bride in Waycross, on the edge of the Okefenokee Swamp, where he managed Snively Groves' box factory. Coon Dog and Avis's son was conceived in an apartment on Mac-Donald Street and raised in the family's new home on Suwanee Drive in the Cherokee Heights district. Ingram was very close to his father. They spent many memorable camping hunting, fishing, and canoeing trips in the swamps, a harmonious age of innocence later chronicled in Gram's song *Hickory Wind*. He also held fond memories of his mother, expressed in his song *Brass Buttons*, written in loving memory of his mother. He would not record this song until his final album, released posthumously, in January 1974, with Emmylou Harris singing harmony.

Gram's introduction to music came through piano lessons, his first composition at age 12 a boogey-woogie number. By listening to a band that the box factory employees had formed, he was also introduced to grassroots American music. At age nine in 1955, he persuaded his parents to permit him to attend a package show at the City Auditorium that featured Little Jimmy Dickens and an unheralded newcomer, Elvis Presley. Presley was a huge rockabilly hero in the local area, directly before he was sold by Sun Records impresario, Sam Phillips, to RCA and became a national singing sensation. After the show, Ingram marched into Elvis's backstage dressing room and stuck out his hand. "Hello, there," he said, "You're Elvis Presley and I'm the little kid who buys your records." He got an autograph for his efforts, a prize indeed in those days, and knew he had discovered his destiny, a comfort that he retreated to, lip-synching to Presley's 45 rpm records as an escape from the drunken fights that became routine behavior for his parents.

Elvis's Sun Records' singles were a distillation of country, bluegrass, and blues, facilitated by Sam Phillips during the now well-documented sessions in the tiny Sun studios where Sam booked guitarist Scotty Moore and bassist Bill Black to egg Elvis onward until they collectively hit a vein of pure gold. Elvis's rockabilly style was born when he sang Bill Monroe's *Blue Moon Of Kentucky*, fusing blues and blue grass into something new. Elvis's early rockabilly seemed to pick up where Hank Williams had left off. In 1956, Elvis hit on the radio with *Heartbreak Hotel*, his RCA debut, and Gram branched out, lip-synching Elvis songs for his peers. Pretending to be Elvis was a hit with the girls.

In December 1958, Coon Dog Connors, after ushering his family to the local train station, where they climbed into a passenger coach headed for Winter Haven and Christmas with their in-laws, returned to his office, thoughtfully spread newspapers on the carpet, put a gun to his head, and blew his brains out. His son was devastated. Gram was dismissed from Bolles military prep school during the following semester for disciplinary problems.

Soon after her husband's suicide, Avis Snively began dating fortune hunter Robert Ellis Parsons, a suave New Orleans playboy. Bob Parsons' behavior would soon bear out claims that he had his eye on the Snively fortune while he was romancing the recently widowed Mrs Connors. Upon marrying Avis, Parsons had the birth certificates of her children legally changed to his surname. Gram Connors became Gram Parsons. Sadly, Avis soon discovered that Bob was paying more interest to the teenage babysitter they had hired to tend their newborn daughter than he paid to his wife. Gram felt his mother's pain and sought outlets to express his own.

In 1958 at age 12, Gram Parsons bought himself a Fender Stratocaster and joined his first band, the Pacers. The Pacers were older boys at Winter Haven high school, and Gram was a pre-teen James Dean rocking out on Elvis, Buddy Holly, and other rockabilly material. To give his stepfather credit, Bob Parsons encouraged his stepson's musical interest. Gram next set out to form his own band, linking up with *Spiders & Snakes* author Jim Stafford to form the Legends, with Stafford on lead guitar, Jim Carlton on bass, and Lamar Braxton on drums. The Legends' pre-British Invasion repertoire included covers of Ray Charles, Chuck Berry, Little Richard, the Everly Brothers, Duane Eddy, and the Ventures. As the group evolved, Gerald Jesse Chambers would replace Roberts on bass and Jon Corneal would replace Braxton on drums. Kent Lavoie, the lead singer of the Rumors, and other musicians came and went from the lineup. Lavoie, like Stafford, would be an achiever in the 1970s when he hit with *Me And You And A Dog Name Boo* under the stage name "Lobo." From this time onward, Gram Parsons' life would dovetail with the careers of an ever-increasing number of the movers and groovers who would combine their talents to forge the country rock genre.

In an interview with a reporter from *The Guardian*, Jim Carlton recalled visiting his teenage friend at his family's mansion in Winter Haven, which has subsequently become part of Cypress Gardens Resort. "Back then," Carlton recalled, "it was a big old lonely place out on Lake Eloise, a garden variety southern mansion with a butler at the door. Even with all the trappings, you felt it was full of old Southern ghosts. We would do acid in Gram's big room, where he had a piano and a Hammond B-3. It was odd, but you'd never see his parents."

Gram formed the Village Vanguards, a Peter, Paul and Mary style folk trio with his girl friend Patti Johnson and pal, Dick McNeer. This trio often played intermission sets at Legends' shows. The Legends earned a regular spot on a local tv show, and when Bob Parsons purchased his stepson a Volkswagen bus to haul their equipment to gigs, the envy of rival teen bands. Unfortunately, Gram's mother and stepfather's relationship continued to deteriorate. Gram failed his junior year of high school, and his Snively relatives intervened, sending the wayward waif from Waycross to the Bolles school in Jacksonville, which was no longer a military prep school, to finish his high school education.

Parsons next joined the Shilos, a Kingston Trio type folk group that he met while judging a talent contest in Greenville, North Carolina, where family friend Buddy Freeman became Parson's first manager. At 17, along with manager Freeman and band members Paul Surratt, Joe Kelly, and George Wrigley, Parsons spent the summer of 1964 in New York City. Freeman booked the Shilos into small Greenwich Village venues like Cafe Rafio and clubs like the Bitter End and Cafe Wha. Right away, Parsons inveigled his way into the company of their musical idols, the Journeymen. He bonded with Journeyman Dick Weissman, an unlikely happenstance for a wannabe teenage folk musician in the Big Apple, but true, nevertheless, and the extent of his influence did not stop there. For example, John Phillips was also moved to arrange a meeting between the Shilos and Bob Dylan's manager Albert Grossman. Nothing came of the encounter, however, and the Shilos returned home to attend high school. Back in Greensville, the Shilos recorded nine or ten tracks at a radio station on the campus of Bob Jones University. No record resulted, and the Shilos broke up. These tracks would later be issued as part of GRAM PARSONS: THE EARLY YEARS VOLUME I (1963-65), released on the Sierra label in 1979.

Gram Parsons graduated from high school on the same day in June 1965 that his mother succumbed to cirrhosis of the liver, a victim of marital neglect and bitter inter-family squabbling over the management of Snively family citrus interests. His step-father wasted no time in consolidating his relationship with his favorite babysitter, marrying her, and piecing off his stepson by pulling strings and arranging a deferment of his draft status. Considerable Snively 'pull' was needed to arrange Gram's admittance into

Harvard University, to study theology. As Gram later admitted in a record label bio: "I did a back-dive into Harvard. They were looking to break out of their traditional mold of choosing students, and I was way out of the traditional mold. I guess they figured they had enough class presidents and maybe they needed a few beatniks."

At Harvard, Parsons wasted no time in forming a group that could gig in the local area. He first bonded with some of the students at the Berklee School of Music to form a folk group he called Gram Parsons and the Like. While working in this band, Gram met up with guitarist John Nuese of the Trolls. Not long after this, former child movie star Brandon de Wilde, who some say could sing harmony with Parsons as well or better than anybody except Emmylou Harris, took an interest in managing the group. When De Wilde secured a recording session in New York, Parsons, Nuese, and Dunlop moved there at very nearly the same moment in time as Emmylou Harris got herself a room in a YMCA in the Village. Gram Parsons' days at Harvard had come to an end, but he would not cross paths with Harris until they met at Clydes four years later.

Discovering the usefulness of his new trust fund, Gram footed the bills, renting a house in the Bronx for the band, now called the International Submarine Band, a name they lifted from a 'Little Rascals' episode. Their heroes were Ray Charles and Buck Owens. Their first 45 rpm record, issued on the Ascot label, was the novelty tune, *The Russians Are Coming, The Russians Are Coming*, a corny instrumental that Johnny Mandel had composed for Canadian film director Norman Jewison's Cold War farce of the same name. The B-side, a driving rendition of Terry Fell's *Truck Drivin Man*, which the band had learned from Buck Owens' version of the song, showed more promise. The second ISB single, *Sum Up Broke b/w One Day Week*, issued by Columbia in 1966, was a better effort but failed to excite deejays.

Gram Parsons had predicted to friends and associates that these releases would soon make him the next Elvis. He was wrong, but his charisma quotient kept on climbing. As Barry

Tashian, leader of Barry & the Remains, a Boston band that had scored a regional hit with *Don't Look Back*, recalled during an interview with *Rock N Reel*, "I met Gram either in Cambridge or in the Bronx . . . Through guitar player John Nuese, who played in the International Submarine Band, Gram's band at that time. I heard that band rehearse in the Bronx, in this big house they were renting — with a rehearsal studio on the top floor lined with egg cartons as sound-proofing. They played Buck Owens' songs, *Buckaroo, Standing In Your Welfare Line*, and *My Heart Skips A Beat*. I was still playing rock 'n' roll with the Remains. Country songs sounded mighty fine to me, and it was really the first day that my attention was turned toward country music. *Six Days On The Road* was another song that they did. The Remains were very busy in their own right. We'd not had word of going on tour with the Beatles at that point, but we had our record contract with Epic, and were recording and writing. I'd moved to New York, and we were just about to get news of the tour with the Beatles. The Beatles were coming over for a 14-city tour, the summer of 1966, and it was the biggest tour of the time." Tashian would later play a significant role in the touring career of Emmylou Harris.

All four members of the International Submarine Band followed Brandon de Wilde to California. They lived in the canyons above Sunset Boulevard, descending nightly upon the clubs on the Sunset Boulevard strip and surrounding area, mostly playing in various configurations under a number of gig-band names, including the Flying Burrito Brothers, a band name that was coined by Ian Dunlop. Parsons and his new girlfriend, Nancy Ross, enjoyed the luxury of an apartment on Sweetzer Avenue. Larry Spector, a manager Gram had hooked up with through his friendship with Peter Fonda, booked the ISB in opening slots for bands like Iron Butterfly.

From this scene, the Flying Burrito Brothers band emerged. "Ian Dunlop and John and Mickey got together with this guy, Barry Tashian of the Remains, and Leon (Russell), and people like J. Markham and Bobby Keyes and J.J. Cale, or whoever was around . . . and that was called 'the Flying Burrito Brothers',"

Gram explained in the liner notes to a Burrito Brothers album. "And I would sit in at the Prelude. They would play all those clubs up and down Lankersham, like the Hobo and the Red Velour. It was Ian's name and I stole it from him when he went to England."

Brandon de Wilde was best known for his nine-year-old role in *Shane*, starring Alan Ladd. His 'connections' led to the ISB recording half a dozen songs for the soundtrack of the 1967 feature film, *The Trip*, starring Peter Fonda, as well as performing live on the set of this Roger Corman flick, now a cult classic. These tracks were replaced by cuts recorded by Electric Flag, which the producers believed to be more appropriately psychedelic for Peter Fonda's acid trip. The Submarine Band was seen on screen in the final cut of the film, briefly, but their music (which included a version of Parsons' *Lazy Days*) lay discarded on the cutting room floor.

Parsons' friendship with Peter Fonda led to the actor recording Gram's *November Nights*. Like De Wilde, Fonda had an itch to become a rock & roll star. Fonda's debut record, *November Nights* b/w Donovan's *Catch The Wind*, was released into obscurity as a 45 rpm single by Chisa Records in late 1967. Fonda soon became a counterculture hero when he teamed up with Dennis Hopper to make the quintessential '60s flick, *Easy Rider*.

Barry Tashian & the Remains also moved to the West Coast during this time. "After the Beatles tour," Tashian recalls, "Bill Briggs — out of the Remains — and myself went out there to join them, moving into the house with them in Laurel Canyon in early 1967. A big old house, nestled in the Hollywood Hills, where we had a great time living and playing together. They were doing a bit of recording. It was an exciting time. There was Joni across the valley. Neil Young and his band. There was a lot happening. Unfortunately, we never got to do anything that was prolific or productive. The following year, we moved back East, but beforehand we stayed out in a big house belonging to Brandon de Wilde. Again it was full of good times; we used to play at the Topanga Corral in the canyon." Remains' drummer N.D. Smart

III would stay on the coast and become a member of the Gram Parsons-Chris Hillman Burritos.

As he had done in the past, Gram Parsons continued to create new acts, always questing for the perfect combination of singers and musicians. For bread and butter gigs, Parsons, Nuese, Dunlop, Guavin, Briggs, Smart, and Tashian banded together in working units along with other musicians who found themselves in limbo in La La Land during the late 1960s. As Barry Tashian describes this musical chairs situation, "We played dates around Los Angeles, playing under different names; some as the Mainstream Blues Band, with a musician from Tulsa, Junior Markham. Bobby Keyes was the sax player in that band, and we were the rhythm section. We'd play Otis Redding, Sam & Dave, and that kind of stuff. Then we had another 'gig band' with Gram, myself, Bill Briggs, Ian, and the drummer from the Submarine Band, Mickey. Under the name 'the Flying Burrito Brothers' we played in several clubs in the Valley — the San Fernando Valley. That was the original Burrito Brothers."

With nothing much happening after the issue of two Submarine Band singles, Parsons began looking farther afield. When he began to miss rehearsals and gigs and take jobs working with Bob Buchanan, Dunlop and Guavin left the group and began to concentrate on their gig band, the Flying Burrito Brothers. Parsons wanted to play more and more country music. Then Lee Hazlewood, who had steered the careers of Duane Eddy and Nancy Sinatra into the mainstream, took an interest and signed the ISB to a recording contract with his new label LHI Records. John Nuese and Gram Parsons reaped the benefit of the groundwork laid out by all four original members. Hazlewood's girlfriend, Suzi Jane Hokom, was the producer. Parsons and Nuese were able to convince Hazlewood to buy into their idea of a hip country album.

In preparation for the recording sessions, Parsons convinced ex-Legends drummer Jon Corneal to forsake his developing career as a session drummer in Nashville and join Parsons and

Nuese as version two of the International Submarine Band. In the studio to record the album that would eventually be known as SAFE AT HOME, the band also enlisted the services of session bassist Joe Osborne and Jay Dee Maness, the house steel player at the Aces Club in Elmonte, an L.A. suburb. The first two sides, Parsons' *Luxury Liner* and *Blue Eyes*, were cut in July at Western Recorders in Hollywood. The next sessions to complete the album did not take place for four months, but Parsons had his hands full, especially when he learned that the beautiful Nancy Ross was pregnant and wanted to bear his child.

Parsons' life had become as complex as it had when his parents had been alive. As Nancy Ross confided to Pamela Des Barres, "I was actively fighting for this little soul in my belly because Gram's manager wanted me to have an abortion on my very own bed. Gram didn't know what to do. He was so young, so scared, and so confused. We couldn't make a go of it. He couldn't give up his kismet, his contract to come to earth and do his mission with his music. He had to choose and that's where the pain started. That tore him up, it tore me up. For me it was Gram and his happiness or Polly and her life." Gram proposed and announced elaborate wedding plans, but when Nancy discovered that she was merely being conscripted into a publicity wedding modeled upon the onstage marriage ceremonies that Hank Williams had orchestrated with his second wife, Billy Jean, Nancy balked. She refused to participate in the spectacle, and she and Parsons continued to drift further and further apart. A $1,000 fee for a wedding dress, which Parsons had commissioned Nudie Cohn's Rodeo Tailors to fashion, went unpaid, and would later surface in the lyrics of one of his songs. Cohn held no grudge. "He was one hell of a good songwriter and musician," he later said of Parsons. "He was also real smart and a nice boy, too. He was a real down-home kind of a guy, and he liked to hang around my store and pick the guitar."

SAFE AT HOME was released in the spring of 1968. Among the tracks recorded were two more Gram Parsons originals, *Do You Know How It Feels To Be Lonesome* and *Strong Boy*. Six cover songs fleshed out the album.

Before the album was released, Gram Parsons jumped ship, joining the Byrds in February 1968, and embarking on recording sessions that would lead to the legendary SWEETHEART OF THE RODEO album. "I'd heard of him, already," Chris Hillman told *Goldmine*. "We had the same manager, Larry Spector, who also managed Hugh Masakela, and a couple of the Monkees. He [Spector] doesn't even rate his name in print because he was a thief. I asked Gram down to rehearse. We may have been looking for a keyboardist, and he played a bit of piano. He came down and was fun. After the rehearsal, he broke into a Buck Owens song." Roger McGuinn remembers the audition differently. "We hired a piano player," McGuinn told *Fusion*, "and he turned out to be Parsons, a monster in sheep's clothing. And he exploded out of this sheep's clothing. God! It's George Jones in a big, sequin suit!"

Initially, McGuinn's vision of a double album set, which traced the history of American music, was bandied around between founding members McGuinn and Hillman and their two new recruits, drummer Kevin Kelley and pianist, vocalist, and rhythm guitarist Gram Parsons. Their decision-making was made easier when Columbia nixed the double album idea. Byrds' records sales were plummeting, not building. With founding members Gene Clark, Michael Clarke, and David Crosby gone, McGuinn and Hillman found themselves in a unique position. They could not afford to look back and merely repeat themselves with another jingly-jangle album of folk rock featuring Roger's Richenbacker 12-string guitar licks. Folk rock wasn't selling like it had in 1965. Looking forward, country music appealed to both of them. Chris Hillman, who had come from a bluegrass background, felt he had a country ally in Gram. Parsons played the devil's advocate, a sil-ver-tongued bullshit artist with a manifest destiny: to create some Cosmic American Music. In the tradition of the Byrds' electrified history, which had kicked off the folk rock craze, it had all the prospects of being a landmark album — if they could pull it off.

Once again, the Byrds' remarkable ability to be at the leading edge of creating yet-another new genre, that of country rock, was realized. Kicking the album off with Dylan's *You Ain't Goin'*

Nowhere linked the experiment irrevocably with the poet laureate of the '60s, who had handed them *Hey Mr. Tambourine Man*, their first radio hit. Parsons' haunting *Hickory Wind*, co-written with Bob Buchanan, was worth the price of the album all on its own. Choosing Cindy Walker's *Blue Canadian Rockies* was a stroke of genius, sung with charm and style by Chris Hillman. The inclusion of Parsons' *Lazy Days*, which he had originally recorded for the dumped soundtrack of *The Trip*, came later, as a bonus track on CD versions of the classic album, culled from out-takes. The Louvin Brothers' *The Christian Life*, Woody Guthrie's *Pretty Boy Floyd*, J.T. Hardin's *Reputation*, and the traditional *Pretty Polly* provided covers that would have easily fit into Roger McGuinn's original historical concept.

The sessions began in Nashville, in the same studio that Bob Dylan had crafted both BLONDE ON BLONDE and JOHN WESLEY HARDING, but were interrupted for a previously booked college campus tour and resumed in the City of Angels. Before they left Nashville, the Byrds were invited to play in the Ryman Auditorium on the Glaser Brothers segment of the Grand Ole Opry broadcast. Columbia executives had to pull some strings to secure this "invitation" that would mark the first time in history that a rock group had been permitted to play the Opry, let alone the broadcast portion of the show. The boys were advised to "get their long hair trimmed." All might have gone well if Gram Parsons had not forgotten that he was in the hallowed Ryman Auditorium — where Bob Wills had been hassled for using a drummer and smoking his cigar on stage. Where Hank Williams had been a no show and eventually drummed out of town. Where truck drivin' man Elvis Aaron Presley had been told to forget about making records and go back to driving truck for a living. Opry audiences were known to be tough, the Opry managers even tougher.

Chris Hillman resurrected the scene during an interview with *Goldmine* magazine's Bruce Sylvester. "I walked in there wide-eyed. Here was the original Ryman stage in the original Opry building. Columbia Records had probably put a little pressure on the Opry to let us on. We were on Tompall and the Glaser Brothers' portion of the live broadcast." Their first number was Merle Haggard's *Sing Me Back Home*, which was at first met with animosity, then received a decent applause as the audience warmed up to the fact that these longhairs could actually play the Hag's song. They had agreed to do another Haggard song as their second offering before taking the stage. That's when things went sour, Hillman recalls. "On the air Tompall said, 'you're going to do Merle Haggard's *Life In Prison*, aren't you?' And Gram said, 'No, we're not. We're gonna do *Hickory Wind*, for my grandmother.' After we finished, Tompall was screaming at Gram, 'How dare you make me look bad on the Opry! Don't you know who I am, blah, blah, blah.'"

When it was released in June 1968, SWEETHEART OF THE RODEO did not set the world on fire, either. Country deejays, used to the smooth, saccharin strains of contemporary Nashville releases and the grittier, red-neck productions heard on Buck Owens and Merle Haggard's Bakersfield Sound records, were not prepared to play long-haired country artists from the rock & roll world. Top 40 deejays were equally puzzled. The Byrds last single to chart in the Top 40 had been their 1967 release of Dylan's *My Back Pages*, which rose no higher than number 30 on the *Billboard* chart. Nevertheless, SWEETHEART OF THE RODEO was an immediate hit with musicians and an unidentified counterculture fan base that would soon embrace all of the country rock releases that it spawned, being championed by many commentators as the record that created "country rock." The album would eventually be listed in *Rolling Stone* magazine's Top 200 albums of all-time.

In May 1968 the Byrds, with Gram Parsons, Kevin Kelley, and electric mandolin player Doug Dillard aboard, embarked on an overseas tour to support their "Sweetheart" release. They played to a sold-out crowd at the Piper Club in Rome, then flying to London, where they played two nights at the Middle Earth club, returning in July, en route to South Africa, with a club date at Blaises Corporation House and a concert show at Royal Albert Hall. After the first show, Roger McGuinn looked up his pals

Keith Richards and Mick Jagger, and introduced Gram Parsons to the bad boys of rock & roll. As Keith Richards remembers it, "Gram blew into town with the Byrds, who were playing Blaises. Gram came back to Mick's Chester Square flat with Roger McGuinn. Their next gig was to be in South Africa, and we told Gram English bands never even went there. So he threw in his lot with the Stones and hung around London."

The Byrds reacted by firing Parsons, who sought 'solace' at Keith Richards' Redlands country estate. This began a musical friendship that led the Rolling Stones to dig deeper into country material. Gram Parsons was "one of the few people who really helped me sing country music," Mick Jagger has remarked. "Before that Keith and I would just copy off records." Keith and Gram also shared their passion for drugs. As Keith later put it to Stanley Booth, Gram "could get better coke than the Mafia." As Mick Jagger's "executive nanny" and notorious road manager Phil Kaufman notes in his autobiography, *Road Mangler Deluxe*, "Gram Parsons thought he had Keith Richards' metabolism. He didn't. Gram really thought he was macho; that he could drink and do drugs and get laid and carry on indefinitely — that he was not vulnerable. And he paid for it. Not only the good die young. I'd say in a lot of instances the dumb die young."

Kaufman had already been through a lot in his fast-paced lifetime. His early adventures as a smuggler led to doing some hard time with Charles Manson. Manson employed him during the recording of his album LIES, then Kaufman worked as a movie stuntman, before he got into the music biz on a full-time basis as Mick Jagger's handler. On the road with Gram Parsons, Chris Hillman, and the Flying Burrito Brothers in 1969 he had earned his nickname, "road mangler." Kaufman would soon play a very large part in the Emmylou Harris's career.

Later that summer, Mick and Keith showed up in L.A. to mix the tracks that would be released as BEGGAR'S BANQUET. Parsons' education of Richards and Jagger in the spirit of country music continued. As Phil Kaufman recalls, "Gram was teaching the Rolling Stones country music. Quite often we'd just sit around the house — Gram, Mick, Keith, and I. They had been to Ace Records and bought every country album they could find: George Jones, Merle Haggard, Dave Dudley, Ernest Tubb — you name it. Gram would say, 'here's an example of this,' and he'd tell me which album he wanted and I'd play the record." As Keith Richards told Parsons' biographer Ben Fong-Torres, "I used to spend days at the piano with Gram, you know, just singing. I did more singing with Gram than I've done with the Stones. He taught me all the Everly Brothers' stuff, and the cross-harmonies and shit like that. He wrote songs, man! He kept going; he would go all day without repeating himself."

The Stones' next album, LET IT BLEED, proved that they had done their homework, *Country Honk* being the most obvious example of Gram Parsons' influence. And when the Stones sent Parsons a tape of *Wild Horses*, in hopes that Sneaky Pete could be cajoled into contributing a pedal steel track, Parsons recorded it on BURRITO DELUXE before the Stones' released it.

When the Stones packed up and left L.A., Gram Parsons picked up where he had left off. He didn't have to look too far to find a partner willing to form a band. In a shuffle of personnel, Chris Hillman quit the Byrds and Gram Parsons moved into a house with him in San Fernando Valley, which became known as 'Burrito Manor'. "We were both coming off bad marriages and crying on each other's shoulders," Hillman told Bruce Sylvester. "We worked in the mornings, believe it or not. We didn't do all-night writing sessions. We were pretty normal at that point. I got up and started this idea — 'This old town's filled with sin, it will swallow you in, blah, blah, blah . . .'" These lyrics to the song *Sin City* went on to refer to manager Larry Spector's "gold-plated door." In addition to the barbed lyrics of *Sin City*, Gram and Chris penned *Christine's Tune*, which was later changed to *Devil In Disguise*, when the girl referred to in the title died. They also wrote *Wheels*, *Hippie Boy*, *My Uncle*, and the surf-guitar inspired country instrumental, *Buckaroo*.

Parsons and Hillman took their band name from Ian Dunlop and Mickey Guavin's gig-band name, the Flying Burrito Brothers.

By December, they had secured a recording contract with A&M Records and begun sessions for THE GILDED PALACE OF SIN with Sneaky Pete Kleinow on pedal steel. Jon Corneal and several other session drummers worked the sessions. Michael Clarke would come aboard for the band's first tour. David Crosby added high harmonies to a cover of Dan Penn and Chip Moman's *Do Right Woman*. There were many highlights, not the least of which was Gram Parsons' aching vocal on Penn and Moman's *Dark End Of The Street*.

For the classic album cover, Gram Parsons made another visit to Nudie's Rodeo Tailors, where he picked out a new outfit for himself and "Nudie suits" for his band mates. When the album appeared in record stores, the Flying Burrito Brothers were depicted as five young Hank Williams wannabes posing before an outhouse adorned with two very foxy ladies. Some record buyers initially bought the album simply because they were intrigued by the unique cover shot and the band's cool name. Once placed on turntables, the music surprised everybody, and, in a single fell swoop, made country cool for hippies. Sneaky Pete's exploratory use of the pedal steel, which included several radical, blistering, fuzzed solos and edgy fills, made Hillman and Parsons' traditional harmonies user friendly to the turned-on generation. THE GILDED PALACE OF SIN was a hip album through and through.

"We were still trying to do my deluxe number," Gram Parsons explained. "A dream of soul country cosmic, what I called in my earlier college days 'Cosmic American Music'. I would do numbers, I mean, besides the Nudie suits. I'd do numbers like buy a bottle of tequila and five turbans, and always insisted on having an organ around so I could do Jerry Lee Lewis numbers and get a big sound." Parsons cited Delaney Bramlett and his wife Bonnie as the inspiration to go cosmic with Hillman in their version of the Burritos. "We were close to Delaney & Bonnie. We were close not only sort of musically, but in our heads we were close. And they were always pulling us aside and saying how much country music meant and it was important that somebody did it." Bonnie Bramlett may have been the original inspiration that drove Gram

Parsons to seek out his own "kick ass" harmony singer. Gram would introduce Emmylou Harris as his "kick ass" to his pals.

When GUILDED PALACE OF SIN was released in February 1969, *Los Angeles Times* music critic Robert Hilburn declared that Parsons' vocals were "straight from the sentimental George Jones heart of country music." Gram could have imagined no greater praise. In the short time that Gram Parsons had been on the West Coast, he had had a hand in recording three of the definitive albums that created the country rock genre and inspired a generation of country rockers.

True to character, Gram Parsons and Chris Hillman became estranged before the band's second album, BURRITO DELUXE, was released. "What made us all angry in the Flying Burrito Brothers was that he was seduced by all the trappings of wealth and fame," Chris Hillman explains, "and he hadn't earned them. He'd suddenly say, 'I'm gonna get a limousine', and we'd go, 'Why? We're going to play five shows in some bar, what are you talking about?'" Gram's drug habits were also taking a toll on his friends, as Phil Kaufman recalls. The Burrito Brothers train tour provided this 'road mangler' with even more headaches. "What a fuckin' disaster. The train from hell. They'd play poker, take mescaline, coke, and Quaaludes, then stagger off the train in some small town in their glittery outfits and all out of their heads. It was deranged. We did a show with the Grateful Dead and someone spiked everybody's drink. You ever seen a steel player on acid? Believe me, you don't want to."

Fired from the Burrito Brothers, Parsons moved into the notorious Chateau Marmont, a castle-like Sunset Strip hotel and bungalow complex where John Belushi would meet his Waterloo 15 years down the long and winding road that was already littered with rock & roll suicides, plane crashes, automobile accidents, and drug overdoses. Here the 'cosmic hillbilly' hooked up with filmmaker Tony Fountz, staying in Fountz' bungalow before moving to a suite of his own. Fountz, in production with a B-movie production based in the Mojave, near Cap Rock, where UFO sightings were reported, had previously bonded with Parsons and led him to the Joshua Tree National Park. Fountz's film production had led to the depictions of the Burrito Brothers in goggles and 'spaceman' gear on BURRITO DELUXE, a mixed bag of debris that fell far short of its predecessor, but a defining moment for the former Ingram Cecil Conners, a.k.a. "Gram Parsons, space man." Long after Fountz had completed filming, Parsons continued to haunt the area, often booking himself into the nearby Joshua Tree Inn — possibly even exploring the nearby Giant Rock Airport, home of George Van Tassel's Spaceport Earth UFOlogy Center. When the Stones took Gram to the Stonehenge, he would respond in kind, hauling Keith out to this newly discovered desert location at Cap Rock to scan the night skies for UFOs.

When he got his own suite in the Chateau Marmont, Parsons began to make plans for a solo album, linking up with producer Terry Melcher, Doris Day's son, and a frequent producer of the Byrds. Marred by cocaine abuse and all night sessions, 10 tracks were eventually recorded but never released.

Melcher remembers Gram Parsons as "such a romantic character. He was one of those people who actually thought it was great to die young." Grams' ex, Nancy Ross, was also convinced that Parsons had it in his deep South "cellular memory" to repeat the tragic fates of his father and mother. "There has never been anyone I've known who had such archangelic charisma," Nancy Ross told Pamela Des Barres. "When Gram was fully present and in his full power, you would have walked off a cliff for him. Early in our relationship, he told me, 'Do you understand what a fallen angel is? It's an angel from the divine realms who comes to earth, loves a mortal woman, is wronged by her, and sullies his grace — thereby falling from grace.'"

John Phillips of the Mamas and the Papas recalls Gram's brush with death during an outing on their motorcycles. Richard Farina had gone out on a bike, and Dylan had been out of action for a year following a messy bike accident. As Phillips recalls in his autobiography, "Gram's chopper was pure redneck — buckskin seats, fringe hanging down. He was the real item. The front fender was loose and he had rigged it together with a coat hanger or something like that. All of a sudden, we realized that we didn't hear his chopper behind us. We turned around and went back about a mile and found Gram and his new friend Maggie lying on the road. There was blood every where . . . I kneeled beside Gram and thought he was gone. He looked up at me and squeezed my hand. 'John,' he said, semiconscious, 'take me on that long white ride.'" Parsons was rushed to hospital by ambulance, but Phillips believes that "he was never the same." Parsons appears to have become determined to live out Hank Williams' live fast, love hard, and die young legacy.

In the late spring of 1971, Gretchen Burrell in tow, Parsons sought out his pal, Keith Richards, renting a flat in Kensington, and when Keith and his lady du jour Anita Pallenberg moved to southern France, Parsons and his young girlfriend followed. There, the Stones recorded what many critics have called their best album, EXILE ON MAIN STREET. Gram was singing when the tape was rolling and can be heard on *Sweet Virginia* and was likely mixed into a vocal blend on other tracks. As Keith would later admit, "he was just there, if you got lost for a harmony . . ."

Among the Stones constantly changing entourage that summer was Dominique Tarle, a young French photographer. Twenty-nine years later, Tarle's photo essay of the making of "Exile" was published in a lavish coffee table edition. *Mojo* magazine reviewer Andrew Male paints this extraordinary portrait of the characters portrayed in Tarle's photo essay. "The narcissistic Jagger, immaculately turned out even in the grubby basement that has been requisitioned as a recording studio; Bill Wyman and Charlie Watts, poker-faced, cool; Gram Parsons, stoned and trouser-less; Mick Taylor with his serious baby-face; Paul and Linda; the impossibly beautiful Anita Pallenberg. The obvious star is, of course, Keef — stoned, magnificently dissipated, 'appy, wiv 'is crooked teef, his woman, his kid, and his drugs. Here he is, showing Gram some chords on the balustraded patio . . ."

From the Riviera, Parsons and Burrell went to England to visit Ian Dunlop, then to Florida, and eventually New Orleans to marry at the estate where his stepfather and his babysitter bride had made their tryst. From there, the newlyweds went on to Maryland and Washington, where Gram Parsons met Emmylou Harris, the singing partner fated to share his final recording sessions before he left her to face the music and he went on to face his maker.

In My Hour Of **D**arkness

Gram Parsons frequently told friends and associates that his next album would be a solo effort on the Rolling Stones' new label, but that deal was never made. Instead, he hooked up with ex-Byrds' manager Eddie Tickner, who worked on an album deal with Warner/Reprise while Parsons worked on his rehabilitation. He began jamming with his pal Rick Grech, who was invited to produce Gram's first solo album, GP.

Barry Tashian was one of the first musicians Gram called on to assist with the new album. "Gram at this point hadn't decided what to put on the album," Tashian later told *Rock 'N Reel*, "so I played him a bunch of songs that included *The Streets Of Baltimore* and *I Can't Dance* ... None of them were originals because I wasn't productive in that area at that time, although I did contribute to *Ooh Las Vegas*, which has always been awkward to me, having been given no credit. I wrote the verse: "Well, the first time I lose I drink whiskey / Second time I drink gin . . ." We all went to Las Vegas to see Elvis. It was a wild night, most of which I don't remember very well except that we saw B.B. King, as well as Elvis. Gram stayed up most of the night, and asked Glen D and James Burton to play on his record." How Gram convinced Elvis' band members to come along for the GP sessions remains a mystery.

James Burton offered little light on the subject when he told Steve Fishell, "Well, Gram said, 'I think I've got a deal to do an album, and I really want you on it.'" Apparently, Gram's reputation alone was good currency among legendary pickers like Burton.

Gram Parsons also invited Emmylou Harris to join him for the GP sessions. As she recalls, "He talked about doing this album, and I didn't hear, and I didn't hear, and then finally one day when I came home there was a ticket to go out to L.A." On the Piedmont Airlines flight to the West Coast her jumbo-sized Gibson SJ-N was damaged. Parsons immediately leant her a little Martin New Yorker.

Emmylou Harris first met Phil Kaufman in the doorway of her Chateau Marmont hotel room. "I was being bombarded by a lot of strange stuff," she recalled during an interview with a British magazine. "L.A. was very exotic to come to, it was my first time there, and everything seemed unusual."

As Kaufman recalls, "I knocked on her door to introduce myself. 'Hi, I'm Gram's road manager. I'm looking after you.' The door opened and there was this beautiful young lady there, with long brunette hair. She was a hippie, folkie girl. Not beads and sandals, but long straight hair. I just called her the 'chick singer' — to this day, we say, 'has anybody seen the chick singer?'" Kaufman remembers that during the GRIEVOUS ANGEL sessions later that year, "she'd sit in the studio and knit, and I'd say, 'Aren't you meant to be singing?' She'd look at me and say, very proper, 'When Gram wants me, he'll call me.' She was very much impressed with him — he had a good track record, having been with the Byrds, and friends with the Rolling Stones. He was impressed with her singing ability, and they spent a lot of time rehearsing their voices together."

"Phil and Gram were very close, like brothers," Harris told the same interviewer. "For all his making light of things, Phil obviously loved him. I also loved Gram very much. He was my best friend and someone who changed my life. Whether we'd have gone on to be more than friends, it's hard to say. All I know is I was devastated by his death. We'd just started to know one another." That tragic moment would come all too soon.

Installed in the Chateau Marmont, Emmylou began her country 101 lessons, the usual Gram Parsons approach, beginning with George Jones, his hero. "Gram showed me the power and the poetry in it and just the purity of it. He did it with a real rock 'n' roll attitude. What's more, he really loved and lived and breathed that music. I was very naive. At the time I met Gram he was consciously trying to quit the junk and he was drinking a lot, but he was trying to kick that, too. People think that his voice was out of shape or whatever, but just listen to his track on *Love Hurts* — it's heartbreaking. He had that same way of understanding a song that George Jones has. I really liked working with Gram. It was a completely new experience for me. I was a little wary at first because of Los Angeles and Hollywood and all, and I was very much East Coast orientated. I was very much on my guard. But Gram was a very real person, and whenever I went out there, I always felt that I was in some kind of protective bubble. It was never Los Angeles itself, but always working with Gram and the music, and I kept myself in a very small circle."

"He was sneaky, in a very sweet way," Emmylou told Holly George-Warren years later. "He brought me a tape and said, 'this is just some stuff for you to listen to. There was Carl & Pearl Butler, the Louvin Brothers . . . I was so blown away by the Louvins, but I didn't know who they were, so I said, 'who *is* that girl?' I thought Ira Louvin was a girl! I'd never heard anybody sing that high. He kind of smiled. He knew he had me then. He knew I was hooked. I think that was kind of a test that I passed. What he gave me was learning how to sing, and how to phrase. He didn't really tell me what to sing. Singing with him, I learned that one of the universal things about country music at its best is the restraint in the phrasing, the economy of the emotion. Just by singing with him — it was almost by osmosis — I learned that you plow it under and you let the melody and the words carry you; all this 'emoting' thing — it will happen on it's own."

Barry Tashian recalls the exceptional session players Gram had assembled, notably "all these clean-cut guys from Las Vegas, from Elvis's band — James Burton, Glen D Hardin, and Ronnie Tutt.

And there was Byron Berline." Persuading Burton, Hardin, and Tutt to cut his album was a minor coup for Gram. The sessions were engineered by Hugh Davies, Merle Haggard's regular engineer, picked up during a visit Parsons and Grech made to the Hag in Bakersfield.

Before they went into the studio, rehearsals were held at Byron Berline's home. "Gram was in pretty good shape," Berline told *Desperados* author John Einarson, "until we got into the studio that first night and he got pretty whacked out. Everybody told him, 'look, you've got another chance, straighten up!'" When the recording sessions got underway in earnest, Rick Grech, although credited with co-production on the back cover credits, faded into the background after suffering a gall bladder attack. Parsons, forced to take charge, did, delegating tasks.

"Glen D Hardin," Tashian notes, "played a big role in those sessions. I wrote out some of the basic charts that showed the chord changes, but Glen D elaborated on those. He was a seasoned studio pro. I was kind of the outsider at the sessions, even though I had known Gram the longest."

"Emmylou," Byron Berline told John Einarson, "was in awe of the whole process and very nervous. She was not as refined as she would be later, but I think she did a really good job. I think she and Gram knew they had something special going on when they started singing for the first time."

"You couldn't really listen to Gram without being affected by him," Emmylou told *Rock N Reel*. "The fact is, he did bring his own poetry to the lyrics, and fused that with a traditional musical style — country. So, he came up with something that was very unique, and very much himself. This how we get art, by people coming up with something new, as they borrow from the past. We have to. You have to take it to a new place, and that's what Gram did."

GP was an album ahead of its time, a vision of where country could be taken if you wanted to go down an uncharted trail. Pedal steel player Al Perkins remembers the way he and James Burton just seemed to click, able to create interwoven conversations among dobro, steel, and Telecaster in original east Texas honky tonk style. "James and I did twin parts," Perkins told John Einarson, "like were heard on country records in the late '50s and early '60s." Gram's renditions of Harlan Howard's *Streets Of Baltimore* and George Jones' *That's All It Took* are right on the money. His own *Still Feelin' Blue* and *A Song For You* fit right in with the classics. Barry Tashian takes control on the rocking J. Geils Bands' *Cry One Time*. The best track by far is Parsons' *She*. Emmylou Harris's voice was inspirational, a "golden memory" for Barry Tashian. Most folks who bought the album were knocked out by Emmy and Gram's vocal blend.

When the time arrived to promote the album after its February 1973 release, Eddie Tickner was able to book a tour that was comprised of a mix of small out-of-the-way venues and major venues — "the better hippie honky tonks of the nation," to quote Emmylou Harris. Joined at the last minute by Phil Kaufman's pal Michael Martin, who bonded with Parsons and became the star's unofficial valet, they hit the road in an ancient Greyhound bus with the star's name prominently displayed in large letters on the sides. The bus was piloted by a veteran driver, "Leadfoot Lance." Parsons had wanted to call his band "the Turkeys" but was voted down and reluctantly settled for "the Fallen Angels."

Emmylou bought herself a road guitar. "With the money I made from the record with Gram I bought myself a brand new Martin D-28," she recalls. She did eventually get her SJ-N fixed and ended up passing the Martin on to Ricky Skaggs a few years down the line. After Parsons death, Phil Kaufman gave her the little Martin New Yorker as a keepsake. It now resides in the Country Music Hall of Fame Museum.

Emmylou looked on with interest as one of the lowest paid touring bands of all time was assembled. Aiming to help out, she suggested as a band member Gerry Mule, her former folk music guitarist from Washington, although he was neither a country player nor a rock player. N.D. "Norman" Smart, ex-Remains drummer, could kick ass. Bassist Kyle Tullis and steel player Neil Flanz were decent sidemen, too. After laying down tracks with Burton, Hardin, Tutt, Berline, Perkins, and Tashian, Emmylou found the road band somewhat less polished. "We must have played 50 songs," she would say later, "but we didn't finish one." Missing were the tick, tac, toe elements needed for live performance. Sure enough, first night of the tour in Boulder, Colorado at the Edison Electric Light Club they got fired — well, almost fired. "Fortunately, before they could fire us," Emmylou explains, "the city ordnance came and shut the club down because Weather Report had played the week before and it was so loud they wanted it closed down." In the audience was Richie Furay of Buffalo Springfield and Poco fame who remembered the show as "one of the most pitiful things I ever saw."

Emmylou's presence on the tour is remembered fondly, however, especially by Phil Kaufman. "When I listen to those old records, her voice is beautiful," he told Lucy O'Brien. "Emmylou was very conservative, and she had her little girl, Hallie, with her. Once in a while, she would go out with the boys, and drink tequila and get sick, and swear off. She never was an abuser. The boys enjoyed her company, though — they were very protective of her. Those years were a blur. We were really honky tonk and heavy in those days."

Kaufman had his hands full dealing with Gretchen Parsons, Gram's wife, who became obsessively jealous of Emmylou. Kaufman has always maintained that Emmylou was innocent of Gretchen's suspicions; she "just wasn't that kind of girl to break up a marriage." For her part, Emmylou has always been reticent on this question. "Gosh," she told Steve Hammer, "well, it always seemed like he let his food cool until it was almost cold before he'd eat it. He was really very funny, and a very generous person. Very bright. I don't think he ever did any damage or hurt any human being except himself."

After that first show in Boulder, Jock Bartley joined the band and Gerry Mule left. The new configuration rehearsed at the Pioneer Inn, a remote biker bar. "We had to go up in the mountains to Nederland, to a club that looked like it was out of *McCabe & Mrs. Miller*, even the women there were wearing guns," Emmylou recalls, for a "real rehearsal, where we picked endings, beginnings, and middles."

The dilapidated Greyhound chugged southward toward Austin, Texas, where Tickner and Kaufman scheduled a second rehearsal before their show at Armadillo World Headquarters. By the time they went on the following night, Kaufman was no longer babysitting a bad band. "We completely blew the roof off the Armadillo World Headquarters," Emmylou recalls.

By the time Gram Parsons and his Fallen Angels arrived in Houston for a four-night stand, the act was clicking on all six cylinders. Steve Earle, hitchhiking in from San Antonio, would have a "life experience," he later recounted. "I am one of several thousand men who have been in love with Emmylou Harris since the mid-'70s. Actually, my infatuation dates back to 1972 when I first saw Emmy, then a member of Gram Parsons' Fallen Angels, at Liberty Hall in Houston, Texas. Liberty Hall held about a thousand folks, a little over half of those in attendance that night were men. We stumbled out on Chenevert Street when the show was over, smitten to a man. Bam! — six hundred lifelong Emmylou Harris devotees." As Steve recreates the show scene, "It was loose, but it was tough. Gram's hair was frosted and his nails were painted red. He sang through his nose with his eyes closed, while the band played catch-up for most of the night. I saw Emmylou for the first time that night. I left a little bit in love and absolutely certain what I was going to be when I grew up."

"It was the end of a long tour for me, and I was kinda down," Linda Ronstadt recalls of her first meeting with Emmylou in Houston. Buoyed by hearing Emmylou Harris sing for the first time, Ronstadt stayed after the show. Chris Hillman and Gram Parsons, all previous transgressions forgiven, were hanging around the backstage area, where Hillman eventually introduced the two women. By night three, Linda was on stage belting out *Sin City* with Gram and Emmy. On night four, Neil Young stepped up to jam. Members of both bands partied through the night at Young's band's suite in an upscale Houston hotel, Ronstadt and Harris harmonizing with Parsons as he pulled out song after song from his encyclopedic repertoire of Everly Brothers, Louvin Brothers, and George Jones chestnuts. Linda's contributions to

Neil's HARVEST album, and her role as a harmony singer in Young's band that summer, parallel Emmylou's days spent with Gram Parsons. Both would go on to successful careers pioneering country rock on their own and eventually transcend the idiom, moving on to careers that have withstood the onslaught of time.

While the tour was taking off, Gram's marriage was collapsing. From a blow on the ear from a wooden coat hanger wielded by his wife while he slept, Parsons suffered permanent damage to his hearing. This frenzied attack is said to have been prompted by his choice of a photograph of himself and Emmylou seated on a Harley for the cover of his next album. Another time, Gretchen and Gram trashed a hotel room during a fight to the extent that the police were called to this domestic violence scene, where Gram was maced, hand-cuffed, and tossed unceremoniously into the local lock-up. "He was thrown in the county jail, in his crushed velour pants and out of his tree," as Phil Kaufman describes the sorry scene. "I put my ponytail up inside my cowboy hat, and went down to get his bail, but I could hear him bad-mouthing the cops from reception, and them beating the shit out of him. It was a very bad scene, one of the worst." Phil banished Gretchen from the tour, putting her on a flight for LA. Before he was done with this relationship, their house in Laurel Canyon would be burned to the ground.

While Kaufman protected Gram from his wife, Gram protected Emmylou from Phil. As N.D. "Norman" Smart confided to John Einarson, "Gram really protected Emmylou. He wouldn't let her get Kaufmanized. Phil's got a heart of gold, but he's as X-rated as you can get. There was a lot of shit going on during that tour that even I didn't know about. Emmylou and I used to do a window patrol on the bus. We'd run through the bus and open up all the windows and get all the smoke out. I'd always look out for Emmylou and her kid."

True to her character, Emmylou's recollections of the tour focus on the good times. "The crowds were there. The rooms were small, but the energy was of a special intensity. It may not have been as audible in Chicago as it was in Austin, but it was always there. And they came to see this young man and to hear the voice that would break and crack but rise pure and beautiful with sweetness and pain." Between Emmylou and Gram, a special magic emerged on stage, as Bernie Leadon of the Eagles notes. "Emmy would be standing there next to him," Leadon told Bill DeYoung, "staring at his face, staring at his mouth, and having the ability to get it by some telegraphic twitch or something — where he was going."

Parsons and his "fallen angels" were praised in the *Chicago Tribune* for their show at the Quiet Night. Then after a show at the Smiling Dog in Cleveland, ex-marine tour bus driver Leadfoot Lance headed the ancient Greyhound toward New York City for a show at Max's Kansas City, hangout of the New York Dolls, the Velvet Underground, and Andy Warhol. Bud Scoppa, aware of the buzz that was building up around Parsons and his new chick singer, headed over to Max's to visit with the cast and crew during their load-in at the club. "When I emerged from the subway," he recalled in his liner notes for the recent Parsons' tribute album, "and spotted the bus — you couldn't miss it, not with those giant painted letters spelling GRAM PARSONS across its flank — parked in front of too-hip Max's, I was delighted by the culture-clash hilarity of the juxtaposition (in retrospect, maybe rednecks and chickpeas do go together). As I stepped inside and climbed the stairs from the restaurant area to the club room on the second floor, I was greeted by a gregarious Parsons, who seemed more robust and lucid than he'd been when I'd last interviewed him the year before (hanging out with the Stones during that period apparently could be damaging to your health and welfare). In his typically gracious way, Gram introduced me to his beautiful, soft-spoken new partner. In so many ways they were as different as night and day, but Gram and Emmylou immediately seemed like a matched set. And, as I found out later that evening, boy, they sure could sing. Watching the two of them, eyes closed, around a single microphone, gave me the overlapping sensations of being in church and gazing through the window of a lover's bedroom. *Love Hurts* they sang in crystalline harmony."

A radio show taped on Long Island at WLIR Hampstead was later released on vinyl in the early 1980s and resulted in a Grammy nomination for Gram Parsons and Emmylou Harris. In Boston on the final night of the tour, Barry Tashian joined in, taking his lead vocal on *Cry One Time*. Backstage, Boston poet Tom Brown handed Gram a poem, "Return of the Grievous Angel," which had been inspired by the band's performance. Parsons would fashion Brown's lyrics into the title song of his final album. To celebrate the end of the tour, Gram set off a fireworks display in a vacant lot outside the band bus. In the synchronicity of it all, Jock Bartley hooked up with Rick Roberts and the two went on to success together in Firefall, with ex-Byrds drummer Michael Clarke gigging out of Bartley's home stomping grounds in Colorado.

Back at home in Laurel Canyon, Gram's entourage was on the increase. Tony Bennett's son, Danny, a groupie hanging out on the fringe, later gushed to the press that "Gram was mesmeric. He'd play songs in the house and everybody would be enraptured, but then you'd see him later and he would be falling about. He was the sweetest guy, but he was torn up about his failed marriage. Gram was most at ease when Emmylou Harris was around. She just seemed to ground him."

Despite the fact that GP had spawned no hit singles and had sold few albums, Eddie Tickner was able to secure a contract for a second Gram Parsons album with the added perk of a budget that included a provision to have his hired gun studio band appear on a limited number of promotional concert shows.

The sessions for Gram Parsons' second album began in August 1973 at Wally Heider's Studio 4 and were completed at Capitol Records. Gram produced the sessions. He was now officially managed by Eddie Tickner and Jim Dickson's "Dickson-Tickner Productions," inheriting the original management team that had put the Byrds on the map in 1965. Expectations were high as the musicians arrived for the first session. Glen D Hardin, once-again hired as music director, had worked up charts and arrangements where necessary. Ex-Dillard banjo player, Herb

Pederson, a real technician when it came to nailing down harmony parts, replaced Barry Tashian.

Emmylou was well prepared, too, having worked on many of these songs with Gram while on tour. "We were really tight from working on the road together," Emmylou recalls. "We did a lot of singing in that time, a six-week tour of the entire country. We traveled in a bus and we did so much harmonizing in the back of that bus. A lot of the material for GRIEVOUS ANGEL was gotten together and perfected in motel rooms, in the back of that bus, and on the stages of places like the Smiling Dog Saloon in Cleveland, Ohio."

The song that had drawn so much attention during the Fallen Angels tour, *Love Hurts*, really is the centerpiece of this remarkable album. Their rendition of the song is the ultimate country rock example of what Emmylou has called "the 'high lonesome', the beautiful heartbreak harmony duets you hear in songs by the young Everly Brothers, Charlie and Ira Louvin, and Felice and Boudleaux Bryant." This sound "seeps through their work together like blood through a bandage," Brian Hilton remarks in his book *Country Roads: How Country Came To Nashville*. Emmylou later told Ben Fong-Torres that in her opinion "our singing came together on two songs, *Love Hurts* and *The Angels Rejoiced Last Night*. I finally learned what I was supposed to do." Reprise did not share her opinion on "Angels Rejoice" and chose not to include this song on the vinyl release.

Gram and Emmylou's *In My Hour Of Darkness*, with Linda Ronstadt lending a harmony to the vocal blend, is a darkly foreboding prediction nestled innocently enough in a supremely uplifting melody and gospel-flavored chorus. As Emmylou recounts the genesis of the song, "We didn't really write songs together. Gram always carried those songs around in his head. He just needed a little prodding to get them out. That's all I did. I helped him here and there. As far as our musical relationship goes, I was the energy source. I was always saying, 'Okay, let's do it!' And he was always the visionary and the real leader. So we really complemented each other because he needed my energy and I needed his direction. I really needed it. I was really very, very happy working with him. I didn't really dispute the credit on *In My Hour Of Darkness*, which he gave to me. ... Gram was in really good shape for that album."

The song has taken on biographical significance in the life and death of Gram Parsons. *In My Hour Of Darkness* apparently refers to the deaths of Gram's two good friends, Brandon de Wilde, who had died the previous July, and Clarence White, who died July 14, 1973, and perhaps the death of Gram's father.

The first verse of *In My Hour Of Darkness* chronicles de Wilde's fatal motorcycle accident on his way to Colorado where he was booked to appear in a dramatic role. During Gram's early years in New York and then in L.A., Brandon had been among his best friends.

> Once I knew a young man
> Went driving through the night
> Miles and miles without a word
> With just his high beam lights
> Who'd have ever thought they'd
> Build such a deadly Denver bend
> To be so strong, to take as long as
> It would till the end
>
> In my hour of darkness
> In my time of need
> Oh, Lord grant me vision
> Oh, Lord grant me speed
>
> — *In My Hour Of Darkness* (Gram Parsons, Emmylou Harris)

The second verse focuses on Clarence's White's death, hit by a drunk driver while crossing the street. A former bluegrass musician as a member of the Kentucky Colonels, White had developed into an electric guitar wizard playing with Nashville West, the Byrds, and other configurations. White and Gene Parsons had come up with the first "stringbender," a mechanical device installed in the body of White's Telecaster by Gene that allowed him to alter his "B" string and simulate pedal steel guitar sounds. Gene still builds and custom installs these Parsons/White string-benders in guitar pickers' instruments to this day. Fender has adopted the invention into a special model Telecaster.

Gram Parsons and Clarence White were pals, too, planning at the time to tour together as a country rock supergroup. Gram and Phil Kaufman attended Clarence White's funeral, where Gram broke into song with Bernie Leadon, inspiring grave-side mourners to join in singing the gospel standard *Farther Along*.

> Another young man safely strummed
> His silver stringed guitar
> And he played to people everywhere
> Some say he was a star
> But he was just a country boy
> His simple songs confess
> And the music he had in him
> So very few possess
>
> In my hour of darkness
> In my time of need
> Oh, Lord grant me vision
> Oh, Lord grant me speed

The third verse could be about his father's suicide, except the details are all wrong. During a visit with his stepfather in New Orleans earlier that summer, Gram and Gretchen had listened to Bob Parsons' confession that he had hastened Gram's mother's death. Gram was sent reeling by this drunken revelation. To many, this mysterious third verse now sounds like an account of Gram's own death, nine weeks after Clarence White's funeral.

> Then there was an old man
> Kind and wise with age

And he read me just like a book
And he never missed a page
And I loved him like my father
And I loved him like a friend
And I knew his time would come shortly
I did not know just when

In my hour of darkness
In my time of need
Oh, Lord grant me vision
Oh, Lord grant me speed

Gram's death has become one of the great legends of contemporary music history, an event he seemed to stage in cosmic American style. "I remember Gram talking to me about a pact he'd made with Phil after the funeral of Clarence White," Emmylou Harris told Lucy O'Brien, "that if one of them died, the other would take the body out to a place called Joshua Tree in the California desert. And, of course, shortly after that, Gram died. Phil kidnapped his coffin from the airport in L.A., and burned it in the desert. My first thought was I wished I could have been there, because I never got a chance to say goodbye to Gram. I respect Phil for doing what he did, it was an act of love and friendship."

"I think that what Phil did was wonderful," she told Daniel Cooper in 1996. "If I had the opportunity to get in that hearse and drive it, I would have been there, and I would have done it. But didn't. I don't have the flare for the dramatic that Phil has. I just sing. He does all the drama."

Gram Parsons apparently died of a drug overdose in Room 8 at the Joshua Tree Inn. Under directions from his stepfather, his remains were shipped to LA for a flight to New Orleans. Phil Kaufman had caught wind of Bob Parsons' plans to bury his friend's remains in Louisiana in order to inherit what few funds remained of the once-grand Snively family fortune. He set out to honor his pal's wish to be set free from the flesh in a fiery flash in the desert. Running on bravado, a case of Mickey's Big Mouth ale, and plenty of Jack Daniels, Kaufman and Michael Martin commandeered a hearse and drove up to a loading dock at the L.A. airport. They claimed the body from airline cargo handlers who were preparing to move it from a truck to a hangar. Kaufman had sussed out the situation, dummied up some fake paperwork beforehand, and told the airport officials that the family's plans had changed. He was there to collect Gram Parsons' casket. On the release documents, he signed his name "Bob Nobody."

Once they arrived at Cap Rock, Kaufman said his goodbyes. "I fooled around a bit," Kaufman comments in characteristic noir style. "Told him his dick was too small, told him he had failed his autopsy, all the sort of deranged shit you do when you are grieving. It was my stupid way of saying my goodbyes." He poured five gallons of gasoline over Parsons' remains. "Hi-test gas," Kaufman later kidded in interviews, because he didn't want his buddy "to ping." He lit a match and tossed it into the casket. Kaboom! "A huge pillar of flame … damned near took off my eyebrows and moustache," Phil exclaims. He raised a bottle and toasted his friend. "'That's it! You've got what you wanted, you bastard,' and, I swear, right then, a dust devil caught his ashes and lifted them into the desert sky. It was unreal. I stayed and watched his body burn. Stayed until there was nothing left but brass and bone." Kaufman and Martin were later charged with theft of a coffin, which Phil referred to as "Gram theft Parsons," and fined $750. As Elvis Costello later put it, "his exit was perfect." The singer's bones and ashes were claimed by Bob Parsons and buried in New Orleans, the inscription on his headstone, the title of Bernie Leadon's song, *God's Own Singer*.

At the time, the press tried to link the event to cult activities, citing Phil Kaufman's past associations with Charles Manson and the presence of the UFOlogy Center at Giant Rock Airport 20 miles south of Joshua Tree. Gram Parsons' death and disposition still fascinate the public. "It is one of the most deeply imbedded pieces of Joshua Tree folklore," any one of the National Park Service employees will tell you. "There's not a rock climber in the country who does not know that story." His life and legend have become the subject of several books, including Randall Riese's *Nashville Babylon: The Uncensored Truth and Private Lives of Country Music's Stars*, Pamela Des Barres' *Rock Bottom: Dark Moments in Music Babylon*, Sid Griffith's *A Musical Biography: Gram Parsons*, Ben Fong-Torres's *Hickory Wind: The Life & Times of Gram Parsons*, and John Einarson's *Desperados: The Roots of Country Rock*.

Later that fall, Pamela Des Barres was the first of thousands to make the pilgrimage to Joshua Tree Inn and Cap Rock. Des Barres spent the night in Room 8. Others, like alt country singer Victoria Williams, who camped near Cap Rock for a week during her first visit to the park, have preferred other cabins and motels. Emmylou Harris and her daughter are known to be among these pilgrims.

Emmylou recognized the seminal influence Gram Parsons has had on her life and the course of contemporary music. "I did feel that I had to carry the torch," she states. "It was incredibly important to me after wandering around aimlessly and then coming upon a style and a music that was bequeathed to me. Gram was my main musical influence. He really gave me the direction. He turned me on to the Louvin Brothers, Charlie Pride, George Jones, Merle Haggard, and Carl & Pearl Butler. When Gram died, I felt like I'd been amputated, like my life had just been whacked off. It was solid wall-to-wall emotion, day-to-day living. I never realized what kind of music was inside me until I met Gram. Then I knew exactly what I wanted to do and where I was going, but then he was gone."

In the liner notes for the Warner Reprise boxed set of her music, Emmylou commented, retrospectively, again on Gram's impact. "He's been tributised, analysed, villianized, idealized, and eulogized until the fact and fiction of his brief Faulknerian life blurs, threatening to overshadow the true legacy left behind." That legacy is the music Gram Parsons played in clubs, concert halls, recording studios, hotel rooms, band houses — wherever his gypsy quest took him, including the hallowed halls of Harvard, the Grand Ole Opry, Keith Richards' villa on the French Riviera, and Room 8 at the Joshua Tree Inn. Gram Parsons was a passionate advocate of soulful country music. As Barry Tashian commented to a reporter from *Rock N Reel*, "Gram never lost his appetite for music. That's what I loved in Gram. He carried a torch for this country music layered with soul." GRIEVOUS ANGEL was released in February 1974 to enduring acclaim by three succeeding generations of musicians.

During the last year of his life, Gram and Emmylou were always seen singing together, much as Cameron Crowe depicted them in his gritty 2000 feature film *Almost Famous*. In Crowe's movie, the actors playing Gram and Emmylou — a scruffy guy in a Nudie suit strumming a guitar and a raven-haired girl seated beside him on a bed in the Chateau Marmont — are seen only briefly by the protagonist as he passes by their doorway. They are singing. Gram and Emmylou are remembered that way — singing together — always.

Boulder to **B**irmingham

"Gram's death was like falling off a mountain," Emmylou Harris told Cameron Crowe during interviews conducted in 1975 to promote her first solo album. "It was a very hard year between his death and the making of my album. A year of throwing myself into a lot of work that my heart wasn't into." As she told Colin Escott over 20 years later, "It was like an explosion ... I was going 'round trying to pick up the pieces." On her album PIECES OF THE SKY she did exactly that, picking up where she had left off with Gram Parsons. "I really didn't have a choice," she said recently. "That music had become so important to me. And I didn't know how to do anything else. It was either that or go back to waiting tables. So I got a little band together in D.C., rehearsed in a garage in freezing weather, and went back to the places I had been as an acoustic act before I'd met Gram, as much to continue the learning process as just to survive."

"Back in DC," Emmylou recalls, "I couldn't go on and I felt like couldn't give it up. What I did was to plunge myself into work on a real anonymous level. I was in Washington. Nobody cared. I just got a band together and started doing the songs we'd done on stage. And I did it, and it wasn't a very inspired thing. It was like therapy. I didn't know how to mourn except to just throw myself back into that music. My way of grieving was to continue that music."

During her grieving days, Emmylou began writing a tribute to her fallen angel that she later told Holly George-Warren "just fell out of the sky. I didn't labor over it — it was kind of there." Bill Danoff helped her craft the lyrics and melody into the song we know today as *Boulder To Birmingham*. "It was written on my own except for the melody to the verses," she explains, "which I couldn't get. I took it to Bill, sang the chorus, showed him the rest of the lyrics, and he just took it from there. I was out in Los Angeles during the Topanga Canyon fire. It was right after Gram's death, and I was really undergoing some strange things. It was really kinda awful being out there. I felt really kinda lost. It's funny, sometimes people respond to a loss or a sadness by crying a lot but what happens to me is that I dry up inside and it becomes very painful. That's what I was going through and that fire didn't help. I felt like I was being burnt alive."

I don't want to hear a love song
I got on this airplane just to fly
And I know there's life below
But all that it can show me
Is the prairie and the sky

And I don't want to hear a sad story
Full of heartbreak and desire
The last time I felt like this
It was in the wilderness and the canyon was on fire
And I stood on the mountain in the night and watched it burn
I watched it burn, I watched it burn

I would rock my soul in the bosom of Abraham
I would hold my life in his saving grace
I would walk all the way from Boulder to Birmingham
If I thought I could see, I could see your face

— *Boulder To Birmingham* (Emmylou Harris, Bill Danoff)

While still a teenager, Emmylou had written to Pete Seeger, asking him if she could legitimately sing folk songs without having suffered significantly in her own life. Gram Parsons had given her all the heartache she needed to write *Boulder To Birmingham*. "I think it was my first song," she has commented, that "I really had something to write about." Writing this dirge helped her reach a tentative form of closure with her lost mentor, as she explains. "Gram showed me that you can bring all your influences together if you have a focal point. I got this point of departure that I didn't have before. With Gram's writing, he brought his own personal and generational poetry and vision into the very traditional format of country music, and he came up with something completely different. I was the audience he wanted to reach — I was his age group, growing up with rock 'n' roll and folk music. He really did bring the whole rock sensibility — not just the attitude and the lyrics, but the whole culture — into this other culture. He really had one foot in each culture, in a very real way. I sort of adopted those things."

During the period, Emmylou's new friends stepped forward to help out. Linda Ronstadt invited her to sing harmony on the Hank Williams' chestnut *I Can't Help It If I'm Still In Love With You*, one shining track on Linda's remarkable 1974 album HEART LIKE A WHEEL, produced by Peter Asher.

In assembling her new band, Emmylou first approached Barry Tashian, driving to Connecticut to visit Barry and his new wife, Holly. When Tashian declined, she was prepared to return to the West Coast, but John Starling advised her to put her band together in the Washington area, where she had her own connections. She followed this route, forming the Angel Band with Tom Guidera on bass and Danny Pendleton on pedal steel, rehearsing in a shed during the winter of 1973 with other local musicians, then securing a house gig at the Red Fox Inn in Bethesda. "We were playing six nights a week," she has recalled, "but the Red Fox was our regular bread and butter gig." At $50 per night, her backing musicians all had day-jobs.

One night, at an after-hours jam session, she met a young,

hotshot picker by the name of Ricky Skaggs. "It was sort of a ritual after a show at the Red Fox," she later told Colin Escott. "We would go play with the Seldom Scene at John Starling's house. Ricky was with the Country Gentlemen then, but one night he was over at John's house for one of those jam sessions. He was already a prodigy on the fiddle and guitar, and I always had it in my mind that I wanted to work with him."

Gram's old gang soon began to champion Emmylou. "Emmylou had gone to Washington and formed a band that wasn't very good," Phil Kaufman summarizes. "Then Eddie Tickner, Gram's manager, took her under his wing. Under his guidance, she got a record deal." As James Burton told Steve Fishell in 1984, "when Gram passed away, Tickner started managing Emmylou. He had the same plans for her that he had made for Gram."

Record executive Don Schmitzerle, a product marketing department head at Warner Brothers' Burbank offices, was a diehard fan of Emmylou's "angelic voice." His first instinct was to badger his label's East Coast A&R rep, Mary Martin, to pursue Emmylou for a recording contract. Warner Brothers and their associate labels were known for signing singer-songwriters like Joni Mitchell, Maria Muldaur, Randy Newman, Jackson Browne, Ry Cooder, and James Taylor. Emmylou Harris, Schmitzerle was convinced, shared the same appeal as this group of "integrity artists."

"Don just told me to get off my duff and go down and see her," Mary Martin commented. "What I saw was primarily this fragile singer with a strong voice. She was vulnerable … that's what I liked about Miss Emmy. There was this sweet girl at the Red Fox Inn on a Tuesday night and everybody drunk and asking for *Orange Blossom Special*. She said something unprintable. Everybody laughed. She could handle an audience. Emmy's just a wonderfully tactful, dedicated, passionate girl. She did have another song on her agenda." At a second Angel Band gig, Tickner cornered Martin in a backstage washroom and pitched a record deal. Martin then made what turned out to be a very timely move. She put Emmylou Harris together with Canadian producer Brian Ahern, Anne Murray's producer. With Ahern on board, Martin was convinced that she could get Tickner's artist a record deal. "The company wasn't crazy about her," Schmitzerle recalled, "but Mary Martin, our company's chief talent scout, and I were, and we finally got our ducks in a row."

Brian Ahern got his start in the music business in Halifax, Nova Scotia in the early 1960s, where he was a jack-of-all-trades. "I started making money playing folk music and electric guitar," he explained in a rare 1996 interview with *Mix* magazine's Rick Clark. "At one point, I actually had three bands going simultaneously. I was working at two different tv stations, CBC and CTV, and at the same time with these three bands and they didn't catch on." Adopting various disguises, he played pop on the tv show *Music Hop* wearing sunglasses, "because the lights annoyed me." He played Celtic jigs and reels on *The Nova Scotians*, where he was "not recognized without the sunglasses," and rock 'n' roll with the Bad Seeds, who had "a record deal in the 'States on Verve." The Bad Seeds didn't get much chart action with their single releases, but when Brian became the music director of *Singalong Jubilee*, he met an artist with the potential to become an international superstar, Anne Murray. "This was all in Halifax, Nova Scotia," he told Rick Clark. "Even though I had all the work I could handle in Halifax, I got bored. I moved to Toronto and starved for a while."

In Toronto, he lured Anne Murray into a studio to record a low budget album for Arc Records. Murray had intended to pursue a career as a gym teacher, but her decision to record with Ahern changed her focus. "I used that record to get her a deal at Capitol Records," he recalls, "where she stayed for 30 years." Anne Murray's career took off when her recording of Gene McClellan's *Snowbird* introduced her to American radio listeners. By 1974, Ahern and Murray had a lock on the Canadian Juno awards, regularly chocking up multiple wins as producer and artist, but the ever-alert producer was always on the lookout for new talent. Accepting Mary Martin's invitation to come hear Emmylou Harris in Maryland, he took along a tape machine, just in case he liked what he heard.

"Mary Martin used to work for Albert Grossman when he

managed Bob Dylan, and she had managed Leonard Cohen and Van Morrison," Ahern explained during an interview in *Mix*. "Mary is a woman of substance. If I had a record company, I'd hire her in a minute. Mary called me up in Toronto, and booked me a flight into Silver Springs, Maryland. We sat at a little table with a portable Uher cassette machine and recorded four sets of Emmylou Harris and her band at that time, at a place called the Red Fox Inn." Back in Toronto, he marveled at her voice on tape. Excited, he agreed to produce her, and plotted his strategy. He had a hunch that if he could pair his new discovery with someone similar to Gram Parsons for the harmony singing, she could easily make the transition to solo artist. He believed that Emmylou Harris had unbelievable potential to become a major star. "I knew if I worked really hard with her," he later confided to Daniel Cooper, "all sorts of things would materialize." His choice for a harmony singer was made easier when Emmylou flew to Toronto to listen to demo tapes, and, incidentally, add her sweet harmonies to a Bob Carpenter record Brian was putting the finishing touches on. Among the demo tapes that Ahern played for Harris was one that Anne Murray's bass player Skip Beckwith had brought back from Nashville, where he had crashed at Rodney Crowell's pad — a hive of songwriting activity.

Rodney Crowell and his sidekick Donivan Cowart were rubbing shoulders and swapping songs with Susanna and Guy Clark, Townes Van Zandt, Mickey Newbury, Billy Joe Shaver, and Richard Dobson, the regulars during songwriter nights at nearby Bishop's Pub. Crowell's acceptance into this crowd had come when he had played *Bluebird Wine* during a songwriter's night at the pub. After that, Rodney recalls that Guy Clark would say, "'Hey, Rodney, play *Bluebird Wine*.' So then I was in. I had a song that Guy would say 'play that'."

Crowell had placed his Guy-Clark-approved song at the beginning of the demo tape he sent north to Brian Ahern. After listening to several other tapes, Harris was growing restless. Then Brian pulled out a demo tape of a new writer that he had just received. "Brian popped the tape into the machine," Emmylou recalls, "and *Bluebird Wine* came on. There was something in Rodney's voice that I really liked. There was something about that song and that energy that I really liked. So we listened to *Song For The Life*, and I said, 'Now, there's somebody who has obviously listened to George Jones.'" Ahern tracked Crowell down in Houston and flew him up to Toronto. "My first production meetings with Emmylou Harris revealed how attached she was to the songs of Gram Parsons," he has recalled. "So I ended up buying Rodney Crowell's songwriting contract from Jerry Reed's company, Vector Music, and signed him to a new contract with my company, Tessa Publishing in Toronto, and flew him into Maryland to meet and write with Emmylou Harris. I had an album to make with her and I knew Emmy liked Gram Parsons songs and that I would need more material with poetry and depth. Rodney went on to join Emmy's Hot Band. That airline ticket launched his career. I still have the receipt in his old itinerary file."

Rodney met Emmylou at the home of John and Fayssoux Starling. "We sat up all night and played songs," Crowell recalled during his "Houston Kid" interview with Bill DeYoung. "We were both into all those brothers — the Everly Brothers, the Louvin Brothers, the Wilburn Brothers, John and Paul, all of those duet singing teams."

Emmylou remembers their meeting with equal fervor. "I felt that he was my soul mate, my artistic soul mate. We would sit there and bang away on the guitars, and he would jump in with the harmony. In the way that Gram would play me songs, and I would jump in on the harmony. Or then Rodney would sing the song and I would start harmonizing with him." Upon hearing Rodney's *'Til I Gain Control Again*, Emmylou knew instinctively that she had hit the "mother lode."

When the deal was sealed with Warner Brothers, Crowell was convinced to move to Los Angeles along with Emmylou and some of the musicians she had conscripted into her Angel Band. As he recalls, "Emmy came and played the Armadillo in Austin, and I sat in with her. And after the gig she said, 'I got a ticket for you to go to L.A. Do you wanna go? So, I moved to L.A. Just like that. *That night*. The next morning, I was gone." Arriving in the City of Angels, Rodney learned that plans were changing daily. As he recalls, "I didn't know what was going on. I just went. And when I got there, I learned that management was going to dissolve the Angel Band and form another band, which I was the first member of — this Hot Band thing."

The decision to go with an all-star lineup forced Emmylou to make a difficult decision, as she explains. "It left me with a terrible problem because at that time I had the Angel Band together. Besides being talented musicians, they were good friends. It was a hard decision, but I fired them."

"In the early days, Emmylou was like a deer. Just real full of earthy energy," Rodney Crowell told Alanna Nash. "And real sweet, real loyal, real trusting, and just full of innocence. But not stupid innocence. The kind of innocence that allows you to be open with everybody. At the same time, though, she was real intimidated by the hoopla of her success, and, as you say, a little bit insecure. Actually, it wasn't that she was insecure. She was just so sensitive. But she was really fun. And, of course, I had a crush on her. But that mellowed into a real deep friendship. She inspired a real loyalty in me."

Emmylou had initially felt uneasiness about working with Brian Ahern, known mainly for his productions with Anne Murray, a direction she had no desire to explore. His instinct to involve Rodney Crowell had been right on the money, and as she and Ahern continued to plot the course they would explore on her sessions, she realized that he had no intentions of cloning. "That was so serendipitous for me," she told Daniel Cooper, "from my original experience with Jubilee, and then hooking up with a producer who knew what he was doing, who knew that I didn't know what I was doing, and respected my instincts, and encouraged me to say what I felt, to say when I didn't feel comfortable — who really very gradually and carefully, without me realizing it, was bringing me out as a recording artist." As she later told Colin Escott, "the working relationship with Brian was good from day one. He knew you had to help the artist develop their confidence and personal style." Bernie Leadon later described Ahern during a *Goldmine* interview as "this real sort of stable-type, even-keeled Canadian guy."

There were also fringe benefits to be had, such as the time that Neil Young dropped over to the Enactron Truck Studio with the tracks for his song *Star Of Bethlehem* and Ahern recorded Emmylou singing a backing vocal for Neil. Contributing tracks to albums by Linda Ronstadt, Little Feat, and John Sebastian, Emmylou established a reputation in the L.A. recording studio scene, which provided Eddie Tickner with a convincing argument when he approached the elite musicians who had contributed to her previous sessions with Gram Parsons. James Burton, Glen D Hardin, Herb Pederson, and Ronnie Tutt signed up for the sessions. Neil Young's pedal steel player Ben Keith signed on. Bernie Leadon, a founding member of the Eagles, made a guest appearance. "I didn't know who I wanted to work with," Emmylou explains. "So I was just gravitating toward what I knew. I knew that Gram had given me that focus and direction, so I wanted everything associated with him as much as I could in that whole process. It was almost more for a talisman than for even musical reasons."

In October 1974, Brian Ahern hired a truck and driver to haul his 40-foot semi-trailer sized mobile studio to Los Angeles. In keeping with the serendipity of Emmylou's career, Ahern had just finished constructing his unique studio on wheels with the help of a Toronto architect. "At the time," he explains, "a typical mobile unit was a cluster of equipment strapped down and wired together in a box on wheels. I wanted to have a working environment, fixed and comfortable inside, but very portable. It had to have at least three rooms with sound-lock doors. In most trucks, the speakers are jammed into one end of the vehicle, and the other 30 feet are behind you. I mounted my gear sideways, so you could look in either direction and have a 40-foot sight line at all times. I lined it with lead, so that if we pulled up next to a radio station, power pole, or a lighting tower, RF would be minimized; although we tell clients we did it so we could mess with Lois Lane and Superman would never know." Brian Ahern's recording truck and custom gear was admired by musicians and technicians through-out the industry. Recording engineers in the truck could hear everything clearly in their monitors as they sat at the Neve con-sole, and they could see the main participants in the large living room via a closed circuit tv hook-up.

"We'd rented an old rundown estate in a private canyon in Beverly Hills," Ahern explained to Rick Clark, "pulled up outside this ranch-style house, and ran umbilical cables from the Truck into most rooms and the pool area. There was no linen, so the first night we were there, Linda Ronstadt and Emmy had to go out and buy us some bedding. They came back with Linda's MGB hatchback loaded for all us recording guys."

Brian also became the invisible member of the Hot Band, learning the songs from Emmylou and closeting himself away with his favorite J-50 guitar and letting the arrangements write themselves in his mind. "During the sessions," he adds, "I'd always have a station set up for myself in the studio so that if the band didn't get the tempo and the feel just right I could 'drive' the track with my guitar work. We recorded almost all of those tracks live. Sometimes we would have to repair or replace a lead vocal. And sometimes there'd be an acoustic guitar sound or feel that I had in my head that we couldn't get live, so we'd go into the Truck, find and situate the appropriate mics and play ahead or behind the beat in certain places to make the feel change with the lyrics. We used J-200s a lot. She'd play sometimes, and I'd play. I mostly used an AKG 224, which has two transducers. It articulates the complex mid-range of acoustic instruments."

Glen D Hardin, hired during pre-production, recalls that working with Emmylou was a 180 degree shift from working with the unprepared and unpredictable Gram. "She was real together, and she had really done her homework," Glen D told Cooper. "We'd sit down and go over songs, and time 'em, and, you know, talk about who's gonna play the instrumental. We had done a lot of homework by the time we sat down to record. And so it was really a breeze. It was well planned and well executed." Glen D was also impressed with the ease Brian Ahern staged the sessions.

"He was like Emmy. He was very well prepared. But even at that, even though we were well prepared, there was a lot of room to make changes, or kind of go with what was happening. It was a very, very easy situation. Although we had a real good intensity level when we worked. We'd work late at night. Till dawn, a lot of times. And we'd drink, and have a good time, and have the fireplace going while we recorded." They also added overdubs to a couple of tracks that had been cut back East and featured Ricky Skaggs on fiddle.

Multi-instrumentalist Bernie Leadon was struck by the Spartan layout of Ahern's Coldwater Canyon operation. "Brian lived in a back bedroom," Leadon told *Goldmine*, "and the rest of the house was all just living space, part of the time, and recording space part of the time. That's how they made the album. It was a constant … they might record at any hour of the day kind of thing."

Herb Pederson was booked to contribute harmony vocals. Pederson fit right in with the team, recognizing Ahern's role as camp director. "He was very particular about arrangements," the ex-Dillard told Bill DeYoung. "He was a very schooled musician from Canada, before he came down here. He did a lot of the rhythm guitar parts that are on there, and he didn't take any credit for them. He was careful of the arrangements, and the key choices, and the times. He didn't want it to be just another country chick singer. Emmylou was very definite about what she wanted to do, too. She was as much a part of that whole thing as he was."

The results that Brian and Emmylou got from those initial sessions, working with cream of the crop pickers like James Burton, Ben Keith, Herb Pederson, and Byron Berline, and a rock steady rhythm section of Glen D Hardin on piano, Ray Pohlman on bass, and Ronnie Tutt on drums set the standard for recording excellence for years to come. Years later, when Tony Brown became the head of MCA Nashville, he noted that "Brian Ahern's Emmylou Harris albums rank up at the top with the great country records that were done by Billy Sherrill and Owen Bradley. Brian's influence on how records are made in Nashville today is more prevalent than some would care to admit."

PIECES OF THE SKY was released on February 7, 1975, preceded by a lead single, Emmylou's rendition of Billy Sherrill's *Too Far Gone* which rose to number 73 on the country charts. The second single, Charlie and Ira Louvin's *If I Could Only Win Your Love*, rose to number 4 on the country charts and made some serious inroads on the pop charts. "Getting a Louvin Brothers song on the pop charts," Emmylou declared at the time, "that really made me feel I had done what I set out to do."

Bluebird Wine was selected to open the album, followed by *Too Far Gone, If I Could Only Win Your Love, Boulder To Birmingham,* and *Before Believing.* The album boasted what would become known as Emmylou Harris's eclectic mix of song selections, including a country treatment of John Lennon and Paul McCartney's *For No One,* which Emmylou had incorporated into her stage repertoire during her stint at Clydes and which was a favorite of Rodney Crowell's. The album's title was derived from the lyrics to Danny Flowers' *Beyond Believing.* The presence of Dolly Parton's *Coat Of Many Colors* and Merle Haggard's *The Bottle Let Me Down,* alongside Felice and Boudleaux Bryant's *Sleepless Nights,* provided a mix that kept critics guessing.

The gem on the 12-inch vinyl disc was *Boulder To Birmingham,* an album track eagerly played by the more eclectic FM deejays from Los Angeles to Alaska. This plaintive song reverberated throughout the audience Gram Parsons, Chris Hillman, and their Burrito brothers had built up, establishing Emmylou as an underground hero and "keeper of the flame."

Los Angeles Times music critic Robert Hilburn praised *Boulder To Birmingham,* citing it as "perhaps the best single piece of music I've heard so far this year." *Stereo Review* critic Noel Coppage wrote, "Emmylou's voice is smooth and it has good range, and a lovely tone that shimmers on the high notes, and she complements all this with a folk-singer's straight-forward phrasing. She puts across the too-rural-to-be-modern air of Dolly Parton's *Coat of Many Colors,* introduces her own *Boulder To Birmingham,* does well by Merle Haggard, the Louvin Brothers — you name it. Even a slow-as-molasses experiment with Lennon & McCartney's

For No One seems to work, profiting as it does from a wondrously economical and deeply felt electric guitar solo from Amos Garrett. James Burton plays with similar economy and fine style." Emmylou's tracks "simultaneously appeal to both country and FM rock audiences," a critic from *Music Retailer* noted. "Accompanied by the Hot Band on record and on stage, which includes the legendary James Burton, Emmylou Harris is capable of moving, highly spirited performances, which can be appreciated in any variety of musical contexts."

Looking back on this era, Daniel Cooper sees Emmylou Harris's debut release as a "quiet repudiation of the studio-slick commercialism overtaking the country rock scene. Not that it was intended or heard that way at the time. For really, in the summer of 1975, there was no way to know that listening to *Boulder To Birmingham* back-to-back with the Eagles' *One Of These Nights* on local FM radio was to hear a frontier skirmish in what would prove to be a 20-year battle for the soul of country radio." From this moment onward throughout her career, Emmylou Harris would be confronted with the "is it country, is it pop" mentality that emanated from Music Row. "Politically," Cooper points out, "the situation was somewhat complex. Emmylou had been signed by a Warner Brothers' New York rep to the label's Burbank office. Conspicuously out of the loop was Warner Brothers Nashville."

Fanning the flames of controversy, Bud Scoppa in *Rolling Stone* declared that "PIECES OF THE SKY is more country than Nashville." Scoppa cited Gram Parsons as "the only true innovator" of country rock, which left out a lot of worthy contributors, most notably Roger McGuinn, Chris Hillman, Sneaky Pete Kleinow, and Chris Ethridge, all consigned to supporting roles in his review. "When the Byrds recorded SWEETHEART OF THE RODEO in 1968," Scoppa continued, "the romance between country and pop was still secret. Now seven years later both country and country-influenced pop are all but mainstream. But 'Sweetheart' itself still seems distinct from the clichéd and shallow music it helped inspire." Emmylou Harris "bypassed Nashville altogether," Scoppa argued, "preferring to work clubs with her band in her present home area, Washington D.C., and to record in Los Angeles with many of the same musicians Parsons used. Nashville has very little to do with the music on PIECES IN THE SKY." As Scoppa concluded, "Harris's exceptional musical and personal appeal should be sufficient to put her in touch with a good many non-country listeners." This certainly proved to be true.

Years later *Goldmine* critic Bill DeYoung summarized the achievement of this album. "The playing on PIECES OF THE SKY was clean and economical, the arrangements tastefully layered, with fiddles and mandolins at every turn. Harris's angelic soprano had taken on the razor's edge of ache and sorrow, what bluegrass musicians called the high lonesome sound. Despite the steel guitars and other embellishments of tradition, PIECES OF THE SKY was more pop than country. But it wasn't rock 'n' roll, either. It had little to do with the Eagles squeaky-clean country rock, which was all the rage at the time, or Linda Ronstadt's sheeny pop country." For DeYoung, although "the album had elements of folk, rock 'n' roll and very traditional country, at the center was Harris's fragile, gossamer voice, breaking from the heartache of *Boulder To Birmingham* and cracking honky tonk wise on Shel Silverstein's *Queen of the Silver Dollar.*"

The album sold well in both country and pop markets, reaching number 7 on the country albums chart, and number 45 on *Billboard* magazine's Hot 200 albums chart. This pleased Emmylou, as she confessed in *Crawdaddy* in May 1975. "I'm just plumb tickled. I feel there is a lot of good country music involved. It's real basic. It's what we were trying for, and I think we succeeded. I can't foresee what's going to happen, but I'm going to continue to do the same kind of material in my show. I think it's fairly representative of myself."

Years later, Emmylou would tell Cecilia Tichi that "what I've always tried to do is blend the real hot electric country music with the real traditional mandolins and fiddles that fill in that mountain and bluegrass side . . . I include folk music and different kinds of ethnic music: bluegrass, mountain, even Cajun and Celtic, because that's where country music comes from." And as she later told a reporter from the *Pittsburgh Post Gazette*, "In the beginning it was really important for me to make people aware of the rich traditions of country music, but not to copy them. So many of my peers disdained country music, threw the baby out with the bath water. They called it reactionary and couldn't see the beauty of it. I wanted to make them aware of it."

In years to come, Emmylou Harris & the Hot Band would play to packed houses and delirious audiences who discovered the beauty of country music in her songs. They would perform not just in the "better hippie honky tonks of the nation" but in the best theater, auditorium, and stadium venues. Emmylou Harris would appear on network tv shows broadcast from New York, L.A., and Austin, Texas. She would become an international star, playing Wembley Stadium in London and trekking across the Continent, carrying the spirit of the honky tonk with her.

The **H**ot Band

In March 1975, Emmylou Harris rehearsed with the other members of her new road band in the familiar quarters of Brian Ahern's Beverly Hills living room. Brian's decision to select studio musicians for Emmylou's recording sessions who would also tour the album was a stroke of genius. "At that time," Ahern explains, "most artists did not record with their bands. I thought this was a waste of energy. Here bands did all the rehearsing and bonding on stage, and went through the exhaustion and the work, only to be dismantled and to watch someone assemble some studio musicians to try to get that natural 'band feeling' back. I thought why not just spend more on a better road band, and then when you finish your tour, you can record with them." Paying these top notch sidemen was an issue, but Warner Brothers agreed to shell out the cash, billing their artist, of course, which would eventually run Emmylou Harris into debt to the tune of half a million dollars, charged against her royalties. "Gram told Emmylou to pay for the best," Phil Kaufman notes, "and she's never forgot it."

James Burton, Glen D Hardin, and Emory Gordy Jr. were playing shows with Elvis at the time, but Eddie Ticknor was able to juggle schedules so that they became charter members of the touring Hot Band. As Emmylou recalls, "We thought, 'Well, they probably won't go out with us, but let's ask 'em. If the record company is really willing to front the money for it. And they were. We got Emory, and we got James, and we got Glen D, and we needed a drummer because I think Ronnie Tutt wasn't available. So we found John Ware." A veteran of Michael Nesmith's First National Band, Ware would stick around for a decade. Rodney Crowell took on a key role, handling the harmony parts that Emmylou had sung with Herb Pederson on the record. "It's interesting that everybody focuses on the Hot Band, and the hot players, and rightly so," Emmylou told Bill DeYoung. "Everybody in the band was so important. But Rodney brought something special to the band — I think he became the spirit and the personality. He had such a wonderful, open, playful quality about him, and yet he was so talented as a songwriter. Everything just fell into place, and somehow it was real pivotal around Rodney."

Pedal steel player Hank DeVito came aboard courtesy of Linda Ronstadt, replacing session man Ben Keith. Bernie Leadon remembers that "before that album was released, Emmylou did a little show at UCLA Royce Hall. She opened for the Earl Scruggs Revue, which was really cool. Emmy's band was just me and Herb Pedersen and her. So we did it all acoustic, and three-part harmonies."

When James Burton drove down from Vegas with his bandmates, the full Hot Band rehearsed for a day at Brian Ahern's place, celebrated Emmylou's 28th birthday with a party at a Mexican restaurant, and headed to San Francisco for three nights at the Boarding House. Their L.A. debut came a few days later at the Palamino Club, North Hollywood's equivalent of the Troubadour. The cramped quarters and muddy sound system were familiar to Emmylou, the former folkie, but a far cry from the challenging roar of the crowd she would soon hear when she opened for Elton John before 60,000 screaming fans in Dodger Stadium. The Palamino was packed by the time Emmylou Harris and the Hot Band hit the stage. Among the notables in the audience, mentioned by Cameron Crowe in his *Rolling Stone* feature story "Long Hard Road," were Bonnie Raitt, Linda Ronstadt, and

Maria Muldaur. The show went over well with the club audience and drew rave reviews.

Some of the people in the Palamino that first night in Los Angeles had surely come to hear the wizardry of Elvis' lead guitar player, James Burton. "James Burton is a poet," Emmylou told *Guitar Player* magazine. "He plays things on that guitar that are so simple, and there is nobody to compare to him." As she recalls, "the first year I played with James Burton, I was so much in awe that a lot of the times I looked on the Hot Band as a vehicle to put the spotlight on James to say, 'Hey, everybody, I hope you realize who you are getting to hear.'" Jimmy Page is said to have carried a picture of Burton in his wallet. Chet Atkins was an admirer. George Harrison, another. As Steve Fishell notes in *Guitar Player*, PIECES OF THE SKY "features some of Burton's most profoundly lyrical playing on songs such as *Boulder To Birmingham* and *Too Far Gone*. The subsequent live dates, driven by James' hot-rod Tele, were nothing short of blazing."

As she launched the tour, Emmylou's domestic life became more challenging. When she had moved with her four-year-old daughter Hallie to L.A. to record PIECES OF THE SKY, she had rented a house in Hermosa Beach, but had never really settled in, furnishing it with little more than beds and linen, because it seemed like she was either in the studio or on the road. At first, Hallie tagged along, living the gypsy life her mother had experienced as an army brat in the 1950s and early '60s. "Hallie's taken to my nomadic lifestyle very well. I couldn't have done it without her cooperation," Emmylou told curious interviewers at the time. "I hate housework. I can get by in the woods with an iron skillet and cornmeal, but I'm lost in a modern kitchen." As her mother's touring grew more hectic, Hallie spent more and more time with her grandparents on the East Coast.

Journalists were struck by Emmylou's beauty. "Photographs don't do Emmylou Harris justice," Edith Carl wrote. "She is lovely, with wide-set eyes, a slightly retrousse nose, a finely sculptured mouth. Her hair, touched with silver, falls around her face, giving her a modern madonna look." They also found her humility refreshing she when referred to herself as merely a "collector of songs." She was also somewhat unconventional — at least in country music circles. On July 4, 1975, Emmylou stepped onto a festival stage in the Berkshires not in the "customary on stage garb" with her "trademark fringed top and tight blue jeans tucked into high suede boots," but in a "printed pink dress, ankle socks, and white sneakers." To a puzzled Edith Carl, Emmylou "looked like a teenager performing at a high school rally."

When asked if she intended to marry soon, Emmylou responded with characteristic reticence. "I need more time to learn what and who is right for me. Who wants to be 45 and still be on the road? I've lived for a long time on $75 a week, and if this doesn't last, I've had a great time. . . . You have to understand that the last two years of my life have been like 20 years squeezed into two," she told *The New York News*. "There really have been an incredible lot of things happening, good and bad. A lot of growing up and a lot of changing."

Emmylou was being somewhat coy, for she had already fallen in love with Brian Ahern. With Hallie, she moved into his Coldwater Canyon house, forming a family unit with Brian and his eight-year-old daughter, Shannon Ahern. "My relationship with Brian is different from the kind of relationship I've ever had with anyone else," she would later tell Kip Kirby. "There was no question in our minds almost from the very beginning whether we would marry because we were just so suited to each other. It was simply a question of finding the time and the circumstances." That moment did not arrive until January 9, 1977, with Emmylou and Brian exchanging marriage vows in Nova Scotia during a simple ceremony with only family invited, far from the scrutinizing eyes of the media. Ironically, Emmylou had sung Charlie and Ira Louvin's *If I Could Only Win Your Love* to Brian during the pre-production of their first album project together.

"Brian's very calm, very strong," she told Kip Kirby. "People who don't know him well are a bit taken aback by him. I think he can be very awesome and quiet. 'Cerebral' is probably a good word to describe Brian. But you know, actually he has the most wonderful sense of humor." Kirby also noted that "those closest to the couple echo the opinion that their relationship is unusually deep and devoted. There is, they tell you earnestly, a spiritual bond and unspoken communication that flows like a river between Emmylou and Brian."

"Brian has allowed me to grow as an artist in a way I never thought I could," Emmylou told *High Fidelity*. "He thinks I'm a great rhythm guitar player. He uses me on sessions! He knows there's a lot more to making hit records than just hitting every note at the right time. I trust his judgement implicitly. Brian really listens to what I have to say and trusts certain of my instincts. We enjoy the time we spend together in the studio. Maybe it's an oversimplification, but I believe it all comes down to trust, not only as producer and artist, but as husband and wife."

Emmylou and Brian extended their family bonds beyond their daughters to include the Hot Band, a sentiment Emmylou has felt for her band members throughout her career. As she once told *Oregon Statesman* reporter Bruce Pollock, "there's so much camaraderie among musicians. It's not hype at all. You talk a language and have experiences that nobody else can understand. I've been opening shows for Willie Nelson for so long that I feel like one of his family." Another time she told Ira Kaplan that "it sounds corny, but it becomes sort of a family. I've been lucky. The people I've worked with from day one have been super-professional, people with lots of humor — we really have a good time. We enjoy each other's company. I love it. I mean, I can have insomnia all night long, but as soon as I hit the bus — my little bunk — I go right to sleep."

In the summer of 1975, Emmylou Harris & the Hot Band found themselves playing large auditorium shows, opening at times for pop star James Taylor, at other times for Merle Haggard & the Strangers. While their appeal to Taylor's audience was simple, reaching the Hag's following was another matter. They opened their act with Haggard's own *The Bottle Let Me Down*, and "after that," Mary Martin told Daniel Cooper, "the crowd was hers." For Rodney Crowell, this situation "was a little strange. I think Merle dug Emmy, but it was, like, when we first came around, first started playing with the Hot Band, we played *loud*, you know. We were, like, a rock & roll band. Merle had a quieter situation. And I think that Merle was a little ticked because here was James and Glen D — guys that played on his records — out on stage with Emmy."

Often overshadowed by James Burton and sometimes dismissed as a surrogate Gram Parsons, Rodney Crowell was Emmylou's confidante and star performer. "I found myself center stage because of fate and circumstances," Emmylou told Bill DeYoung, "but I always felt that I was sharing the stage with Rodney. And the whole rest of the band. I always thought of myself as a member of that band. Being a harmony singer was such an integral part of what my real musical education was about." She later told Holly George-Warren that Crowell was "like the kid brother than I never had. I consider him my musical soul mate, in a way. He brought all those great songs, and we loved singing together."

"It wasn't my level as a musician, or even a singer, that earned me that place," Rodney Crowell confided to Bill DeYoung. "I think my songwriting certainly earned me a place there, but I think that I was an extension of Emmylou's creativity at that time. So, I collaborated with her on songs, and just on, 'this is what it is'. This is what's cool about this music. So it was a good place to be." Rodney continues, "When I was workin' with her on the road, it was the most important thing in the world to make sure that this thing happened for her. And she was really generous with her experience and her time with me. I would have to say I owe one of my biggest debts of gratitude to Emmylou for taking me around with her, and letting me gather up a lot of experience for myself while she was forging her own career. She let me get in touch with my talents. A lot of people wouldn't have done that."

Their collaboration produced the songs *Amarillo*, which Emmylou had begun with Tom Guidera, and *Tulsa Queen*. She also recorded Rodney's *'Til I Gain Control Again, You're Supposed To Be Feeling Good, Ain't Livin' Long Like This*, and *Leaving*

Louisiana In The Broad Daylight. Later, when he had left the band, she would tell interviewers that she felt "lucky to have him all to myself for a couple of years." Like "a kid in a candy store," she could pick and choose from his backlog of well-worked songs as well as new tunes that he would play her out of sheer enthusiasm.

Amid the heady rush of the tour, Emmylou awaited public response to her debut album. "I was pretty nervous about it," she later admitted. "I didn't think anybody was gonna 'get' the record." She was on AM country stations with *Too Far Gone* and on FM stations with *Boulder To Birmingham*, but when the moment first came that she heard she was charting, she could hardly believe her ears. When a label rep called her on the road and told her that she was on the pop charts at number 120, she was bowled over. "I said, 'What?'" she recalls. "I mean, never in a million years. 120, that was okay, just to be on a pop chart. To be on any chart. I couldn't believe it." When her second single, *If I Could Only Win Your Love*, rose into the Top 5 on the country chart and the Top 60 on the pop charts, she got her first reality check. As she recalls, "It was like night and day. It was, like, all of a sudden I went from just this person that had a private life that nobody really knew who you were to being this other person."

When she was on the road, Emmylou missed the protective presence of Phil Kaufman. After torching Gram Parsons' body at Cap Rock, Kaufman had left L.A. "I got out of the music business for a while," he explains, "came to England with my 4-year-old son, and worked for Harley Davidson. In 1975 I saw Emmylou when she came to England, playing a concert with the Hot Band at the Hammersmith Odeon." That brief 1975 European tour awakened a fan base in England and Holland that would build over the years. When Kaufman returned to California a few months later, his friend in Coldwater Canyon gave him a call. Emmylou "asked if I'd be her road manager again. I said, 'Yeah, boy, you know it.' I've road-managed her on and off for 25 years. We're pals. With her, I've been through three marriages and several different hair shades." As Emmylou recalls, "It was great to have him back. We didn't miss a step. He comes off like the clown with the jokes and wisecracks, but he uses that in doing a good job. I feel very safe knowing Phil is running things."

During a whirlwind visit to Nashville, where she appeared on the Opry during the taping of the radio show's 50th anniversary special, Emmylou Harris found herself judging a talent contest at the Exit / In before performing a showcase set. Five years later, *Country Music* magazine's Kip Kirby reminded Emmylou of that "Queen of the Silver Dollar" talent contest. "The thing that really got me was I'd picked out a winner," she laughed. "It was a guy dressed up in drag! — and they overruled me. I thought if you were gonna do something like that, anyway, it might as well be *funny*, and someone told me Shel Silverstein originally wrote the song about a *guy*. But Brian was with me and we eventually ended up having a good time that night, as I remember. One time, Lowell George and I were exchanging what we called our 'little horror stories' about that kind of thing. And he said that *he* had to go around to radio stations dressed up in a *chicken suit* to promote Little Feat's DIXIE CHICKEN. I don't know if it was true, but it made me feel a lot better myself. All in the same trip I met Dolly, and sat in and played with George Jones at his club, downtown, and then went back to my hotel room and threw up from all the excitement."

Emmylou was invited to sing a harmony vocal on Guy Clark's debut album, OLD NO. I. The invitation to record on Clark's early album sessions was facilitated by Rodney Crowell's long-time friendship with both Clark and producer Neil Wilburn. Emmylou made many new Nashville friends that day, including Guy's wife Susanna and one impressionable young musician by the name of Steve Earle. "The first time I met Emmylou," Steve recalls, "she came in to sing on Guy Clark's first album. She gave me half of her cheeseburger. I wasn't the same for weeks." A year later, Emmylou and Brian were both featured on Guy Clark's second album, TEXAS COOKING, Ahern on guitar and Harris on harmony vocals.

Other Nashville cats caught on, too. Chuck Flood, a Warner Nashville friend of Mary Martin, went beyond the call of duty to plug Emmylou's singles to country radio deejays. Warner also hired NFL football stars to woo deejay support for Harris. Being invited to rub shoulders with the likes of the Dallas Cowboy Ray Toomay or Oakland Raider David "the ghost" Casper was motivation enough for deejays to spin Emmylou's early 45 rpm singles. Publisher and songwriter Frank Dycus, who was managing Porter Wagoner's recording studio at the time, sent Dolly Parton's demo tape of *Coat Of Many Colors* to Emmylou, which she would record on her next album. Bill Ivey at the Country Music Foundation sent Emmylou songs from the Louvin Brothers' back pages.

On July 28, 1975, Emmylou entered Nashville's Quadraphonic Sound studio, invited to a recording session with her hero, Bob Dylan. Typical of the way Dylan has approached his recording career, taking on new musicians for each new album in the effort to reinvent himself, he had just assembled his band to record DESIRE. While playing at the Bitter End in Greenwich Village, Dylan had met drummer Howie Wyeth, bass player Rob Stoner, singer-songwriter Steve Soles, and Village veteran Bob Neuwirth. Together, they would form the core of the Rolling Thunder Review that would soon set out on a gypsy journey with Joan Baez, Roger McGuinn, Ramblin' Jack Elliott, Mick Ronson, and many others. At the session on July 28, Wyeth and Stoner met Scarlett Rivera, a young fiddle player Dylan had discovered busking on Bleeker Street in New York City, percussionist Sheena, and Emmylou Harris.

Bob Dylan had stopped Emmylou in her tracks long before she met him in the flesh. "He really fired me up as a teenager," she recalls, "and pulled me into the possibility of poetry in lyrics, his intensity. I think Dylan represented that pivotal point when I first got into music. His records can bring me to tears. I think he should get the Pulitzer Prize for literature, and someday he will. All of us children of the '60s feel something very special for Bob Dylan. It's not only musical, nor is it really political. He just somehow opened doors and made us aware of other possibilities."

Her music-business friends encouraged Dylan to invite her to these sessions for DESIRE. "Dylan just wanted a girl to sing," she recalled during a BBC radio interview, "and he asked Don DeVito if he knew of anyone. And Don said, 'Well, there's this girl, Emmylou Harris.' I thought he wanted me to sing on a country song, but it turned out he must wanted me to sing, period." As she later admitted, "I was a little nervous about meeting Dylan. I think it would have been completely different if we'd have met before in a social situation. As it was, I just walked into the sessions and shook hands with him and started working." But she soon learned that singing with Bob Dylan was a lot like singing with Gram Parsons. "His phrasing changes a lot," she recalls, "but Gram did that a lot, too. Gram and I had the same feel for phrasing, but I still watched him all the time, so I did the same thing with Dylan. That's where all that humming comes from. You can hear me humming on some of those tracks. I didn't know they were going to use that."

Dylan worked quickly, tossing her songs with little or no preparation and going for feel and emotion rather than perfection. He was more interested in her response than in planning perfect thirds and fifths in the harmonies she and Rob Stoner were coming up with. "I didn't give much conscious thought to what I was doing," she told *Rolling Stone*, "because it all happened so fast and he's really a dramatist in his singing, and I didn't think of myself as doing anything else than just singing with him, and trying to follow him. I *am* real familiar with the way Dylan sings. I get familiar with the way people sing, and the way people pronounce words and syllables is so important to me — even more important than the parts. It's a matter of that *feel*."

Three songs were recorded that first day in the studio. *Romance in Durango* and *Abandoned Love* appeared on the album, while an out-take of *Golden Loom* later surfaced on Dylan's BOOT-LEG SERIES 1-3. On July 30, *Isis, One More Cup Of Coffee (Valley Below), Joey, Mozambique, Hurricane, Oh, Sister, Black Diamond Bay,* and *Rita Mae* were recorded during a remarkably productive session that is said to have gone until five or six in the morning. Emmylou marvels at how intense this recording experience was. Dylan was "very energetic," she explains. "We'd do several feels on one song. You know, bam, bam, bam. Very intense working all the time, but laid back at the same time. It was different. But I had to work very hard because I'd never heard the songs before, and they were pretty much one takes."

Emmylou's harmonies would shine in the final mixes of five tracks, drawing praise from critics for her efforts on both *Mozambique* and *Oh Sister*. DESIRE was released in early 1976, preceded by a single, *Hurricane b/w Rita Mae*, featuring Emmy on the B-side. The recording sold a million records and was listed as the number one album for 1976. DESIRE liner notes author and "Co-director of the Jack Kerouac School Of Disembodied Poetics," Allen Ginsberg, declared that the poet laureate of the Woodstock generation had recreated himself.

On New Year's Eve 1975, Emmylou first heard *Romance In Durango* on her car radio while driving to the home of John and Fayssoux Starling. She turned it up. She couldn't believe it. She parked in the driveway and ran back to John's car, which had just pulled in behind her. "I'm on the radio! I'm on the radio with Bob Dylan!" she screeched. "I couldn't believe it," she recalled later. "I liked *Romance In Durango*, but my god — there I was singing with Bob Dylan — and the song was in Spanish. I was always bad in languages at school, and the first record he gives me is in Spanish." She had thought her tracks were off pitch and had even asked Dylan if she could "come in and fix my parts." When she walked away from the sessions, she recalls, "I really didn't think he'd use any of it." But there she was, day after day, on the radio with Dylan, as stations played more tracks from DESIRE. "Sometimes I cringed," she has admitted, "when there were a few notes that I thought I could have hit a little better. But that's just me being microscopic. Believe me, it was all live. No overdubs. First takes. The very first time I'd sung *One More Cup Of Coffee* it was recorded. Lyrically, it's my favorite Dylan album."

The opportunities to play with other celebrated artists kept on coming. On September 9, 1975, a summit meeting between three of the hottest acts in the country music business took place at the end of a narrow residential street, just off Coldwater Canyon

Drive, where civilization ended and gave way to forested hillsides. Here Emmylou Harris and Linda Ronstadt met with their favorite singer, Dolly Parton, for the first time. Linda and Emmylou had sung together on several occasions, most notably on the Hank Williams song *I Can't Help It (If I'm Still In Love With You)* that garnered a Grammy Award for Linda. People had begun to call them the Everly Sisters. Now they would add the voice of Dolly Parton to create three-part harmony on a planned album project, to be produced by Brian Ahern. The three women began to call themselves the Queenston Trio.

Brian Ahern's Happy Sack Productions partner Bob Hunka met Dolly at LAX. "Emmy had met Dolly the previous month," Hunka recalls. "So she decided to cook dinner for all of them; chili, I think." After dinner, Emmylou pulled out her guitar. "We started harmonizing," Linda told *USA Today*. "We went 'Wow, we ought to record this." Hunka remembers that the first song they sang together that night was *Light In The Stable*, which later appeared on Emmylou's Christmas album of the same name.

The much-anticipated album never materialized for reasons Linda did not reveal until 20 years later. "I think we had pretty much a whole record," Ronstadt explained in a 1996 *Goldmine* interview, but "there were some real problems there. I think Brian is an excellent producer. I don't think he was really on track with that album. . . . It was actually a difficult thing for Emmylou to be married to the producer," Linda speculated, "because there were times when she didn't agree with him, and I think she felt she had to agree with him. And things would get farther than they needed to. I think that really hurt Brian, and Emmy, and for all of us that was an aborted production. But it was mine and Dolly's decision, on the phone, to stop it. We didn't feel the record was worthy of what we wanted to have. *Mister Sandman* was one of the problems. We didn't sing it in tune. It wasn't a good version of it. I thought the version she did that was all hers was dramatically, infinitely, better."

Dolly has confirmed Linda's assessment. "The big part of it," Dolly said, "was that we didn't have time to do it properly. It put so much pressure on us, it scared us to death."

Dolly PARTON · Linda RONSTADT · Emmylou HARRIS

Trio

Emmylou harris   Linda ronstadt   Dolly parton

Trio II Two

All three women eventually utilized the tracks they had recorded as the 'Queenston Trio' on their own albums. Dolly's harmonies on Linda's *I Never Will Marry*, Linda's harmonies on Emmylou's *When I Stop Dreaming*, and Linda and Dolly's harmonies on Emmylou's *Even Cowgirls Get The Blues* showed so much promise that country fans wished and hoped they would hear more. However, fans who attended Dolly's September 1979 concert in Los Angeles would be the last audience to hear all three perform together that decade. Linda went on to star in Gilbert & Sullivan's *Pirates Of Penzance* on Broadway. Dolly built Dollywood, made it in Hollywood, and released some very lushly produced pop records. Emmylou Harris continued to release country records. They remained friends, often adding harmonies to one another's solo recordings.

Despite Linda's reservations about Brian Ahern, Emmylou thought otherwise. "I was very lucky to do all of those records with Brian," she reflected years later *in Mix*, "because I learned to be completely relaxed and open to the recording process, I really feel that I became a recording artist during that time. Brian tends to have a lot of faith in the intrinsic instincts of an artist. It is because of this sympathy that he attempts to make the artist blossom intact, rather than trying to fit the artist into his particular sound."

Blossom she did on ELITE HOTEL, her next album, which featured her first number one country hit, a fresh version of Buck Owens' *Together Again*. "I was just off in my own little world, singing my songs," Harris later confided to Daniel Cooper. "But the first thing I knew, I had a number one country single, and Nashville just couldn't do enough for me."

Don Schmitzerle had taken a lot of flak at Warner Brothers for the cost overruns in recording PIECES OF THE SKY. Finals costs were $70,000 on what was projected to be no more than $10,000. This problem was mitigated when Brian Ahern revealed that he had recorded far more tracks than would be needed for one album. "There was stuff in the can after that album because we over-recorded," Ahern later told *Mix*. "I felt that if we could skip the lame first album and jump to album number two, so to speak, the music would be better and the record company and the artist would save lots of time and money. So, in a sense, her first album was a second album. Once the record company realized what a good idea it was, we always had about 20 songs going. When we had enough ideas to justify a session, we would do it. And then when it came time for an album, we would pull out a group of songs that seemed to fit together." ELITE HOTEL was released 10 months after PIECES OF THE SKY.

The B-side of *Together Again* was a stunning country adaptation of the Beatles *Here, There, And Everywhere*, recorded in the bluegrass tradition without the use of drums or percussion. The track was gently anchored by the finger-picked acoustic guitars of Brian Ahern and Herb Pederson, nestled in a string arrangement created by Nick DeCaro. The color was provided by ex-Speckled Bird Amos Garrett, a Canadian who also played lead guitar on Maria Muldaur's signature tune, *Midnight At The Oasis*, and by Willie Nelson's 'harmonicat' pal, Mickey Raphael. Garrett and Raphael's sparse but sweet contributions were glued to the track by Hank DeVito's shimmering steel. Emmylou's vocal was heartfelt, sweetened by harmonies here and there from Fayssoux Starling and Dianne Brooks. This B-side would hit number 65 on the *Billboard* pop chart.

ELITE HOTEL solidified Emmylou's signature sound, which everybody now identified as this "voice" and this "hot" band. James Burton again stood out. As Steve Fishell notes, the album "captured the full spirit of the band, mixing live cuts with studio tracks. Burton's melodic genius is captured throughout. The album highlights compositions by Rodney Crowell, Buck Owens, Hank Williams, and Gram Parsons' *Ooh Las Vegas* with its exploding guitar support." Fishell describes Burton's intro as "rapid-fire staccato, a riff that had guitar players from Florida to Alaska scrambling to emulate his efforts." "I always wanted to play banjo," Burton told Fishell. "I just love doing stuff like that. I feel good when I play something that I'm excited about. I used the same thing on Gram's version of the tune." Fishell joined the Hot Band several years later.

Emmylou's "brought forward" version of Don Gibson's *Sweet Dreams*, her second number one country hit, reminded most fans of the late Patsy Cline, but was closer to Gibson's original version. Her remake of Peanut Montgomery's *One Of These Days*, a single for George Jones in the '60s, hit the number 3 spot on the country charts. It was Emmylou's mother's favorite song.

Once again the Hot Band was true to name on stage. *Washington Post* critic Alex Ward noted that "songs like *Ooh Las Vegas*, *Feelin' Single, Seein' Double*, and even Hank Williams' dusty but serviceable, *Jambalaya*, take on a vibrancy and a spirit when Harris sings them on stage that they don't have on vinyl. Harris's backup group, the Hot Band, more than lives up to its name."

Although James Burton left the Hot Band at the end of the year, he continued to record at Brian Ahern's living room studio on Emmylou Harris sessions, as well as a number of outside projects Ahern produced for other artists, including Rodney Crowell's debut solo album and albums by Jonathon Edwards, Mary Kay Place, and Jesse Winchester. Burton told Fishell that for Winchester's *Nothing But A Breeze* "Brian wanted me to play a bottleneck on my Tele, but it's hard to do because of the arch in the round neck. I didn't have a dobro bar with me, so I asked around and somebody there had a Zippo lighter. I laid the Tele on my lap like a dobro, and played the solo with the Zippo for a slide. It was pretty neat." Burton's favorite studio guitar was still his trademark pink paisley Telecaster that a pal had hot-rodded for him. "The front pickup is stock, but the back pickup is a dual winding that Red Rhodes did for me. I was just looking for a boost, but not necessarily a change in the sound of the guitar." Emmylou contributed backing vocals to Winchester's *Nothing But A Breeze*, and no doubt witnessed Burton's Zippo solo.

Mary Kay Place, co-star of the cult soap *Mary Hartman, Mary Hartman*, in which she portrayed wannabe C&W singer Loretta Haggers, a character modeled on Dolly Parton's public persona, chose Brian Ahern's Enactron Truck Studio to record TONITE! AT THE CAPRI LOUNGE, LORETTA HAGGERS, her debut album. Place won an Emmy Award for her role as Loretta Haggers and hit the Top 10 with the tracks she recorded with the Hot Band, *Baby Boy*, a number 3 country hit in 1976, and *Something To Brag About*, a number 9 duet hit with Willie Nelson the following year. Emmylou, Dolly Parton, Anne Murray, and Nicolette Larsen contributed harmony vocals to the Mary Kay albums.

Emmylou was in demand as a backing vocalist, logging sessions with Little Feat and John Sebastian, as well as Linda Ronstadt — her name as cool as her harmonies when discovered among liner notes on many, many albums in the '70s. So cool, in fact, that Brush Arbor penned and recorded *Emmylou*, a novelty song that paid tribute to her by chronicling the escapades of an Emmylou Harris groupie who follows her from Houston to the Palamino Club. Typically frothy lyrics common to novelty numbers close off the verses: "Well, I love Olivia's eyes / And Ronstadt's really nice / But heaven is a girl named Emmylou." Meanwhile, Emmylou's old pals Bill Danoff and Taffy Nivert hit number one on the pop charts with *Afternoon Delight* that year, teamed with John and Margo Carroll as the Starland Vocal Band, their only Top 40 hit, on John Denver's Windsong Records label.

By late spring, ELITE HOTEL hit the top of the country albums chart and peaked at number 25 on the *Billboard* Hot 200 albums chart, with sales nearing the half million mark that would soon designate gold status, a remarkable achievement for a country woman artist. In fact, all of Emmylou's '70s albums would eventually be certified gold. At the time, no country queen had ever sold a million copies of a single album, and Dolly Parton would have to record a lushly produced pop album to do so.

In a story about Emmylou that ran in the February 26, 1977 edition of *The Nashville Banner*, Bill Hance noted that "Warner Brothers can't make her records fast enough. The kids love her, both city and suburban. They've labeled her 'an angel in honky tonk clothes' and a girl 'with a voice as pure as a mountain stream.' Last week she was named a Grammy winner."

Emmylou won her first Grammy Award for Best Country Vocal Performance, Female on ELITE HOTEL. "I'm excited about the Grammy," Emmylou admitted. "But I look at it with mixed feelings. If you win, it just means you got more votes. I sort of take it with a grain of salt. The real thrill is being nominated with the stars — the people I consider the stars, people like Tammy and Dolly." Emmylou also showed high regard for Tammy's 'man', George Jones. "He's probably my favorite singer," she told Jack Hurst at the time. "But I'd like to see his vocal abilities more appreciated by a wider audience. I always thought he was right up there with Ray Charles as a singer, and perhaps the recognition will come, eventually. But his talent does not depend on recognition." Jones, who had never won a CMA award, let alone a Grammy, would not win his first CMA award until 1980.

Willie Nelson's association with the Enactron Truck and Brian Ahern's living room studio resulted in Emmylou Harris & the Hot Band touring with Willie and his Family Band, on and off, for the next few years. "Willie often came in to sing and overdub guitar," Brian Ahern recalls. "He was always willing to play, and he's great to work with. One day I got really impatient with that old guitar of his, the one with the hole in it, because it wouldn't stay in tune. I said, 'Willie, this isn't going to work.' He just looked disappointed and left. A couple of days later, he pulled up in a big limo, and walked in with a $30,000 gut string classical guitar, ready to do that overdub. He did it, climbed back in the limo and left."

When Willie was fixing to record his landmark STARDUST album with Booker T. Jones, they used Ahern's facility to rehearse and record. "The years that Emmylou was with Brian Ahern in California were wonderful," Bryan Taylor points out, "because of the Enactron Truck. They could just record, record, record. They didn't need to pay studio rental fees. He had the truck plugged into their living room, and their residence became the gathering point for a monstrous amount of talent. Somewhere, no doubt, there is an archive of master tapes of some very cosmic music that will probably not see the light of day. When you get all those musicians, from the Byrds, the Dillards, the Flying Burrito Brothers, the Eagles, from Elvis's band, plus Linda Ronstadt, Nicolette Larson, and Willie Nelson, all hanging out at your house, pickin' and grinnin', I bet you there was some marvelous stuff played. Just to be sitting there in a chair in a corner of that living room would have been wonderful."

James Burton's replacement, nimble-fingered British guitarist Albert Lee, brought a cheery, energetic, on-stage presence to the act, while continuing the standard of excellence Burton had established. A veteran of the Thunderbirds, Country Fever, and Head, Hands & Feet, Lee had kicked around the L.A. area for several years playing with the Rick Grech era Crickets, Don Everly, and Joe Cocker before joining the Hot Band. Unknown to the American media, he would immediately impress reviewers. Like James Burton, Albert Lee is a guitar player's guitar player. Jimmy Page lists Albert as an early influence. His long-time association with the Everly Brothers made him especially interesting to Emmylou. Meeting Don and Phil in England during the 1960s, Albert looked them up when he arrived in L.A. and bonded with Don. "He made me feel at home," Lee recalls, "took me to Disneyland, and we got to be really good friends. Then they split up and Don and I were playing local bars in Los Angeles. It was such great fun."

When Albert met Emmylou Harris, he sang her *Country Boy*, which would become his signature tune and a giant hit for Ricky Skaggs. "She said, 'Ah! That's great, we've got to do that in the next show,'" Albert told BBC deejay Nick Barraclough. "So, we worked it up at the next rehearsal, and from there on it was in Emmy's show, I did it every night." Albert Lee left the Hot Band to pursue a solo career in late 1978, but he continued be a frequent guest in Coldwater Canyon, where he recorded his debut solo album. "I corralled the talents of Brian Ahern, and Emmylou & the Hot Band," he recalls, "and re-cut *Country Boy* with Emmylou and Ricky Skaggs, and I think it was a great version. What a band!"

On tour with Willie Nelson & his Family Band in August 1977, Emmylou Harris & the Hot Band were in Memphis the day that Elvis died, scheduled to open for Willie that night. They remember being besieged at the venue by journalists badgering the King's former band-mates for quotes. The show went on as over 3,000 people gathered across town outside Graceland to mourn the King. More than 80,000 people flooded the streets of Memphis before the day of the funeral. Without steady employment after the King's tragic death, James Burton would team up with John Denver.

Later that year, Emmylou Harris & the Hot Band opened for Willie at a performance in Columbia, Maryland attended by President Jimmy Carter and his wife, Rosalynn. The presidential couple arrived via helicopter. They were Willie Nelson fans, but they loved Emmylou Harris, too.

LUXURY LINER was her next album, released in January 1977. The album kicked off with the title track, an up-tempo Gram Parsons number from his Submarine Band days that featured John Ware, Brian Ahern, and Emory Gordy's driving "train-feel" beat, Ricky Skaggs' hot fiddle licks, Albert Lee's rollicking electric guitar, and some tight ensemble playing as Skaggs and Lee locked in with Glen D's piano and Hank DeVito's pedal steel. Emmylou served up her first Townes Van Zandt offering, *Pancho & Lefty*, an existential story about an outlaw friendship in old Mexico. The next track was a haunting rendition of Kitty Wells' 1955 hit *Making Believe*, before side one ended in a lone star state of mind with Susanna Clark's *I'll Be Your San Antone Rose*. Side two began with a rocking version of Chuck Berry's *(You Never Can Tell) C'est La Vie*, which would remain a show favorite for years to come. Also covered was Gram Parsons' *She* and the Carter Family's *Hello Stranger*, with Emmylou supported by Nicolette Larson and Fayssoux Starling. The album finished with Emmylou and Rodney's *Tulsa Queen*, featuring James Burton. It was her finest effort thus far.

With the release of LUXURY LINER, Emmylou's career became a subject of contention between pop and country critics. Pop critics wanted her to move away from her well-worn country groove and follow the course of Linda Ronstadt and Dolly Parton into a pop idiom; country critics saw her moving the opposite direction, into more traditional country music. *Rolling Stone* critic Ben Fong-Torres' review of LUXURY LINER, entitled "Emmylou:

Country without Corn," set the tone for one side in this debate. "LUXURY LINER," he commented, "is perhaps the best that Emmylou Harris can do, the tunes, fetchingly melodious though rarely eventful, offer a variety of styles. Harris embraces each with a tremulous warmth that except for its lack of definition might be her trademark. And here's the rub. Her vocals are pretty vapid." While Fong-Torres was looking for a more strongly defined pop sound in Emmylou's voice, country reviewers saw Emmylou "crossing over backwards, from pop to country."

Emmylou's response to the critics was characteristically diplomatic and non-combative. "Harris is unconcerned," Kip Kirby noted in *Country Music* magazine. "She tries not to pay attention to critics who nail her in reviews, especially the ones who accuse her of staying in a rut."

"I think that's a negative way for them to look at it," she told Kirby. "Artists search all their lives trying to discover where they belong, and then the press comes along and picks on the very fact that you've found a style and are happy with it. What do they expect you to do — change your style completely and go into something altogether different? ... The records I do, I do for myself," Emmylou asserted, "and for the people who listen to them." Years later she told Alanna Nash, "People say, 'She's a pop artist', and somebody else will say, 'She's a country artist.'... What turns me on about the music I do is the purity of it. And the 'traditionalness' about it is what is pop about it."

Emmylou made her position even clearer in a subsequent interview with Ben Fong-Torres in *Rolling Stone*. "I've been real fortunate in being able to do exactly what I want to do," Harris told Fong-Torres, "the record company being supportive of that, and the public being supportive enough to where nobody decides that anything should change. I've done it without a pop hit, 'cause all of my hits have been country and there's been no crossover. All the same, I'm sort of out in the middle there, somewhere, without any category. ... It came down to me realizing that I want to play with this band, and if I have to open, I'll open. I don't care." Elsewhere she added, "People assume I'm more successful than I am. I'm not a big money act, but I'm at a point where I can play to a very loyal audience. My tours are successful in that there are good turnouts at small halls. And then I can always go on the road with Willie Nelson. What more can you ask?"

The forces of traditional country music, not contemporary pop, did come to the foreground in Emmylou's next two albums, her fourth and fifth on the Warner Brothers label. Possessed of a razor sharp intellect and a wry sense of humor, she shot from the hip, telling interviewers, "I'm getting out of my rut into a deeper one."

In November 1977, Emmylou's recording of Dolly's *To Daddy* was released as the lead single from QUARTER MOON IN A TEN CENT TOWN. In December, it headed for the top of the charts, eventually stalling at number 3 in January. But the follow-up, Delbert McClinton's *Two More Bottles Of Wine*, went all the way to the top, Emmylou's third number one, while the album climbed to number 3 on the country chart and number 29 on the *Billboard* Hot 200 album chart. Definitive versions of *Ain't Livin' Long Like This* and *Leaving Louisiana In The Broad Daylight* proved immensely popular in Emmylou's shows. Another notable track was her version of Jesse Winchester's *Defying Gravity*. Her fans were especially fond of her duet with Willie Nelson, *One Paper Kid*, a song she performed with the Red Headed Stranger on their tours together. Critics from coast to coast endorsed the proto-feminist *To Daddy*, with Rodney Crowell providing harmony vocals, which Emmylou played solo in her shows, coming back after the band had bowed out to strum her J-200 and deliver Dolly's song as a final encore, a truly grand finale to an evening of pure magic making.

The third single pulled from QUARTER MOON IN A TEN CENT TOWN was Susanna Clark and Carlene Carter's *Easy From Now On*, a number 12 country hit for Emmylou in the fall of 1978. This was followed by Warner's re-release of *Too Far Gone*, which received far more air play that it had back in 1975. Then in May 1979 the label released Emmylou's duet with Buck Owens, *Play Together Again, Again*, a sentimental pairing with the garrulous host of *Hee Haw*.

On board for one session were Garth Hudson and Rick Danko, legendary members of the Band. Garth's accordion and Rick's fiddle added a Cajun flavor to *Leaving Louisiana In The Broad Daylight*. Hudson also blew baritone sax on *Burn That Candle*. Hudson and Danko dropping by to record in the living room studio was the result of Emmylou's invitation two years earlier to perform on Robbie Robertson and Martin Scorsese's *The Last Waltz*, the film documenting the Band's final show at Winterland Arena in San Francisco. That Thanksgiving Day 1976 show featured Bob Dylan, Joni Mitchell, Muddy Waters, Eric Clapton, Neil Diamond, Van Morrison, Neil Young, Ron Wood, Ringo Starr, Paul Butterfield, Ronnie Hawkins, Dr. John, and the Staple Singers. As Robbie Robertson explained his choice of guest performers, "For me the idea was to gather all these players that make up whatever it is that you call rock 'n' roll. … And whether it's Emmylou Harris paying respect to the country thing, or the Staple Singers with gospel music, and Muddy Waters with Chicago blues, and Eric Clapton with the British blues, and obviously Bob. Joni Mitchell and Neil Young were cohorts of ours from Canada, and also representatives of the folk singer evolving into a new music, and Neil Diamond represented Tin Pan Alley. It just all added up."

Most of the music sets were recorded live in Brian Ahern's Enactron truck during the concert. Although Emmylou was on a European tour and thus not unable to make the date, her performance was added a few days later. Robertson and Scorsese had their way with her in a simulated performance of *Evangeline*. She sang with Robbie and the Band, their appearance shrouded by smoke machines that consumed barrels of dry ice.

This appearance on Martin Scorsese's landmark documentary film also won Emmylou some fans in high Hollywood places. As Bryan Taylor notes, "Martin Scorsese, Kevin Costner and Stephen Spielberg are all Emmylou Harris fans. That's why in *Back To The Future* you hear *Mister Sandman*. Spielberg does everything he can to include Emmylou Harris's voice in every movie he does. Those Hollywood guys don't care whether she is country or not, they don't care what her label is. They just love her voice."

Much loved in Hollywood, Emmylou had also made a name for herself in Europe. "Emmylou's really a bigger star over there than she is here," Brian Ahern told *High Fidelity*. "Her concerts always sell out. Fans run up to her in the street. In Holland, Belgium, England, Ireland, France, even Germany!"

By now Emmylou Harris had become recognizable by the public. On one long North American tour, Emmylou & the Hot Band made a visit to Mount Rushmore. In the attempt to protect her anonymity, Phil Kaufman and her crew created a new name for her, Sally Rose, the name used in recording her country opera starring this persona six years later. As Emmylou told the story to Alanna Nash, "Originally, the character of Sally Rose came from a time in 1978 when we were in Rapid City, South Dakota, which is one reason for the stuff about Mount Rushmore. We had a night off, and we were in a bar, just enjoying ourselves as regular people out for the evening. And whenever somebody thought they recognized me, Phil being very protective of me, would say, 'Oh, no, that's not Emmylou — that's Sally Rose.' From there, we started taking it that she was my sister or a background singer in my band, and between us she just got to be one of those imaginary characters who become part of the jargon of the road." During one tour, Sally Rose & the Buds performed the opening set of her shows.

A move from Coldwater Canyon to a suburban bungalow provided Emmylou and Brian and their daughters with a more normal family life separate from the studio action. Brian moved the recording site of Happy Sack Productions from their living room to a San Fernando Valley warehouse that had previously seen use as a sign-making factory. Donivan Cowart, Rodney Crowell's Nashville sidekick, worked there as an engineer.

In the February 1978 issue of *Rolling Stone*, Ben Fong-Torres painted a picture of their new domestic set up. "The Emmylou of not long ago, who spent most of her interviews sounding haunted by Gram and uncertain about being on her own, has come back with the old whammo and turned it all around. Now, at age 30 she is married, mother to two girls, her own eight-year-old Hallie and Ahern's 10-year-old Shannon, and settled into a new house in Studio City in Hollywood. It's an unassuming little house, the kind any upwardly mobile young couple in California would be happy to snag these days. She and Ahern are beginning to fix it up and fit furniture in, a some-how mix of Danish and Italian modern, and Art Deco antique."

Fong-Torres also offered this portrait of Emmylou. "Emmylou is in a red t-shirt (advertising the now-defunct Smiling Dog Saloon in Cleveland) and rolled up jeans, white tennis shoes, and white socks." A photo of Harris displaying her shoes, socks, and rolled up jeans, shot by David Alexander and displayed alongside the text of the article, shows an obviously happy Emmylou to advantage. "Her fabled good looks — I've heard of deejays who've kept her LUXURY LINER album cover in front of them for entire shifts to keep themselves inspired — are not played up off-stage," Fong-Torres continued. "Her long, dark hair has an instantly noticeable amount of gray strands, and hers is a 'commune-sweet-commune' beauty. She is soft-spoken but not fragile, quiet but not shy. As on stage, she seems eager to please, and soon after meeting her one realizes that the name Emmylou fits." Ben Fong-Torres would remain closely involved in Emmylou Harris's life, although at a distance, as he wrote *Hickory Wind: The Life and Times of Gram Parsons*, published in 1991.

Blue Kentucky **Girl**

Emmylou Harris & the Hot Band's transition to acoustic instrumentation came about because of a change in personnel after the recording of QUARTER MOON IN A TEN CENT TOWN. Rodney Crowell and Albert Lee left the band to launch solo careers, Emory Gordy Jr. was replaced by Mike Bowden, and Glenn D Hardin by Tony Brown. Emmylou's old friends Ricky Skaggs and Barry Tashian were added to the act, while Frank Reckard appeared out of nowhere to handle the electric guitar chores.

Ricky Skaggs' presence in the Hot Band encouraged Emmylou to widen her horizons. They had first met in Washington D.C., when Ricky was playing for the Country Gentlemen before forming his own Boon Creek bluegrass act with dobro ace Jerry Douglas. Emmylou's old local club circuit provided Skaggs and Douglas with paying gigs when they were not branching further afield. Ricky and Emmylou first met during her stint at the Red Fox Inn with her newly formed Angel Band group. "Emmy tried to get me to join three times before I went," Ricky relates. "I wanted to stay in bluegrass and learn as much about the music as I could, but when Rodney Crowell left, I had an incentive to join her because I knew I'd be able to sing a lot. When I went with Emmylou," he told Rick Wall, "my name recognition started growing because of her popularity."

A child prodigy, Ricky had played on tv with Flatt & Scruggs at age seven. "I started out playing mandolin when I was five," he told Linda Fahey. "My father bought me a mandolin, and I grew up listening to the Stanley Brothers, Flatt & Scruggs, and Bill Monroe. I got to play with Bill Monroe when I was six. I met Ralph Stanley when I was nine. So I was ruined after that. Those guys influenced me so strong and so deeply that my music took roots in those early days. When I was 15, I started working with Ralph Stanley and got to meet quite a few people. I worked for him for about three years. I met Emmylou Harris right after that, and started working for her."

At first, Ricky merely laid down tracks during her sessions. His first contributions came with his fiddle playing on *Making Believe* and *Queen Of The Silver Dollar* on PIECES OF THE SKY. His fiddle work on *Luxury Liner* and *C'est La Vie* contributed to the exuberance heard in these recordings. Once he signed on to play in the touring Hot Band, his enthusiasm for bluegrass influenced the direction Emmylou and Brian took on their next album, BLUE KENTUCKY GIRL. Playing in the Hot Band opened the doors for Ricky, who signed his own recording contract in 1981.

Ricky Skaggs' solo debut was an instant success, sparking further interest in the traditional country music Emmylou Harris had been playing all along. Critics called their music "neo-traditional" and heralded Emmylou and Ricky as founders of the "new traditionalist movement," to be joined soon after by the likes of George Strait, Kathy Mattea, and Randy Travis in a revitalization of the genre.

After John Starling quit the Seldom Scene and moved to Montgomery, Alabama to pursue a medical career, Emmylou, Ricky Skaggs in tow, dropped by to visit whenever she was in her birth state. "We had a little pickin' party," she recalls, "John, Ricky, and me. Boy, that's amazing, to be able to sit around when those people get together." She was enthusiastic about the future of bluegrass, telling the *Florida Sun Sentinel* that "there's such a world-wide market for it. I mean, we found a guy in Stockholm who has the most amazing bluegrass record collection I've ever seen. We spent the whole night making tapes. My bass player, Emory, and Ricky and I were over at their place for dinner and he just kept bringin' out records and bringin' out records."

Rolling Stone compared Ricky Skaggs' country debut to Gram Parsons' GRIEVOUS ANGEL. Every country fan loved the way that Ricky combined his upbeat cheerful personality with sad sounding topics. By 1985 when he released Albert Lee's exuberant *Country Boy*, he already had eight number ones under his belt. This song that he had learned while playing in the Hot Band would be his ninth.

Albert Lee's career as a solo artist never did take off on the Top 40 charts in the United States. His debut, HIDING, produced by Brian Ahern, continued his cult status, though, and he went on the road with Eric Clapton. Albert and Rodney Crowell also put together a gig band that provided work for themselves and their friends when Harris and Clapton were not on tour. They called themselves the Cherry Bombs.

The Cherry Bombs had begun as Rodney & Albert. Over time their Redondo Beach gigs evolved from an initial lineup of Crowell, Lee, Gordy Jr., DeVito, and Ware to include some of the hottest musicians on the West Coast. But "the Cherry Bombs didn't become the Cherry Bombs," Rodney Crowell told Bill DeYoung, "until we brought Larrie Londin out from Nashville to the Record Plant in Sausalito." After that, musicians from far and wide began dropping by to play with Larrie Londin, every musician's favorite groove drummer. Among those who showed up prepared to play all night long was hot licks guitarist Vince Gill. The band's fan base included Vince's wife Janis and her sister Kristine Oliver of the Sweethearts of the Rodeo.

Frank Reckard was an excellent choice to fill Albert Lee's spot in the lineup. Frank remained in the Hot Band for many years, known as the little guy with the big guitar sound. He played a Gibson that had been equipped with a Parsons/White stringbender, twanging out his versions of the signature guitar parts created earlier by Burton and Lee. "Look just to the left of Emmylou Harris on stage and you'll see lead guitarist Frank

Reckard," Gary Vizoli recalled in a preamble to an interview, "small in stature, perhaps, but oh, so large in talent. The man whose fingers seem to fly effortlessly across the frets is more than just a master of hot licks. His interests span opera, history, books, even the desert and mountains."

"None of us were in Emmy's original band, which was full of legendary players," Reckard told Vizoli. "So we've all had to deal with that, replacing people who are more famous than we are. If any of us are competing, it's with people who aren't in the band anymore. We all get along splendidly. ... We know an awful lot of songs. In fact, if Emmy wants to pull out some other chestnuts we can do those also. There's a list of songs that are in the current repertoire but she never does the same show. There are songs we do every night, and a concert does have to have a structure. Emmy likes to do those ballads, and when she does a lot of them in a show, they get balanced with some up-tempo numbers. So there's a shape to a concert that can't be tampered with too much. Different audiences want to hear different things. For example, things they've heard on the radio. And if she is aware of that she'll do as many singles as she can. Other crowds aren't as concerned about that so there can be a different variety of material. On a certain night sometimes Emmy will write a show that really works on how everyone is feeling. A certain order of songs on a particular night, one person can be having a really wonderful time that rubs off. That's part of what I think my job is, to try and look like I'm having a really good time."

Rodney Crowell's exit from the Hot Band was made with Emmylou's blessing. "I wanted him very much to go out and sprout from that tree of artists and writers who came from that country place but who were infused with their own poetry of their own time, their own music," she told *Goldmine*. "That was going to push the frontiers of country music and infuse it with something very much current, and their own. He had the vision to do it, he had the songwriting talent, and he had the voice. I always thought that Rodney was a great singer, a very underrated singer."

Crowell credits the Hot Band for his growth as an artist. "I was young and impressionable," he later told Bill DeYoung, "and I learned a lot. I think that's the period when I became a record producer, because working with Glen D and James Burton and Emory and all those guys, it was a group of arrangers. I could only claim that I was a songwriter and a little bit of a vocalist at that time. But being around those guys, I actually learned to arrange. And combining my sense for songs and what I learned about arranging, being in that band, has really served me pretty well for a while."

From his boss, Crowell learned integrity. As he told Alanna Nash, "I got involved with Emmylou at a very formative stage in my career. It could have gone in any direction at the time. But there's a sort of dignity that Emmylou had about what she did that I kind of absorbed. Personal pride in her work, you know? I think she believes very strongly that what she's doing has a quality. She did back then, and I picked up on that. And I've turned that into my own form of expression as to how I go about doing the things I want to do in music."

Through Emmylou, Rodney met the artist he would produce and then marry, Johnny Cash's daughter, Rosanne, at a party at Waylon Jennings' house, where he was performing with Emmylou. "Me and Emmylou were kind of performing for everybody," he recalls. "We sang duets for them while Rosanne and Willie Nelson sat under a pool table." When Rosanne was signed to Columbia, Rodney produced her major label debut in the Enactron Truck. Rodney's productions of Rosanne's records would yield 11 number one hits during the 1980s. His own solo career took much longer before it finally caught fire in 1988 with a string of five straight number ones. For a decade, his albums were raided by artists like Bob Seger, who had a blockbuster pop hit with *Shame On The Moon*. He got the break he deserved with the critically acclaimed DIAMONDS & DIRT, produced by Hot Band alumni, Tony Brown.

Tony Brown commuted from his desk job on Music Row, playing some Hot Band gigs and sitting in with Rodney and Albert. "The first thing I noticed about Rodney was his eyes,"

Tony recalled when describing his colleague, Rodney Crowell. "It was almost like you could see into his brain, they were just very clear and amazing." Years after that first meeting, following their success as co-producers of DIAMONDS & DIRT, Tony told Bill DeYoung that "people ask you what makes stars. Some people have that, and most people don't. And Rodney has it. He's probably Gram Parsons reincarnated." The ever clever DeYoung has noted that critics had first called Rodney "a surrogate Gram Parsons," then called Ricky Skaggs "a surrogate Rodney Crowell."

In the midst of these transitions in February 1979, Emmylou and Brian learned that they were to become parents of a third child. Parenting together held the promise of resolving some of the step-parenting family issues they sometimes struggled with, especially when Emmylou was on the road. The news that Emmylou was with child was viewed as a blessing in disguise. This would bring them together for the longest single period of their marriage. During her pregnancy, workaholics Brian and Emmylou nevertheless recorded the material for no less than three albums, including LIGHT OF THE STABLE, her Christmas album, with special guests Linda, Dolly, Willie, and Neil Young.

Emmylou was considered for a role in Willie Nelson's on-the-road movie *Honeysuckle Rose*, starring Nelson, Amy Grant, Dyan Cannon, and Slim Pickens, but her condition — coming to term with daughter Meghann during the time production schedules were being put in place — worked against her, and she settled for playing herself singing live on stage during a Willie Nelson & Family Band date in Texas. *Angel Eyes*, a duet with Willie, and her solo performance of Willie's *So You Think You're A Cowboy* were included on the soundtrack album. Par for the course, Brian Ahern and his Enactron Truck Studio were employed to record the film's soundtrack on location in San Antonio, Texas.

Emmylou also recorded a soundtrack duet with Roy Orbison for Alan Rudolf's film, *Roadie. That Lovin' You Feelin' Again* was recorded by Brian Ahern. "One thing you'll notice about Roy's records, especially the older ones," Brian told *Mix*, "is that there are few solos of any kind, or as he calls them 'rides.' Sometimes he might have a riff as in *Pretty Woman*. During this session Skunk Baxter was designing an electric guitar solo. Roy took me aside and said softly, 'B.A., I don't like rides. I'd rather we just called a break, and you and I sit in the control room, and we'll write a third part or some kind of bridge.' So, he bounced stuff off me and I told him what I liked. We worked it into the arrangement and bang — there was another Roy Crescendo!"

"The high point for me as a record producer happened while I was working in a studio I built in North Hollywood," Brian recalls. "Roy Orbison called to tell me he had won his first Grammy. After all he'd accomplished, he finally got a Grammy. He was emotional and weeping." Emmylou and Roy shared the 1980 Grammy award for Best Country Performance, Duo or Group.

"I was a little nervous about working with Roy Orbison," Emmy has admitted. "Because there are just a few people that are larger than life, and he was one. But you know, what's great about singing is once you're actually doing it, you're not thinking about the fact that you're singing with Roy Orbison, you're just singing. And you're carried away by the song, and by what you're doing. I suppose Fred Astaire and Ginger Rogers felt that way. I seem to have an innate ability to follow people. Duet singing is something I don't think about, I just jump in."

Emmylou's fifth album, BLUE KENTUCKY GIRL, was released on May 13, 1979, a radical departure from her previous releases. The album was so down-home and straight-up traditional that reviewers marveled at its simplistic immediacy. "I've always pictured it like walking into a club and hearing songs like these, played by a little bluegrass band where the fiddle player stands up to take his solo break," Emmylou commented later. This artistic vision was illustrated on the cover where Harris appears standing — as if facing an audience — in a black suit jacket and long black skirt above white western boots. She is holding a big old black Gibson J-200, previously owned by Lenny Breau's dad, Hal 'Lone Pine' Breau, which has white beading around its oval contours, and a red rose inlaid below the pick guard. She's just standing there before the footlights in front of a painted stage-set backdrop that depicts a frontier saloon complete with poker tables, card sharks, city slickers, and cowboys, plus a pair of gussied up ladies of the night.

"We wanted an album with no Beatles songs, nothing that could even remotely be called pop," she told interviewers. "I'm considered a pop artist, but I don't really get played on pop stations. I've never had any pop hit singles. I consider myself a country artist, but country artists consider me pop." As she later reflected about her motive in releasing a 'new traditional' album at the time, "Country kind of lost it's way for a while. ... "I'd be on the road in some town, and I could listen to the radio for an hour and not know if I was on easy listening or country — until a Merle Haggard cut came on. But people don't want their country watered down. Country needs to be full-strength, hardcore, honky tonk stuff. That's what's rich; that's what the lifeblood is."

After the mechanical bull craze spawned by the *Urban Cowboy* movie, country radio fans would once again begin to hear more mandolins and fiddles, pedal steels and dobro stings. George Strait's eight-piece Ace in the Hole Band would remind people of Bob Wills & the Texas Playboys' swing style and Lefty Frizzell's honky tonk sound, the closest thing country fans had heard to Merle Haggard for years. George Strait was no urban cowboy; he had a ranch deep in the heart of Texas. Along with Ricky Skaggs and Emmylou Harris, he would spearhead the new-traditional movement.

There were a few new names among the harmony vocalists on BLUE KENTUCKY GIRL, notably Tanya Tucker, Don Everly, Sharon Hicks, and Cheryl Warren, as well as the more familiar Emmylou album alumni lineup of Fayssoux Starling, Dolly Parton, and Linda Ronstadt. On the vocal blends for songs like Dallas Frazier's *Beneath Still Waters*, Gram Parsons' *Hickory Wind*, the title track, and Rodney Crowell's *Even Cowgirls Get The Blues* the alchemy of this remarkable collection of songs is wrought. The show-stopper is *Beneath Still Waters*, a melancholy ballad, liquid and languid in its painful realization of a romance gone wrong.

Emmylou had carried this perfectly faceted gem of a song around in her back pocket for years, simply waiting for the right situation to record it. As she recalls in the liner notes to her Rhino Records anthology, "When I was living in DC, there was, like, a secret George Jones Society of people who would trade tapes like people trade baseball cards. Anytime you came across something that he had recorded, it was, 'Well, have you heard this?' In one of those sorts of trades, I got this tape. *Beneath Still Waters* just seemed so classic, so simple, so straightforward, and the imagery was beautiful. Also, the melody was so lovely. We cut it in our living room. I think it's the second take. It just was perfect."

"BLUE KENTUCKY GIRL made the record company nervous," Emmylou explains in the liner notes to her Warner/Reprise boxed set. "And it was a failure for the first six months it was out. Warner Brothers did a cardboard cut-out of me for stores, but there was so little interest that they just recalled it. It was so embarrassing. It wasn't until it won the Grammy that it began to pick up some steam." By February 1981, sales of the album topped 500,000. Emmylou had another gold record to hang on her living room wall, alongside gold records of LUXURY LINER and her "greatest hits" package, PROFILE: BEST OF EMMYLOU HARRIS. The body of work Emmylou Harris and Brian Ahern had created was both a creative and a commercial success.

In October 1980, Emmylou was named Best Female Vocalist by the watch guard of all things Nashville, the Country Music Association. This CMA award was a remarkable feat for an outsider, an L.A. artist, not yet one of their own. "This latest accolade follows a Grammy award," Leigh Dillinger noted in the *St. Paul Dispatch*. "Behind the acclaim that's finally come to her are years of persistent work, and a reverence for and thorough knowledge of her musical roots. Harris has chosen to remain on a course set years ago when she sang with Gram Parsons. Yet if Parsons was the person who opened her ears, it was Harris herself who opened her mind and heart to the country sound. Though many of Nashville's performers now downplay the twang in their songs,

Harris is as pure as the most traditional country artist." Emmylou soon after starred in Johnny Cash's CBS Spring Special broadcast from the Grand Ole Opry stage. One by one, she was joining the legends of country music on the concert stage.

New **T**raditional

Emmylou Harris's next album was her most 'left field' production to date, harkening back to the days when hillbilly music was broadcast on the Opry broadcast, played with no drums at all. ROSES IN THE SNOW was pure bluegrass, acoustic string-based music, not merely bluegrass elements stitched onto a traditional country band. Since country & western bands had become electrified in the late 1940s, this music played by the Carter Family, the Gully Jumpers, Bill Monroe & his Blue Grass Boys, the Fruit Jar Drinkers, and Roy Acuff & his Smoky Mountain Boys on Opry broadcasts was revered but largely ignored.

For Emmylou, this album was an attempt at educating her fans in the art of traditional country music. "I try to make records for people who maybe wouldn't normally listen to country music," she told Kip Kirby. "I mean, there's a whole young rock-oriented audience out there who listens to me sing *Coat Of Many Colors* and *To Daddy* . . . and they like it. BLUE KENTUCKY GIRL and ROSES IN THE SNOW are different directions for me. But there's a beauty and fragility in those albums that I think people will find irresistible if they sit down and really listen."

Released in May 1980, just as its predecessor was gaining sales momentum, ROSES IN THE SNOW kind of snuck up on folks. It was a bold move to put out a bluegrass album in those days. As Brian Ahern explains, "We started doing a bluegrass/acoustic project, but marketing and management started to worry about the lack of commercial potential it would have. I stayed adamant and stubborn about it, and this acoustic album went higher on the pop charts than any of Emmylou's records, and it was probably the most economical. Instead of having a drummer, I played a big Gibson Arch Top Super 400. That was the drummer. Most of the albums or sessions that we did had some little rule that would set it apart from the other records. In this case, it was a big rule, no drums and no electric bass. There might have been an occasional cardboard box or foot pedal, but most of the rhythm came from that big Gibson, and no click track." Once again, Warner was concerned about this new direction being taken Emmylou. "They basically wanted 'Son of Elite Hotel'," she told *Mix*. "We really had to stick to our creative guns."

"I think it was Ricky's being in the Hot Band that moved us in the direction of doing ROSES IN THE SNOW," Emmylou told Bill DeYoung. As she added during an interview with Holly George-Warren, "there was always some bluegrass in the Hot Band, even though I was doing hard country. Before Ricky joined the band, Albert and Rodney and Emory would do a little bluegrass warm-up before the show, and we'd play it on the bus. We'd put a few songs in the show. Things like *Satan's Jeweled Crown* came from sitting in a living room with John Starling learning that song and then bringing him out to sing on the track. All that bluegrass was intensified when Ricky joined the band."

"I've been headed in that direction for a long while," she reminded Bruce Pollock while discussing this new bluegrass album. "Going out on tour with the Buck White band opening for us, and singing with Sharon Hicks and Cheryl Warren, really brings it out. And, of course, so does the addition of Ricky Skaggs. In bluegrass circles, he's like one of the Beatles."

Emmylou was no stranger to bluegrass, as she reiterated in the liner notes to Rhino Records' deluxe edition CD re-release of the album. "I played the same clubs where the Seldom Scene played.

After the shows, we would always get together and jam. I learned a lot of songs, I sang a lot of harmony. I met Jerry Douglas and Ricky. It was like going to bluegrass school." With Douglas and Skaggs on board, the sessions for ROSES IN THE SNOW featured two of the top pickers available.

Adding one more element of authenticity to the album was Emmylou's choice of the album title song. In a bluegrass section record bin at Tower Records, she discovered Delia Bell and her song *Roses In The Snow*. Emmylou later produced an album for Delia Bell, with Holly Tashian helping out on the vocals.

"It was a risky thing to do," Emmylou responded when asked to summarize her feelings about ROSES IN THE SNOW, "not just from the standpoint of my own constituency, but from the standpoint of real bluegrass people who might resent me doing it." But Emmylou Harris had never been averse to taking a risk.

Emmylou was particularly pleased with the production values of this album, as she told Alanna Nash. "Brian is able to get the sound of the instruments. He really knows how to record voices and instruments and put it all together. So that album was acoustically, to the ear, a real masterpiece of engineering and mixing."

ROSES IN THE SNOW shot up the pop and the country chart, too. Her rendition of the traditional *Wayfaring Stranger* and Paul Simon's *The Boxer*, the singles put out by Warner Brothers, surprised everybody by hitting into the Top 10 along with Emmylou's duet with Roy Orbison before the year was out. Emmylou was pleased by the response to her risky bluegrass project. "I'm lucky I'm able to do exactly what I want to do. I have an audience that will buy everything that I put out, and seems to appreciate what I'm doing. I have very strong country air play. If I didn't have all that, I wouldn't be where I am today. It's that visibility that the country market gives me. I do consider myself a country artist, but I'm an eccentric country artist."

In November 1980, this eccentric country artist performed a triumphant concert at the Opry House, opening her 90-minute set with Willie Nelson's *Sister's Comin' Home*. Ricky Skaggs and Sharon and Cheryl White made cameo appearances. "The seven-piece Hot Band alternate between a spare, rock steady backup presence and formidable extended solo sections," *Nashville Banner* staff writer Mark Howard wrote in his review. "They left the stage while Miss Harris performed a solo version of Dolly Parton's weeper, *To Daddy*, and returned with acoustic instruments to perform selections from ROSES IN THE SNOW . . . featuring *Wayfaring Stranger* and *The Boxer*, but the audience came alive when Skaggs walked on stage, following a glowing introduction from Harris. Skaggs was perhaps the only person in the Opry House who could sing with the same range as Miss Harris, and their rendition of A.P. Carter's *The Darkest Hour Is Just Before The Dawn* was stunning."

Sentimental voting pushed the soundtrack from the Hollywood film *Coalminer's Daughter*, starring Sissy Spacek, past ROSES IN THE SNOW in the CMA balloting that year. As Colin Escott noted, this split in the voting for the album category ensured that Emmylou was a shoe-in for the CMA's Best Female Vocalist award. But after being nominated for three years running, Emmylou didn't think she had a snowball's chance in hell. "I wasn't going to go," she later admitted to Alanna Nash. "I was on the road, and I actually had the day off, but I was way the hell up in Milwaukee or someplace, so I figured I had an excuse. I mean, you know, I didn't think I was going to win." Then she got a call from Eddie Tickner. "I've bought a new tuxedo," he told her, "and I'd like you to go to the CMA with me." She didn't get it at first, then she did. "Well, Eddie," she said, "you've never asked me to do anything, so if you really want me to go, I will." She has never regretted that decision. She was tickled half to death to be named the CMA's Female Vocalist of the Year for 1980.

EVANGELINE was Emmylou Harris's 10th Warner Brothers release, a return to her country rock style. The stand-out track was undeniably the re-make of the Chordettes' 1954 chart-topping hit *Mister Sandman*, a track rescued from the doomed project with her Queenston Trio sisters. The album kicked off with Rodney Crowell's *I Don't Have To Crawl*, a song that spoke of a brave woman's brave resolve to quit a messy relationship.

Acoustic guitarist Tony Rice, along with Ricky Skaggs on mandolin and Albert Lee on electric guitar, reprised Les Paul's
early 1950s multi-tracked guitar parts for the Les Paul & Mary
Ford classic *How High The Moon*. Dolly Parton and Linda Ronstadt provided the backing vocals that pioneer producer Les
Paul had crafted by multi-tracking his wife's voice. Waylon
Jennings contributed a harmony vocal to *Spanish Johnny*, the
tragic tale of a mandolin player who commits murder and meets
his Waterloo.

The controversial track on the record turned out to be John
Fogarty's *Bad Moon Rising*, a Creedence Clearwater cut that
derived its lyrics from the Book of Revelation. Again, Emmylou
was caught between a 'rock' and a 'hard country' place. The least
popular tracks were a Trio version of the Band's *Evangeline* and a
resuscitated *Hot Burrito #2*, which many felt lacked the chili sauce
that had spiced Chris Ethridge and Gram Parsons' original version. The jury was also out on James Taylor's *Millworker* and the
set-closer, Rodney Crowell's *Ashes By Now*. Nearly everybody
who reviewed the album liked Emmylou's rendition of Little
Feat's *Oh, Atlanta*, a southern-fried rocker that one critic called "a
honky tonk kicker."

When Warner decided to release *Mister Sandman* as a single,
Emmylou replaced her singin' sisters parts with her own vocals,
though the 'Trio" version remained on the album. The single has
become a hot bit of Emmylou Harris memorabilia.

EVANGELINE, released on January 28, 1981, was certified gold
nine months later on October 9, 1981, by far the fastest selling
gold album of her six-year career as a solo artist. On the road to
tour her new album, Emmylou breathed life into *Hot Burrito #2*, a
searing overdrive Hot Band performance driven by the dueling
guitars of Frank Reckard and sit-in guest Albert Lee, who became
available when Eric Clapton was unable to tour. Touring had
become problematic for Emmylou as well. A grueling schedule
during the filming of a music video with renowned film director
Ethan Allen had contributed to her fatigue. As she told local
Van Nuys Valley News reporter Milt Petty, "at some point you have

to say no to people. I mean, I was out touring a month after Meghann was born."

"I don't really live anywhere," Emmylou began to complain. "My daughter is on one coast, my husband is on another." To ease the domestic burden, she hired a housekeeper. "I can't believe I waited so long to hire someone," she admitted during interviews. "I used to try to do *everything* myself. I was a real vegetable, trying to record, be creative, be a wife, be a mother, go on the road, take care of business. . . . I thought I was going to go right out the window until I hired Elena." By 1980, Emmylou also had an assistant, Vanessa Hendricks, whose duties included being "a combination costumer, social secretary, make-up artist, and confidante."

"I can put up with all kinds of things when I'm traveling and performing that would destroy a normal person," she noted. "On the road nothing really rattles me." Her road-hardiness was tested during a concert at Wembley Stadium in London. Mervyn Cohn's Wembley International Tours were known to industry insiders to be challenging. "It wasn't the most enjoyable tour I've ever been on, but no one forced me to do it," Emmylou told *Country Music People*. "I knew ahead of time it was going to be hard and not like any other tour I'd done. True, I wasn't prepared for the four-hour waits at the airports and the luggage being carried inside the plane with us. And I had Meghann, my baby, with me, so I was freaked out by a few examples of the corner-cutting that I thought bordered on dangerous. But you know, hey, the audiences were there, what can you say?"

Emmylou was also a good employer, a character trait that kept her on the road. "Right now I want to just keep things together," she told *Minneapolis Star* staffer Jon Bream. "I would like to work less. But I promised this band a certain amount of work. It takes us 25 weeks to make what some other groups make in two or three nights." During an extended engagement opening on the road for Willie Nelson, Emmylou's voice finally gave out. "We were playing his birthday party in Baton Rouge, along with George Jones, Asleep at the Wheel, and Johnny Paycheck," she recalls. "One of the reasons why I think I lost my voice was that there were so many people I wanted to say hello to." She had to resort to a cortisone shot, and after that began to take better care of her vocal instrument. "It was really just exhaustion," she said at the time. "I never was one to give myself room to rest." As Colin Escott notes, "the voice always known for its startling purity was now raspy in some registers. The rasp was actually far from unbecoming and suited some songs surprisingly well."

In the winter of 1980, disaster struck the house on Lania Lane in Coldwater Canyon in the form of a two-foot-high muddy wall of moving hillside. The house was destroyed. Fortunately, Brian had already moved the Enactron Truck and his tape vault to his new Magnolia Sound Studios in North Hollywood, and most of their household effects had been moved to their three-bedroom bungalow in the Encino-Studio City area, made in a leisurely manner over the past two years.

Although home and studio were now separated, Emmylou and Brian continued to live a busy musical life. While interviewing Emmylou at home in August 1980, Kip Kirby noted the "incessantly ringing phone" and a "steady progression through her front door" of friends and associates that "drift in and out. Emmylou's daughter Hallie (pronounced Holly), and Brian's daughter, Shannon, live with them. And now there's Meghann, the pride of the clan, old enough to crawl and investigate the world with fixated curiosity. ... Emmylou lives in a sunny household of organized confusion, frantic comings and goings. Everybody in the family seems to have at least a hundred projects happening at the same time. Things have improved considerably since Emmylou broke down and hired a housekeeper. Now, at least, there is a center in the chaos, an eye in the hurricane."

In 1980 Emmylou portrayed Jesse James' mother, Zerelda James, on British songwriter Paul Kennerly's concept album, THE LEGEND OF JESSE JAMES, starring Levon Helm as Jesse James, Johnny Cash as Frank James, Emmylou Harris as their mother, and Charlie Daniels as Cole Younger. Emmylou can be heard singing three of Kennerly's songs on this remarkable album, *Heaven Ain't Ready For You Yet, Wish We Were Back In Missouri*, and on a finale duet with Levon Helm, *One More Shot*. A single, *Wish We Were Back In Missouri*, was issued by Kennerly's label, MCA Records.

This role fell into her lap courtesy of Albert Lee while she and the Hot Band were touring in England. "Albert had left the band," she recalls, "but he was traveling around with us and sitting in. He asked me if I'd heard WHITE MANSIONS, a concept album about the Civil War. I said I hadn't. And he said that the same guy who wrote that had written the story of Jesse James. He gave me the tape. When I played it, I thought it was the best thing I'd heard. It was all Paul's demo tracks. The songs, the feel, were all there. It had been so long since I had heard something so unusual and so different. Even the demos were a major work. I'm as proud of my work on that album as I am on anything I've done."

Paul Kennerley dropped the song *Born To Run* from the Jesse James project and Emmylou picked it up for her next album, CIMARRON. Brian Ahern's production of the song was stunning. "We recorded *Born To Run* somewhere between four and five in the morning," Steve Fishell recalls. "I was new to the Hot Band and Emmylou and Brian encouraged us to try new sounds. I was thrilled to solo on a 1920s acoustic Hawaiian guitar on that track. I remember leaving the studio in North Hollywood somewhere around 6:00 a.m., just in time to hit L.A.'s early morning rush hour traffic, and feeling on top of the world."

Born To Run soon became a staple in Emmylou's stage repertoire. Fashioning the best of the leftover tracks from their '70s sessions into the set list for CIMARRON, Brian and Emmylou employed a full-spectrum of Hot Band alumni, including James Burton and Ricky Skaggs together for *Another Lonesome Morning* and *The Last Cheater's Waltz*. Frank Reckard was on board for *Rose Of Cimarron* and *Spanish Is A Loving Tongue*, Emmylou's exquisite duet with Fayssoux Starling. Barry Tashian, Frank Reckard, Mike Bowden, and John Ware appeared. Newcomers Steve Fishell on pedal steel and slide and Don Johnson on piano back her on Paul Kennerly's *Born To Run*, Bruce Springsteen's *The Price You Pay*, and Chip Taylor's *Son Of A Rotten Gambler*. The album received two thumbs up from *Rolling Stone* for Townes Van Zandt's *If I Needed You*, a duet Emmylou performed with Don Williams, which hit the number 3 spot on the *Billboard* country chart in November 1981. This track was co-produced by Brian Ahern and Don Williams' producer Garth Fundis in Nashville, marking Emmylou's first solo recording made outside of California since she had recorded GLIDING BIRD in New York City two decades earlier. *Born To Run*, a tale of wanderlust perfectly suited to the romantic gypsy image of Emmylou that her fans held in their minds, soared into the Top 5. Emmylou featured the song during her very first *Austin City Limits* show, which kicked off the PBS live music showcase's seventh season.

Next up on the agenda was the release of Emmylou's 11th Warner Brothers album, LAST DATE, recorded live as Brian Ahern rolled his Enactron Truck Studio along for Emmylou's "Real to Reel Tour" of Southern California club dates in the summer of 1982. Their rule of thumb for this live album was to choose material that Emmylou had not included on her previous studio records. She wanted the world at large to hear her wonderful Hot Band, albeit a latter day lineup featuring Barry Tashian, Frank Reckard, Don Johnson, Steve Fishell, Mike Bowden, Wayne Goodwin, and John Ware. Emmylou's insistence that she was just one of the players in the band was reinforced during an interview with *Musician*. "I don't think of myself as a band leader. I still think of myself as a member of the Hot Band. It's always been a very democratic group."

These live tracks portray an idealized night out with Emmylou Harris & the Hot Band. We hear Reckard's hot-rodding Gibson at its best on up-tempo numbers like Hank Snow's *I'm Movin' On*, and zesty licks from Steve Fishell, Wayne Goodwin, and Don Johnson, as well as Emmylou's heartfelt rendition of *(Lost His Love) On Our Last Date*, Floyd Cramer's 1961 instrumental hit that Conway Twitty later crafted lyrics for, both tracks being Top 10 hits pulled from the package. Emmylou's typically eclectic set list also includes great club performances of Don Everly's *So Sad (To Watch A Good Love Go Bad)*, Neil Young's *Long May You Run*,

Bruce Springsteen's *Racing In The Street*, and a bluegrass-flavored rendition of Carl Perkins' *Restless*.

Hank Cochran's *It's Not Love (But It's Not Bad)*, a number one hit in 1972 for Merle Haggard, and a Buck Owen's medley, *Buckaroo and Love's Gonna Live Here*, paid tribute to the Bakersfield Sound. Emmylou learned the lead guitar part for Owens' number one instrumental hit, *Buckaroo*, written by Bob Morris, and picked the lead part on her new pink, paisley Telecaster well enough during a show in Fresno that it made the cut — a rare excursion on electric guitar for someone accustomed to playing a rhythm guitar role on a Gibson J-200. No Emmylou Harris & the Hot Band set would be complete without a Gram Parsons tune. There are four included on LAST DATE: *Return Of The Grievous Angel, Juanita, Devil In Disguise*, and Joyce Allsup's *We'll Sweep Out The Ashes In The Morning*, which Gram and Emmylou had recorded on GP and performed in his shows.

Emmylou and her harmony singer Barry Tashian were not the only Gram Parsons admirers among the band members. John Ware's liner notes poem for the CD edition in 1999 begins: "Emmylou, B.A., Mary Eddie & a vision / Gram grows / Glenn D, James, Emory, Hank, Rod & me / Lania & Hunka & The Truck & Donivan / bluegrasscountryrock & blue suede earth shoes . . ." Further along he notes, "Emmylou and the Hot Band had wonderful chemistry on stage. The great nights, and there were many, were magical. Something like levitating on stage." Steve Fishell had worked up some of the arrangements with Emmylou. When he left the band, he moved into studio production, crafting albums for Pam Tillis, the Mavericks, and other acts. Like Rodney Crowell, Fishell says that his success as a producer was due to the time he spent in the Hot Band. "Even though this is a live recording," Steve notes, "anything I know about the recording studio, material selection, song arrangements, hearing a performance when it happens and just plain working under intense pressure I learned on this project. Emmylou and Brian allowed me to peek behind the curtain and face the wizard." This outstanding record was lovingly re-mastered by

Brian Ahern and Doug Sax at the Mastering Lab in Hollywood and reissued in 1999 in CD format by Eminent Records.

The year 1982 ended in a whirlwind. On October 10th, Emmylou Harris and Linda Ronstadt headlined a benefit concert on the UCLA campus, sponsored by Democratic nominee for the state assembly, Tom Hayden, his wife, Jane Fonda, and Governor Edmund Brown, a candidate for the U.S. Senate. A month later, Emmylou Harris & the Hot Band were in Dublin to play a party hosted by the Guinness Stout factory that kicked off their European tour. In Amsterdam, she performed on several tv shows, including a Christmas Special.

An idealized "Couples" profile of Brian Ahern and Emmylou Harris appeared in *People* magazine that November under the title "Singer Emmylou Harris and Producer Brian Ahern Make (and Record) Beautiful Music Together." "A singer is just a singer, until your voice is captured with just the right nuances and transferred to disc," Emmylou told Carl Arrington. Ahern praised Harris in return, telling Arrington that "she has integrity — she's one of those stars who won't budge. There's no way to eliminate the natural friction that exists, but when Emmy and I have disagreements it's always negotiable." Speaking very much as many couples do, Emmylou finishes off where Brian's sentence ends, adding, "he tells me when I am screwing up, and I tell him when I want something different." Mildly embarrassed by the sprawling opulence of their three-bedroom Encino home, they told Arrington that their pet name for their abode was "Camp Pretentious."

"Emmylou still has a wanderlust that she satiates frequently with long stretches of international concertizing," Arrington noted. "Brian likes to stay closer to Los Angeles, the better to watch over the children and their state-of-the-art recording studio. She collects friends and great songs, he collects art grotesque. Among his prizes is a pair of bloated bullfrogs playing musical instruments."

Ironically, this story was published mere months before Emmylou got the seven-year itch. As she later said to Bill DeYoung, after CIMARRON "Brian and I were coming to the end of our . . . I know it wasn't our last record, but I think we had maybe maxxed out. We were starting to max out on our ability to be able to work together." They filed for divorce. "The lowest point in my career was when I had to file for divorce," Brian later confided to Rick Clark. "It was more than the breakup of a marriage. My identity was caught up in being the producer of this quality body of work, which was about to come to an end. The last record we did was WHITE SHOES." For seven good years their time spent together was the best of possible worlds.

Concerning their relationship, Emmylou has also been gracious, seldom forgetting to acknowledge Brian's role in her life and career. "I was the central character in an event," she suggests. "Brian certainly is responsible for my sound, my style, and for putting together the musicians of the Hot Band, and putting their sound on record. I think his records have changed the way people make records."

Critics labeled WHITE SHOES her rock & roll album. Released in December 1982, a month after the label had issued PROFILE II: THE BEST OF EMMYLOU HARRIS, her last date with Brian on record featured T-Bone Burnett's cool *Drivin' Wheel* and Paul Kennerly's serene *In My Dreams*, a superlative production of a very good song that would win Emmylou her fourth Grammy. In April 1983, at the end of a long tour, she met with Kennerly during his visit to Nashville, intending to seek help with a song cycle she had been chipping away at since the late 1970s. A new chapter in her personal and musical life was about to be written.

Keeper of the **F**lame

By the summer of 1983, most of Emmylou's California friends had moved to Nashville. This community included Rodney Crowell, Rosanne Cash, Albert Lee, and their Cherry Bombs gig band that had evolved out of the Hot Band, with Tony Brown moonlighting from his desk job in Nashville and playing in both units for a spell, along with a floating lineup that included drummer Larrie Londin, Emory Gordy Jr., Hank DeVito, Richard Bennett, and Vince Gill. "We would play for anything from a dollar a night to whatever our fee was," Tony recalls, "just to be in that band." Tony had been hired to work in RCA's A&R department by Joe Galante. He signed Alabama and his new act hit on the radio with a continuous string of number ones. Next, he signed Vince Gill to the label. Ex-Hotband member Emory Gordy Jr. produced Gill's albums.

When Jimmy Bowen left his job as head of Warner Brothers' Nashville operation and took over MCA Nashville, he hired Tony Brown away from RCA to become his VP of A&R and put him in charge of the department. "Tony was a young, dynamic kid on his way up," Bowen wrote in his autobiography. "It intrigued me that Tony, like me, had been accused of being too hip for Nashville. He had grown up in Greensboro and played in tent revivals. He toured with the Oaks and spent a couple of years on the road in Elvis's band, right up until the King died in 1977. He played with Emmylou Harris's Hot Band, and her protégé, Rodney Crowell." With Tony Brown being given carte blanche at MCA, doors were opening for others who were "too hip for Nashville." The whole climate on Music Row was changing. Lyle Lovett was signed to Curb on a joint Curb-MCA deal. Soon after, Tony signed Nanci Griffith and Patty Loveless. With Emory Gordy Jr., he produced Steve Earle's GUITAR TOWN, an album that has been called the "first alt country album" and a "bridge between the Texas outlaw music of Willie, Waylon, and Billy Joe Shaver, and the Americana hybrids of the 1990s."

Tony Brown remembers this production as his personal favorite. "That's the one I go back to," he told *Encyclopedia of Record Producers* contributor Melinda Newman. "I love it better now. It was one of those things — me, and Emory Gordy, and Richard Bennett were really trying to make our mark. We finished it and nobody liked it but the press. And the press turned our company and Nashville back onto it." It helped when people on Music Row were reminded that "Guitar Town" was the CB handle for Nashville, although some diehard traditionalists still feared that Steve Earle & the Dukes were trying to blow up the country music business with their big Duane Eddy-style twangy guitars and their British Invasion style *Hillbilly Highway* approach to Top 40 country hit-making. The next act in line for a major label deal was the Sweethearts of the Rodeo, Janis Gill and her sister Kristine Oliver. Like Steve Earle, they had a rockabilly edge and sang hillbilly harmonies. All of a sudden, fresh new faces were replacing the old guard.

Rodney Crowell's solo career hadn't taken off yet, but as a producer for Rosanne Cash, Bobby Bare, and Sissy Spacek, and as a writer of number one hits for other guys, Rodney was doing swell. Three Rodney Crowell compositions — Waylon's *Ain't Livin' Long Like This*, the Oakridge Boys' *Leaving Louisiana In The Broad Daylight*, and Crystal Gayle's *'Til I Gain Control Again* — hit the top of the country charts. All three songs had been recorded initially by Emmylou Harris. Rosanne Cash rose to the Top 25 of the pop charts with *Seven Year Ache*, the Dirt Band scored a Top 15 pop hit with Rodney's *An American Dream*, Juice Newton hit into the Top 5 with Hank DeVito's *Queen Of Hearts*, and Bob Seger scored with Rodney's *Shame On The Moon*. Everyone who had recorded with Brian Ahern in his Enactron Truck seemed to be crossing over.

Everybody except Emmylou Harris. True to her character, she was looking for a more eccentric direction. Emmylou had been intrigued by Paul Kennerly's concept albums, and in turn the British songwriter had taken an interest in her own songwriting, especially her Sally Rose songs. They began to work together in April 1983 on the songs for THE BALLAD OF SALLY ROSE. "Paul is a very disciplined writer," she later told Jack Hurst. "I just brought all my not-even-half-finished songs. I'd have, like, a chorus, or a beginning to a verse. He made us start at 10:00 in the morning, take a break for lunch, and quit at five. It was just like, get your briefcase, get in the car, go to the office, 'Okay, what's the problem with this song? What's this word? And you'd get out your rhyming dictionary, and you'd work, work, work. And it would be very boring. But then at the end of the day, you'd stand back and look at it, and it would all come together. We finished six songs in 10 days." They put the album together, took it apart, put it back together, several times over. At one stage, there were three female characters, but they were collapsed into one Sally Rose.

To focus on this songwriting relationship, Emmylou moved to Nashville in the fall of 1983. Word of her arrival was out before she got her bags unpacked, trumpeted in *The Tennessean* by the well-intentioned Robert K. Oermann. Happy Sack Productions spokesperson Franny Parrish told Oermann that Emmylou "wants to write, and so many of her friends, like Rodney Crowell and Rosanne Cash, are there. One reason she's taking an apartment and not staying in hotel rooms is that when Meghann comes, Emmylou wants her to have normal surroundings. She's in the throes of a lot of changes. She's had a great affection for Nashville, and has lived there before. It's been years since she has sat down and wrote. About eight months ago, she started again. And when she's on a roll, when she's got that streak, she wants to be in Nashville. Emmylou has been working on a particular concept with Paul Kennerly, and when he comes to the States to write, he goes to Nashville." As Parish continued, "Paul gives her guidance and suggestions on her songs. And she gives him co-composer credit. It's so exciting to see that. She is a very generous person. The whole project is tremendously exciting. It's a new career direction."

Nashville cats held Paul Kennerly in high regard. "Paul is such an inventive and talented craftsman, and I can well imagine that she learned a lot through that process," Barry Tashian comments. "I remember visiting them out at this little barn where Paul used to live, on Mel Tillis's property. They just sat and pounded out all those songs." During this period, Paul Kennerly handed Ray Charles & B.J. Thomas their number 14 hit, *Rock And Roll Shoes*, and the Judds their number one hit *Have Mercy*.

Emmylou's move to Nashville was timely. She was getting over the agony of her separation from Brian Ahern, shaking off the ghost of Gram Parsons, and forging a new career as a songwriter, tutored by Paul Kennerly, about to become her next musical collaborator and third husband. Emmylou answered curtly to questions about her divorce, explaining to Bob Claypool backstage after a show at Gilley's in Houston that "it's taken me a long time to grow up and be a person who's in charge of my life, and I'm still working on it." Claypool sensed her troubled state of mind when he raised the question of Gram Parsons and the demands her fans placed on her to perform music by the grievous angel. "There are other things I could be doing besides this," she told Claypool. "I mean the whole reason that I'm out here doing this is not because I think I'm so hot, but because it's something I believe in. And if they don't know that, and don't respect that, then they don't have any right to shout out his name like that because they don't have any understanding of what he was all about or what I'm all about. But I really appreciate the enthusiasm of people who wanna hear Gram's songs because

I still have a bitter disappointment that the world doesn't know his music. I thought all I had to do was remind them, and it would take over from there, but it didn't happen that way."

As it was, Gram Parsons was along for the ride every night she took the stage, his vibrations still echoing from his blonde Gibson J-200 that Emmylou used as her main stage instrument. Phil Kaufman had first given this guitar to Nancy Ross, the mother of Parsons' daughter, Polly, but she passed it along to Emmylou. "I ran into Nancy," Emmylou recalls, "and she wanted to sell it. I bought it without even seeing it. She told me it was in a warehouse in pieces. The bridge was off it but it was intact. It turned out to be the ultimate road warrior guitar. I played it for years, and it got stolen, but we actually got the whole truck back. The people who stole it couldn't figure out how to break into the back, so they abandoned it on a street in New York. I was happy to get that guitar back."

Still haunted by Parsons' legend while on the road and unable to establish a calm home life in Los Angeles for her daughters following her divorce from Brian Ahern, Emmylou needed, in her words, "to change the scenery. Maybe it's from being a service brat. I guess I'm one of these people that whenever adversity hits, I move." As she later told Robert K. Oermann, "I really believe that Nashville is a healthy place for music, a healthy place for living in general. There's a different feel to Nashville than L.A. This is a real family-oriented town. It's alright to be a mother here. You're not in a minority here. A lot of my friends here are like me, with children, and the slower pace suits us. I feel it easier to fall into a healthy flow. I mean, I get up at *seven in the morning!* I have a hard time staying up for *Barney Miller*. That's my favorite tv show."

She recalled that "when I first started visiting Nashville, which wasn't very often, I found that everyone here seemed to be delighted with my success, delighted with the records. Everybody had just sort of assumed that working on the traditional side of country wouldn't work commercially. And when they found out that it did, we all sort of shared in the excitement. But here was music that I had admired from afar, and embraced. To stand on the same stage as Tammy Wynette was being catapulted into a whole different world. Everyone was so gracious." Elsewhere she noted that Nashville is "a fairly conservative town. Yet you've got one of the most creative places in the world. I think you'd have to go back to maybe Paris in the 1920s to find the amount of talent concentrated in such a small area."

In May 1985, Emmylou Harris was elected President of the Country Music Foundation, the non-profit organization that oversees the Country Music Hall of Fame Museum and related concerns, a position she held for several years. She worked in many capacities to support the songwriter community, eventually becoming praised, as one colleague stated, because she "embodies everything Music City would like to believe about itself: beauty, grace, gentility, and an unerring ear for good music."

At the CMF, Emmylou continued her mission as a "collector of songs." As she described the Hall of Fame during an interview with a British reporter, "upstairs are the artefacts, you know, Patsy Montana's boots and Elvis Presley's gold Cadillac, and Ronald Reagan's pardon of Merle Haggard." She enthusiastically described the records that the Country Music Foundation had begun to issue, beginning with a Hank Williams album that had come about "with the discovery of these old Hank Williams demo tapes that I believe Polygram gave to us. We put them out on an album and it did so well that we started looking for other things to put out like JIM REEVES: LIVE AT THE GRAND OLE OPRY."

Emmylou never has been one to air her dirty linen in public. When pressed to discuss her personal life at this time, she always managed to change the subject to her new concept album project, telling interviewers that at this stage in her career, "it's not enough to find ten good songs and make a *good* record. It's time to add another dimension."

The release of her long anticipated concept album was met with critical acclaim from almost every quarter. Writers warmed to the story that went along with the concept album, fashioning by-lines that told the world that Emmylou was "back into writin' again." Her half-hearted denials of the autobiographical nature of "Sally Rose" were often cited. "Well, it's *partly* autobiographical," she admitted to Russell Smith in a full-length feature published in *The Dallas Morning News*, "in the sense that certain things that happen to Sally happened to me. But there are lots of it that are not, so it's not cleverly disguised autobiography. But there are definitely some parallels in there."

The song *Sweetheart of the Rodeo* offered a poignant portrayal of Sally Rose, one fans associated with Emmylou Harris, the Queen of Remorse, as one critic quipped. The story line Emmylou and Paul came up with for their album was not wrought with happy endings.

I hear the sound of sorrow in the wind
Blowing down from every mile I've ever been
Calling me out on some road that just won't end
Where the sweetheart rides the rodeo again

Waiting for the sweetheart of the rodeo
They're comin' down from Tonopah to Tupelo
She'll come to town to ride the rodeo
Like she's slidin' down the walls of Jericho
There goes the sweetheart of the rodeo

I stepped into the light you left behind
I stood there where all the world could see me shine
Oh I was on my way to you to make you mine
But I took the longest road I could find

—*Sweetheart of the Rodeo* (Emmylou Harris, Paul Kennerly)

In the song *Rhythm Guitar*, a "high-rolling singer from Tupelo" meets Sally, "the prettiest thing that he had ever heard / Playin' rhythm guitar and singin' the third . . ." If this did not offer a clear autobiographical reference to Gram Parsons and Emmylou Harris, then the lyrics to the last song in the cycle,

Sweet Chariot, clearly are, as Sally sings, plaintively:

> Oh, my darlin', I have searched the desert and the sky
> Just to find you, and take the mourning from my eyes
> When I lost you, I suffered and you were sanctified
> We are all born to live, we are all bound to die.

— *Sweet Chariot* (Emmylou Harris, Paul Kennerly)

In the chorus, Sally visits Joshua Tree, revealing Gram Parsons as the male protagonist of THE BALLAD OF SALLY ROSE.

> Swing down sweet chariot
> The flesh will fall and the bones will rot
> But my sorrow will carry me not
> My heart is bound, my soul is chained to the rock
> Rock of ages cleft for me
> I swung down my hammer out in Joshua Tree
> It rang on the mountain and rolled to the sea
> And it will ring from the rock

"I've never been terrified of making an album except this one," Emmylou confessed. "I felt stripped bare. I had scraps, notebooks, cassettes. Paul felt the pieces of the songs were good, and said, 'Finish them and we'll put it all together in a story later. It was incredibly disorganized." Emmylou was fighting the most intense period of self-doubt she had experienced since the dismal days she had spent in Nashville in 1970 during the dissolution of her first marriage before retreating to her parents' home. "I thought I had nothing else to offer," she confided to Hawkeye Hurst. "I felt if I didn't get the writing part of me going again, I had just done everything. I mean, I could continue to find good songs and make good records, but if I was going to keep on I was going to have to prove myself to myself. I doubt if any artist worth his salt doesn't go through something like it sometime in his career."

Emmylou credits Paul Kennerly for not only helping her finish her songs but also for being there for her in her moment of darkness. "I don't know why," she said to Hurst, "but British people seem to be able to cut through explanations and categories and get right to the heart of what's good about something. He helped me that way, and he got me back into writing, which I'm sure nobody else could ever have done — as well as getting rid of this idea I had nothing else to offer." The bond forged between Emmylou and Paul during the creation of this album led to their marriage a year later.

THE BALLAD OF SALLY ROSE proved to be cathartic for Emmylou Harris. She put the spectre of Gram Parsons to rest and reclaimed her sense of self that had become mingled with the Fallen Angel's troubled spirit. She was no longer just the "keeper" of his flame. She ignited her own fire as a songwriter.

> We worked the road as hard as we could drive her
> But now I am the only survivor
> From night to night at every place I play in
> The sweetness of your song remains
> I'll be the keeper of the flame
> 'Til every soul hears what your heart was sayin'
>
> — *White Line* (Emmylou Harris, Paul Kennerly)

With this album, Emmylou Harris had written her way out of her road-weary writer's block and into Nashville. Getting Sally Rose out of her system may have been a necessary step to moving on. She had done what she could do for the cause. For Gram Parsons' vision, she had been the keeper of the flame.

The album was released in January 1985. The three singles taken from THE BALLAD OF SALLY ROSE were less successful than Emmylou was accustomed to on radio. *White Line* made it into the Top 15, but *Rhythm Guitar*, even with Waylon's trademark Tele chuggin' on the rhythm track, didn't make it into the Top 40, and *Timberline* failed to enter the Top 50. That her concept album was not a commercial success did not bother Emmylou. "It doesn't matter if people don't like it," she claimed, "the important thing is that I've broken the ice and gotten my new life started."

What was missing, some observers claimed, was inspired production. Paul Kennerly had made his concept albums with producer Glyn Johns, who had produced the Rolling Stones, among others. Emmylou Harris had worked with one of the best in the business, Brian Ahern. Why they decided to go it on their own in the studio, neither of them possessing technical skills or innovative production tricks, posed a mystery. Paul Kennerly defended their actions, explaining in *Stereo Review* that "we never thought of ourselves as actually 'producing' it. We just got on and did it, because we had written it, and it just didn't seem necessary for someone else to do it. Looking back on it, though, it was a hell of a responsibility. I mean, I didn't want to let her down, but we had an excellent engineer, Donivan Cowart, and he'd worked with Emmy before."

Emmylou seemed determined to produce her own records. She had been to producers' school in Coldwater Canyon, and she had been taking notes. As she told Alanna Nash, "I definitely wanted to have women singing on it. It's not a feminist thing. It's just a sound you're going for. Women singing with women sound different than women singing with men." In addition to Dolly Parton and Linda Ronstadt, she needed someone to handle the high parts. Gail Davies came to mind. "I called Gail and said 'help!'" she explained to Nash. "She has a wonderful, high, 'head', voice. And she came in and just did a great job on those things." She also admired Gail's independent spirit shown in her efforts to produce her own work without male assistance. As Bryan Taylor remarks, "Gail was one of the first women in country to stand her ground and demand to be allowed to produce her own records. She was a friend of Emmylou. But women producing their own records was unheard of and it cost Gail her career." Producing her own album in Nashville was no mean accomplishment for Emmylou Harris.

The second Harris and Kennerly collaboration, THIRTEEN, released a year later, didn't exceed the level of excellence Harris and Ahern had established with their remarkable run of 10 albums, but Emmylou's fans paid attention, especially to her rendition of *Mystery Train*, the song Sam Phillips updated from the Carter Family's *Worried Man Blues* during a Junior Parker session and then handed to Elvis Presley to record. As Greil Marcus, author of *Mystery Train: Images of America in Rock 'N' Roll Music*, notes, Elvis transformed a desolate song of misery into a defiant rebellion against a dark past — thus giving birth to rockabilly. Thirty years down the line, Emmylou Harris turned this rockabilly train to nowhere into a lament for Elvis, a diesel driven express steered by fleet-fingered Frank Reckard that might have been a real contender as a hit if her label had released it as a single. Paul Kennerly and Rodney Crowell's *I Had My Heart Set On You*, augmented by Duane Eddy's twangy guitar growl, stalled at number 60, while Merle Haggard and Bonnie Owens' *Today I Started Loving You Again*, released three months later, lost momentum at number 43. Also well-received were the songs Emmylou and Paul wrote for the album, especially *Sweetheart Of The Pines*.

When Emmylou Harris and the Hot Band hit the tour circuit that summer, she sported a new-look short haircut, a lavender satin jacket, black blouse, and, as one journalist noted, "bodacious lavender and black print leggings." Always a touch eccentric, Emmylou had reinvented herself once again.

The Queenston Trio

On Dolly Parton's 40th birthday, January 19, 1986, recording sessions for the album TRIO began at George Massenburg's west Los Angeles studio, the Complex. Dolly Parton, Linda Ronstadt, and Emmylou Harris were back in the saddle again, after refining their singin' sisters act over the 10 years since they first tried their hand at collaborating on a record.

The idea to revive the project came from Linda, who flew into Nashville to meet with Emmylou and Dolly. "We met in Linda's hotel room," Emmylou recalls, "and just laid the whole thing out in a matter of a few hours." In order to narrow their song selection, they chose American Mountain music circa 1907 as their repertoire, best exemplified by The McGarrigle Sisters' *I've Had Enough*. "The McGarrigle Sisters' song is really the most on target," Linda explained at the time. "It's Canadian traditional music, but it still sounds like little pioneer mountain girls, and that's what we wanted. The McGarrigles just had to be on the record. They're like our sisters, because they write in that period. Everything radiated from there, including the white lace dresses we wear on the back of the album."

They aimed to capture the spirit of music that people had sung in their mountain homes and make it their own. As Emmylou told

Daniel Cooper, "Each generation has to reinvent itself poetically and artistically. And you draw on the past. And you love the past. And you learn about the past. But it's important not to just make that music. I think you have to somehow add something to it. Otherwise, just play the jukebox."

They began with a clean slate, hiring George Massenburg to produce the record. Moonlighting dentist John Starling was enlisted as musical director. When the three women had chosen their songs and recorded their bed tracks, Herb Pedersen was called upon to lend a hand with some of the vocal arrangements.

"All three of them were pals," Pedersen recalled in *Goldmine*, "and they didn't want to be the one to say, 'You should sing this,' or 'You should sing tenor, and I'll sing bass.' So I kind of came in and would listen to what the arrangement was, and then suggest, 'Well, maybe Dolly should sing this part because it's more in her range, and it won't be such a strain for Linda, and Emmy can sing the baritone.' It depended on the tune and the key." The trio took their time, determined not to rush into putting out a release they would later regret, overdubbing in Nashville and L.A., until their harmonies were as near perfect as possible. Throughout these sessions they kept things simple. "I just sat 'em in a circle and listened," Herb Pederson told Robert K. Oermann. "They didn't need much, just a little adjusting here and there. It's amazing how great they sound together. Their voices are so distinct, yet they blend so well."

Singing together, their voices were greater than the sum of the parts. Linda Ronstadt mentions the creation of a mystical "fourth voice" when they harmonized. "The three of us just made a whole new sound," Dolly comments. According to Emmylou, "this album is more of an event than anything we've done. It's a collaboration of three people who like each other and love this music." Linda saw herself as the cosmic glue that held their harmonies together. "I'm like an emulsifier," she said during one interview. "I can blend with anybody. I can blend with Godzilla. I can blend them together and I can blend with either of them. They blend well with each other, too, but when my voice is in there, it adds a kind of thickness that makes it a little bit smoother."

When TRIO was released in March 1987, the simplicity of the music was received enthusiastically. The album opens with David Lindley's mandolin trill as the singin' sisters launch into the lyrics of Dolly Parton and Porter Wagoner's *The Pain Of Loving You*, backed by Mark O'Connor on viola, Steve Fishell on pedal steel, Kenny Edwards on Ferrington bass, Russ Kunkel on traps, and Albert Lee on acoustic guitar.

Track three is the Teddy Bears' 1958 pop hit *To Know Him Is To Love Him*, composed by Phil Spector upon contemplating the words inscribed on his father's headstone, taken *back* to 1907 in this rendition. Ry Cooder contributes a tremolo guitar part, David Lindley plays a Kona Hawaiian guitar, Kenny Edwards and Russ Kunkel keep it simple in the rhythm section. Restraint, restraint, restraint, which is what Gram Parsons had always emphasized as the key to singing a country song. Among other gems are the Trio rendition of Jimmie Rodger's *Hobo's Meditation*, evoking images of the dirty thirties when legions of America's homeless men hit the rails, and Dolly Parton's mountain girl hymn, *Wildflowers*. Linda Ronstadt's no denying vocal on Linda Thompson and Betsy Cook's *Telling Me Lies* is sweet misery.

Perhaps the two most memorable tracks of all are Kate McGarrigle's *I've Had Enough* and Dolly Parton's mom's arrangement of the traditional *Rosewood Casket*. The set ends on John Starling and Emmylou's arrangement of the traditional *Farther Along*, the song Gram Parsons and Bernie Leadon sang at Clarence White's funeral years ago. Emmylou's personal favorite from the album was Jean Richie's *My Dear Companion*, which the singin' sisters performed on the CMA Awards show. "It's not old," she conceded, "but it sounds timeless, and has real mountain roots."

The cute promotional package — paper cut-out dolls of the three 'songstresses' clad in scanty lingerie, their tiny cardboard cut-out outfits equipped with strap-on tabs, on the back of the album sleeve — was very Dolly. But the front cover photo, with the trio posed in a simulated corral against a big sky backdrop, studded with craggy Arizona buttes, recalls Gram Parsons and Chris Hillman's Flying Burrito Brothers' GILDED PALACE OF

SIN cover photo shoot and spoke of Linda and Emmylou's homage to the Fallen Angel. They are dressed in designer cowgirl outfits made by Nudie Cohn's son, soon to become known as Manuel of Nashville.

Their TRIO album spawned four Top 10 singles: *To Know Him Is To Love Him* (number one), *Telling Me Lies* (number 3), *Those Memories Of You* (number 3), and *Wildflowers* (number 6). An appearance as Johnny Carson's guests provided an opportunity to perform three Trio songs on network tv. A video of their version of Phil Spector's *To Know Him Is To Love Him* was produced and directed by *Star Wars* filmmaker George Lucas, Linda Ronstadt's close companion. The three women were filmed sitting around the fireplace in Linda's West Coast home chatting and cutting out valentines to the strains of *To Know Him Is To Love Him*. "It's a song that came into the room one day," Linda told interviewers, "and ran right into Emmylou's mouth. When she sang it, it sounded like a prayer. It was so natural for her style that we put it in."

TRIO was nominated for the Grammy album of the year award but defeated, ironically, by U2's THE JOSHUA TREE, produced by Daniel Lanois and Brian Eno. While this album title did not draw its inspiration from the legend of Gram Parsons, Emmylou would team up with U2 producer Daniel Lanois several years down the road on her WRECKING BALL project. For their part, Dolly, Linda, and Emmylou were happy enough to accept a mini-gramophone for Best Country Vocal Performance Duo Or Group to place on their bric-a-brac shelves in their houses in Malibu, Nashville, and Sevierville. Sales of TRIO surpassed one million records.

Emmylou's next album was the hastily assembled ANGEL BAND, another artistic statement, which enjoyed little commercial success. The album featured stark, acoustic country gospel music, mixing authentic religious songs of days gone by with newly written material like Allen Reynolds' *Someday My Ship Will Sail*.

During this period, Emmylou's talent as a songwriter was

acknowledged when she was invited to participate in the first women's *Austin City Limits* Songwriter's Special show, along with Gail Davies, Pam Rose, Mary Ann Kennedy, and Lacy J. Dalton. After Emmylou's third *Austin City Limits* show in the summer of 1988, she ended up jamming with Rosie Flores at the Hole in the Wall, a Guadalupe Street hot spot near the KLRU television studio. As John T. Davis notes in *Austin City Limits: 25 Years of American Music*, "it wasn't long before Harris found herself on stage playing and singing in the small, smoky bar, to the manifest delight of the audience. The tequila began flowing, empty shot glasses began to accumulate on guitar amplifiers, and, as Harris ruefully put it years later, 'The bottle let me down — the whole bottle! I must say I'm a pretty puny drinker (but) it *was* the Hole in the Wall.'"

Inspired by hearing Bruce Springsteen's NEBRASKA, an album that he had re-recorded at home on a 4-track cassette machine after trashing an over-produced studio version of the material, Emmylou was inspired to issue demo recordings that had been made for the ANGEL BAND album with coloring added here and there, with Vince Gill sweetening the mix with some high lonesome harmonies. Paul Kennerly is said to have told her to "get back to just singing without the purpose of making a record." ANGEL BAND is a record that Emmylou Harris could truly say she made for herself.

With sales of her records declining, Emmylou made changes in her management, replacing Eddie Tickner with Willie Nelson's manager, Mark Rothbaum, and then later on with Monty Hitchcock. "Eddie and I had been through so many wars together, and I think I'd worn him out," she told *Country Music People*. "Also, I felt it was just time for a change, but we parted amicably, and I still look to him for advice because he was like a father to me. Now, I'm managed by Mark Rothbaum. He's whipped my touring into shape so that I'm able to make a living at it. When he came in, there were no relationships and he could just say to the band, 'Look, I'm sorry, but this is the way it's going to be,' because it got totally out of hand and I was just working to pay everyone's rent and not take a pay check home myself. That tends to take the fun out of it."

During the late 1980s, Nashville taste was changing again, moving away from the new-traditionalist movement Emmylou had launched to brash "new country" sounds. Emmylou's solo efforts were no longer hitting into the Top 40 on the charts and she was in danger of being put out to pasture by country radio programmers. Emmylou's *Back In Baby's Arms*, recorded for the Hollywood movie *Planes, Trains & Automobiles*, was included on the MCA soundtrack album, but a single release failed to draw much interest at radio. A duet with Earl Thomas Conley, *We Believe In Happy Endings*, produced by Emory Gordy, fit the bill, though, and hit number one on the country charts in the fall of 1988. She added her trademark harmonies to Barry and Holly Tashian's 1989 album TRUST IN ME and participated in Folkway's Woody Guthrie/Leadbelly tribute, A VISION SHARED. "You want to be available for things like that, and I enjoyed singing *Deportees*," she told *New York Daily News* reporter David Hinckley. "It's a beautiful song; I used to sing it myself, from the Judy Collins version." She was also happy to report to Hinckley that "I have been able to limit my touring to the summer, so I can be home with the kids (Meghann 9, Hallie 18) during the school year. I want to wake them up in the morning, cook their breakfast, be there when they go to bed at night. There's no substitute for your real presence. I don't know why we ever bought that stuff about 'quality' time. I don't know how they see me, to be honest. I hope I'm just mom. I think I am."

In 1989, Emmylou recorded and co-produced BLUEBIRD with Richard Bennett, a state of the art "new country" album, complete with a Top 10 hit, *Heartbreak Hill*, which she had co-written with Paul Kennerly. The album seemed to refresh her career. Critics and fans raved about her rendition of Johnny Cash's *I Still Miss Someone* and Rodney Crowell's *You've Been On My Mind*. An album highlight was John Hiatt's *Icy Blue Heart*, with Bonnie Raitt sliding into view on guitar and vocals, a song well-suited to the superb talents of these two leading ladies of the women's rights movement in popular music. Also of note was the liquid, melodic rendition of Kate McGarrigle's *Love Is*. A flourish of electric and acoustic instrumentation featuring Richard Bennett, Steve Fishell, and Glen D Hardin — with Kieran Kane on mandolin and Kate McGarrigle on accordion, Emory Gordy conducting his own string arrangements, and Donivan Cowart and Barry Tashian harmonizing with Emmylou — provided a fresh, invigorating Hot Band sound.

One of her most peculiar collaborations during this period was a series of concerts played with the Columbus Symphony Orchestra. As *Columbus Ledger-Enquirer* music critic Ric Barker commented, "I don't know whose stroke of genius it was to invite Emmylou Harris to perform with the CSO, but I give them my High Concept in Music Award. I don't know which was most effective, gathering the Good Ole Boys and ganging up on them with a dose of classical music or herding the High Brows and hitting them with country music." After a program of lite classical music, Emmylou would take to the stage. "Singing selections that ranged from Buck Owens to the Beatles," Barker continued, "Harris crooned with her clear, folksy style to the delight of everyone. Some of the selections were a bit frightening to read in the program. ... For example, Harris's cover of the Donna Summer disco classic *On The Radio*. I for one was scared trying to imagine a symphony orchestra backing up a country singer who was singing a disco tune. I mean that would be like the Sex Pistols backing James Brown at the Grand Ole Opry. But you know something, it worked. Ms. Harris sang the song as a ballad and it was beautiful. Another scary moment was her rendition of *Diamonds Are A Girl's Best Friend*." A critic in Louisville quipped that Emmylou sang this song "in a Lou Reed-like half growl, half yowl."

Collaborative projects continued to fall into her lap, as was the case when Emmylou and Paul Kennerly were invited to participate in the Nitty Gritty Dirt Band's 1989 reprise of their 1972 album WILL THE CIRCLE BE UNBROKEN. Paul Kennerly recorded his *Mary Danced With Soldiers* with the Dirt Band.

Emmylou rocked out on *One Step Over The Line*, singing along with Johnny Cash, Levon Helm, John Hiatt, Rosanne Cash, and the NGDB. At the end of side one she can be heard saying breathlessly, "I think we brought the living room back to music!" Her infectious spirit and upbeat personality were a contributing factor to the success of WILL THE CIRCLE BE UNBROKEN II.

In 1990, Warner Brothers released DUETS, a compilation of Emmylou's numerous duet recordings, including her 1983 outing with John Denver, *Wild Montana Skies*, her duets with Roy Orbison, Neil Young, the Band, Earl Thomas Conley, and Don Williams, as well as *Things About You*, recorded with Southern Pacific, *Love Hurts* with Gram Parsons, *All Fall Down* with George Jones, and *Green Pastures*, a duet with Ricky Skaggs from ROSES IN THE SNOW, and *The Price You Pay*, cut with Chris Hillman and Herb Pedersen's Desert Rose Band.

The gem in the set was a new recording, *Gulf Coast Highway*, a duet with Willie Nelson, written by Nanci Griffith, and produced by Brian Ahern. "I heard that song," Emmylou recalls in the liner notes to her boxed set. "It made me pull off the road, I was crying so hard. It hit me with a sledgehammer, and turned me into a Nanci Griffith fan. I kept the song in my mind as something special, and when the DUETS project came about they wanted me to record two new tracks with the idea of getting a single. Brian was going to produce a duet album with me and Willie that never happened, and I wanted to do *Gulf Coast Highway* on it, so we ended up cutting it for DUETS with Brian producing."

Emmylou's BRAND NEW DANCE was released that same year amid the clamor of early Garthmania. Brooks and the 'hat acts' that followed him into the big, noisy stadiums had taken charge of record sales. But Emmylou Harris's sales to date were nothing to sneeze at. She had recorded eight gold records, sold 12 million copies of her albums, and won five Grammy Awards. She had become the most requested harmony singer by other country acts. She had shaped the new-traditionalist movement, restoring country music to its roots. "I don't want to appear immodest," she told *USA Today*, "but I'm flattered if people credit me, because I like a lot of the stuff that's happening lately. Back then, I assumed other people would pick up the music right away. But it just didn't happen that way, and it was lonely and depressing for a long time."

Emmylou had even taken her new traditional country music behind the Iron Curtain just before the Cold War ended. As she told *Knoxville News-Sentinel* entertainment writer Betsy Pickle in 1990, "We played Budapest last year, right before the Communist regime was abandoned, and that was wonderful. They had a country music festival there, and we headlined that. They were telling me that there are even bigger markets in, like, Czechoslovakia, so I'd really like to tour. I'd love to go to Russia. You feel you're on a crusade — you gotta take the music of Bill Monroe to these people."

Live at the **R**yman

In the early 1990s Emmylou Harris found herself cast off Top 40 country radio by a new breed of market analysis-driven programmers who narrowed the format and lowered the horizon. 'New Country' music directors intent on targeting the 18-25 demographic stacked their play-lists with records by younger artists. No one over the age of 40 need apply. All of a sudden, you no longer heard Willie Nelson, Waylon Jennings, Dolly Parton, George Jones, or Emmylou Harris on the radio.

"My albums aren't selling very well," Emmylou confessed to *People* magazine in January 1991. "That's disappointing. I'm not going into oblivion, but I don't get much air play." A Grammy winner in 1988 along with her TRIO partners Dolly Parton and Linda Ronstadt, Emmylou had also hit number one with *We Believe In Happy Endings*, a duet with Earl Thomas Conley, that same year. In 1989 she had scored Top 20 hits with *Heartbreak Hill* and *Heaven Only Knows*, but as the decade turned and Top 40 radio tastes changed, she had to look elsewhere for outlets for her music.

Emmylou's immediate solution was to dissolve her legendary Hot Band and form an acoustic ensemble, the Nash Ramblers, eventually playing the dusty Ryman Auditorium in Nashville, which had not been in use since 1974 when the *Grand Ole Opry* was moved to a modern theme park facility in the suburbs. "You've got to shake things up, flex new muscles to where it's spontaneous and exciting again," she told *People* prior to her Ryman shows. "There were no new worlds for the Hot Band to conquer." At age 44, she was arguably at the height of her powers, looking forward to another comeback. In this spirit of refocusing her energies, she stopped dying her hair. "With so many other things in my life," she explained, "was this really something I needed to worry about? What you need most as an artist, is to just sit down, play the guitar, think about what you're doing next."

Emmylou had bounced back before — and she would again. "Here's what's great about Emmy," Rodney Crowell told *People* magazine's Jim Jerome. "She had this little pink fringed cowgirl jacket. Somebody stole it. It came back. Another time, somebody stole all our equipment. Her Gibson J-200 guitar came back. So, anyone who's criticizing her today — she's charmed. She'll be back."

By the time Emmylou Harris & the Nash Ramblers hit the stage of the Ryman Auditorium on 30 April 1991 for the first of three shows, she had become the President of the Country Music Foundation but not an Opry regular. In order to use the historic Ryman stage and the Opry emblem for her tv special, Emmylou had to join *The Grand Ole Opry*. "They had wanted me in," she recalls, "but there was always some practical reasons why not, but then the time was right." Welcomed aboard by Roy Acuff, she and the Ramblers would champion the string-based music that had been an Opry staple in the beginning. "It was one of those things that fell together pretty effortlessly," she told Jay Orr.

Serendipity saw her taking the stage on the 99th anniversary of the building that had previously been known as the Mother Church of Country Music. Standing on the worn plank flooring of the Ryman stage that night, she was nervous as all get out. "At a few strategic moments in my career," she admitted later, "I have experienced nervousness, and that was one of them. ... I had to remember the words to 17 new songs," she explained to

Nashville Banner entertainment writer Jay Orr. "And I had to perform them in a way that was going to be a record. Plus, they were videotaping."

The audience was limited to 200 seats for the show due to "Metro codes regulations for the rickety Ryman." Performing a mixed bag of acoustic arrangements that traced the history of popular American music from Stephen Foster and Bill Monroe to Bruce Springsteen's *Mansion On The Hill* and Steve Earle's *Guitar Town*, Emmylou quickly shed her initial jitters, drawing strength from the hillbilly dust that had settled in the farthest nooks and crannies of the stately old auditorium during the exciting days when Hank Williams, Faron Young, Kitty Wells, and Patsy Cline had made their legendary Opry debuts.

"It was just the idea that I was on the stage of the Ryman," she confided to Orr. "It's a kind of awe. When all is said and done, it's probably the most wonderful stage acoustically and ambience-wise that I've ever played on. People who have seen me play live have told me that it's the best they've heard me and the band sound." Emmylou's rich vocals were augmented by a flurry of hot picking — by Sam Bush, Jon Randall Stewart, and Al Perkins — that was spurred on by dog-house bassist Roy Huskey Jr. and drummer Larry Atamaniuk.

Her medley of Nanci Griffith's *A Hard Life Wherever You Go* and the classic '60s elegy *Abraham, Martin, and John* was a fresh take. "I can't really say anything about *Hard Life*, except that when I first heard it, I was so moved," she explained to *Ottawa Citizen* critic Charlie MacKenzie. "It touches on how people can be so cruel to other people, and how, if we don't change and learn to be kind and understanding to one another, we'll have nothing to leave the children, and all we have are the children. *Abraham, Martin, and John* brings back feelings I thought I'd forgotten — the great loss we felt when John Kennedy and Martin Luther King and then Bobby Kennedy were assassinated. It's easy to forget what a traumatic and emotional time that was — when you believed that the world could be a better place, that you could make a difference and things could be changed. I still believe the world can change, and that people can change, too. It has to come from each individual."

Emmylou & the Nash Ramblers breathed a life force back into the long neglected venue during these historic shows, which were released on CD as AT THE RYMAN and broadcast on CMT. The excitement generated by their performances also influenced the fate of the 100-year-old building as Opryland managers debated whether to renovate or demolish the building with an eye on the potential real estate value of the downtown Nashville site. Four years later in February 1995, when Emmylou & the Nash Ramblers returned to the Ryman for their last scheduled show together, the venue had been lovingly restored. Choosing to put together a bluegrass band and play both the Ryman and the Opry broadcast may not have put Emmylou back on the radio, but her return to country roots during her five years spent touring with the Ramblers was widely appreciated. AT THE RYMAN won a Grammy Award for Emmylou and her band.

With the Nash Ramblers, Emmylou once again let her band members shine. "Every musician who ever got to play with her," Bryan Taylor, who spent five years working with Emmylou at Monty Hitchcock Management in the 1990s, notes, "got to stretch their wings and be as good as they could be. Jon Randall, who had his own career recording for RCA, is a great guitar player. He played in the Nash Ramblers, and now he is playing for Lyle Lovett. Jon is a monster guitar player, every bit as good as Vince Gill, but hasn't got the breaks that Vince got. I remember Jon telling me that when he was 22 or 23 Emmy recruited him for the Ramblers. She just, right from the first day, started throwing stuff at him. Jon gives her a lot of credit for his ability that he has now because she demanded in a very nice way that he handle everything she threw at him. And she trusted him to do it. She's always done that with her players. It's not like working a band for some hat act out of Nashville where you lay in a very tightly confined way, where you play certain notes. Her players always got to stretch their limits. As a creative person, that is all you can ask for. Her shows are always evolving. It doesn't matter if you see her twice on the same tour, because the set list is always evolving. And if you are there on a good night, it is magic." Al Perkins' stinging dobro, Sam Bush's trilling mandolin and spirited fiddle, Roy Huskey's double bass, and Larry Atamanuik's percussion all stood out clearly in the mix and provided more space for Emmylou's vocals.

When Emmylou Harris & the Nash Ramblers hit the road, concertgoers discovered a renewed Emmylou. "Her genius, and it is exactly that," Pat McGraw noted in *The Denver Post*, "is her ability to list toward the traditional, almost folk, end of country while giving the music a rock edge, all the while, though, Harris somehow continues to appeal to mainline traditionalists as well." Show highlights included Emmylou's *Prayer In Open D* and Al Perkins and Sam Bush stretching out on a *Sailin' Shoes/Crossroads* medley. On the first leg of the tour, the O'Kanes opened the shows with their upbeat hillbilly honk. A benefit show for the Make A Wish Foundation and the Leukemia Blood Bank at the Judge Roy Bean Amphitheater in Fairhope, Alabama, drew an exceptionally enthusiastic crowd. "It was like a World Series game and the Fourth of July all rolled into one," local journalist Ken Cramton noted. "Emmylou is from Birmingham, and this is homeland for her," Monty Hitchcock explained to Cramton. "Country music comes from a lot of things, and Emmylou is all of these. She plays 'Emmylou music'!"

Notable television appearances from this era include the PBS "Greatest Streets" production *Edinburgh's Royal Mile with Emmylou Harris*. Emmylou explores the famous Royal Mile, Edinburgh's oldest street, connecting Edinburgh Castle with the Palace of Holyrood House, where Emmylou invokes the ghosts of John Knox, Mary Queen of Scots, Robbie Burns, and Sir Walter Scott among the cobblestones, nooks, and crannies. She discovers a garden concert of Burns' songs, then comes upon street musicians playing traditional Scottish ballads, before being swept up in the carnival atmosphere of a fringe festival. She moves on to sip tea with a Member of the Scottish Parliament and tours the national library, where she peers intently at preserved manuscripts of Scott's literary writings, showing a genuine interest in her Celtic roots.

Bringing It All Back Home, a BBC Documentary, featured Emmylou Harris, Mary Black, and Dolores Keane. The CBS special *Women of Country Music* showcased Emmylou Harris, Kathy Mattea, Trisha Yearwood, Pam Tillis, Patty Loveless, and Suzy Boggus. In 1995, Emmylou was featured on the BBC Scotland tv special *The Transatlantic Sessions* along with Kate & Anna McGarrigle, Iris Dement, Michelle Wright, Mary Black, Dick Gaughan, Kathy Mattea, Dougie MacLean, Jerry Douglas, and Donal Lunny. A BBC-TV show titled *Are You Sure Hank Done It This Way* excited Emmylou because the British producers' choice of material was nearly as eclectic as her own choices. "I was in heaven," she told Michael McCall. "I was just in heaven. I thought — this makes so much artistic and creative sense. Why can't I turn on my radio in America and hear music like this? Maybe you can on these new Americana stations. I'm assuming that's what they're headed for — the Lucinda Williamses, the Joe Elys, the Dead Reckoning crowd, but also bringing in Bruce Springsteen. My vision of country music has always been much broader."

Film producers were also in pursuit of Emmylou, as Bryan Tayor recalls from his time working for Monty Hitchcock, Emmylou's manager. "It was a great opportunity for a guy from Canada to go to Nashville and work in Emmylou Harris's organization. That was heady stuff. The first months I worked in the office down there we had very important people calling — Michael Keaton, Tom Hanks, Steven Spielberg, Paul McCartney, Keith Richards . . . All those people called wanting to do something with Emmylou Harris. To me, it just shows the respect that she has ... throughout the artistic community. She is an icon." Emmylou has always turned down these Hollywood offers. "She has turned down a lot of movie roles, a lot of endorsements," Taylor notes. "She turned down something like a million dollars for the Revlon endorsements because she didn't see the artistic integrity of it. And she stood her ground. There was a film made in the 1990s, *A Family Thing*. James Earl Jones was in it. Robert

Duvall was in it. They chased her like crazy for the role of Robert Duvall's wife in that movie. You look at what she *has* stood up for over the past 15 years. She uses her name and her celebrity for good causes, for the landmines issue, for example, that has cost her a lot in cancelled gigs, jobs she had to give up or not book because of her involvement with landmines." Emmylou would record *I Love To Tell The Story*, as a duet with Robert Duvall for the soundtrack album for his movie, *The Apostle*, but she had passed on an acting role. They performed their duet live on *Late Night With David Letterman*.

Now an avid baseball fan, Emmylou sang *Take Me Out To The Ball Game* at numerous major league ballparks during the summer of 1993 and told interviewers that she was an Atlanta Braves fan. "It was the guys in the Ramblers that got me into it," she told Mike Boehm. "Only in the last couple of years have I gotten really into being a baseball fan. The guys are very much into it, and you start to learn a lot about it, you see the poetry of the game. And if you're out for extended times in the summer, the only thing on television that isn't going to give you a headache is baseball."

Baseball also brought back fond family memories of an annual backyard game held at her parents' home. "We have a Whiffle Ball game every summer. The tree is second base, and we have to have special rules when the ball gets caught in the branches." When her father died in 1993, her mother Eugenia came to stay with her and her daughters in their recently acquired new residence, a 67-year-old colonial-style house set back a comfortable distance from a tree-lined Green Hills neighborhood street. The white brick house was within five minutes driving time of one of the best studios in the world, the Exit/In, the Bluebird Cafe, and her favorite bookstore. "Inside, the house is lived-in but well-kept," Brian Mansfield reported in *Request Magazine*. "A careful eye might notice the most recent Grammy award for the 1992 album AT THE RYMAN: EMMYLOU HARRIS & THE NASH RAMBLERS. But the 'material tapes' scattered throughout the house are what give away its owner's occupation. 'Whenever I hear anything that interests me,' she says. 'I might end up with several cassettes, and all of a sudden I see a few songs that start to look like they belong together.' Harris collects art like she collects songs. The sitting room boasts framed drawings by one of Harris's daughters, a carving of Doc Watson, and a statue of rodeo woman Prairie Rose, given to Harris by her third husband, songwriter Paul Kennerly. A brightly colored angel creation by the Reverend Howard Finster peeks out from behind the hearth. An unframed canvas of watercolor flowers painted by Nanci Griffith's sister-in-law leans against a bookcase." Other visitors to the house discovered a comfortably laid-out music room. Eugenia baked cookies for guests and meals for the musicians and technicians who worked her daughter's recording sessions. Her second daughter Meghann was now spending her vacation months with her father and her first daughter Hallie was working at a record store in Nashville.

Emmylou Harris's next album was COWGIRL'S PRAYER, an eclectic mix of something old, something new, something borrowed, and hopefully something blue enough to put her back on the radio. After AT THE RYMAN, she had left Warner/Reprise and signed with Elektra/Asylum. Released in September 1993, her debut on Asylum was a Top 40 country 'Hail Mary' pass. The title came from the lyrics of Leonard Cohen's *Ballad Of A Runaway Horse*. "Linda Ronstadt sent me this song," Emmylou explains, "and urged me to record it. I've been a fan of Leonard Cohen's since my folk days." COWGIRL'S PRAYER was her bravest selection in years, an album filled with sparkling jewels such as Lucinda Williams Cajun-flavored *Crescent City* and Tony Joe White's *High Powered Love*. Choosing David Olney's *Jerusalem Tomorrow* was not only a risk for a country artist, it also required a good deal of nerve to pull it off. "I felt it was worth taking a chance on something completely different, stylistically," Emmylou notes, "and giving it a flat reading actually gives the song more power." The rarest gem was Emmylou's own *Prayer In Open D*, a no-holds-barred performance of a song that had been aching to escape from her for many years.

In her shows with Spyboy, one of the most remarkable moments came when the musicians would leave the stage briefly and Emmylou would pick up her open-tuned Gibson guitar and perform her own *Prayer In Open D*.

There's a valley of sorrow in my soul
Where every night I hear the thunder roll
Like the sound of a distant gun
Over all the damage I have done
And the shadows filling up this land
Are the ones I built with my own hand
There is no comfort from the cold
Of this valley of sorrow in my soul

　　—*Prayer In Open D* (Emmylou Harris)

High Powered Love and *Thanks To You*, singles released from the album, received a mixed response from radio, as Emmylou noted. "*High Powered Love* got *some* interest from radio. It didn't hit the Top 40, but it got close. And considering the lack of interest in me by radio over the last few years, that was a nice surprise. It was nominated for a Grammy and the video was very well-received, too. *Thanks To You* came out as a single. At some stations it just skyrocketed, and then other stations just wouldn't play it. And we put out *Crescent City*. I'm very pleased with the album and very proud of it." The music video of Jesse Winchester's *Thanks To You* also made it to number one on CMT's Top 10 Videos.

Soon after the release of COWGIRL'S PRAYER, the Trio — Emmylou, Dolly, and Linda — sang *Where The Grass Won't Grow* on Brian Ahern's production of George Jones' BRADLEY BARN SESSIONS, a career retrospective of the Possum's hits. Emmylou also contributed to Steve Earle's comeback album, TRAIN A COMIN'. She had become a Steve Earle fan back in the 1980s after hearing him play at the Bluebird Café. "One night there was a sign in the window that said 'Steve Earle & the Dukes'. It was Steve and a couple of people. ... He did that song *Devil's Right*

Hand, and it was the best thing that I heard in so long. It was like a reaffirmation. So I became a fan." Emmylou recognized Steve Earl's role in the 'alt-country rebellion' that was about to take place in Nashville. "He's consistently come up with great stuff. I think that he's back now, healthy and whole, and come back even stronger than he was before. He certainly is one of our finest songwriters."

Emmylou's impact upon the career of Nanci Griffith was equally powerful. Nanci gives Emmylou credit for encouraging her to create her splendid album OTHER VOICES, OTHER ROOMS. "Emmylou Harris and I spoke of the beauty and clarity of the late Kate Wolf's music," Nanci recalled in her album's liner notes. "We spoke of both the sadness in her passing and the lack of new voices singing Kate's songs. Emmy said songs need new voices to sing them in places they're never been sung in order to stay alive. So, it was with Emmy's words of wisdom and encouragement that the seed that Rod Argent planted was nourished and grew into this project."

A "Girls Night Out" show with the Nashville Symphony in early 1995 resulted in Emmylou being named winner of the symphony's Harmony Award. Doyle R. Rippee, chairman of the Nashville Symphony Association, recognized that "her contribution to music appreciation in Nashville is unsurpassed, and her exceptional talent often defies classification." Past winners included Steve Winwood, Vince Gill, Amy Grant, and Wynonna & Naomi Judd.

In February, Emmylou Harris & the Nash Ramblers came to the end of the road with a triumphant concert at the newly restored Ryman. Emmylou was pleased with the restoration, as she told Tom Rowland from the *Nashville Banner*. "I think they did an extraordinary job because they kept the integrity of the building, the soul of the building, intact. Steve Buchanan told me that they recreated their chandeliers from photographs. That attention to detail, that's important. I think those things mean a lot, that attention to the past, and yet bringing it into the 21st century as a performing hall. And it still sounds great."

At the Ryman, Emmylou Harris & the Nash Ramblers took the stage to the strains of the Playmates' 1958 hit *Beep Beep*, the novelty song about a Nash Rambler racing a Cadillac. Three-and-a-half hours later, they were still there. As Emmylou had said during her opening address to the Ryman audience, "We've got a lot of songs to play, so I hope you have no place to be. This place feels like a neighborhood party. I recognize so many people." Her big, black poodle, Bonaparte, ambled onto the stage at one point during *Luxury Liner*. Special guest Bill Monroe dropped by to perform *Blue Moon Of Kentucky* and *Kentucky Waltz*. Emmylou closed the show with *Crescent City* and *C'est La Vie*, the 34th and 35th numbers of the night. An encore performance of *Calling My Children Home*, with Roy Huskey Jr. on board, and *Jambalaya*, with Keiran Kane lending a hand on mandolin, ended the evening. Backstage, Barry and Holly Tashian, Carl Jackson, Steve Fishell, Brian Ahern, Eugenia Harris, Meghann and Hallie, and other friends and colleagues congratulated Emmylou.

In April 1995, Emmylou embarked on a European tour with Hot Band alumni. The tour began in Ireland and moved on to Scotland, England, France, Germany, Sweden, Denmark, Holland, Norway, and Spain. Photographer Nubar Alexanium caught up with the tour in Dublin. "She is so simply, supremely committed to music," Nubar observed. "Every night on tour, Trisha Yearwood and Marty Stuart opened for her, and I would notice her leaning against the wall at the edge of the audience, listening to them carefully. For Emmylou, music was as compelling as the events that inspired it. 'I was listening to Gavin Bryar's *The Sinking Of The Titanic*,' she told me one day. 'It's based on the final hymn the band was actually playing as the ship went down. Man! I sobbed through the whole thing.'"

Later in the year, Emmylou taped a CBS Special celebrating the 70th anniversary of the *Grand Ole Opry* before a capacity crowd of 4,400 at the Opry House. The lineup for the show included Allison Krauss & Union Station, George Jones, Patty Loveless, Vince Gill, Ricky Skaggs, Chet Atkins, the Whites, Ray Price, Clint Black, Travis Tritt, Pam Tillis, Connie Smith, Marty

Stuart, Jerry Douglas, Mark O'Connor and many, many others. A bluegrass finale, featuring 60 fiddlers playing *Uncle Pen*, was staged as a tribute to Bill Monroe, with the entire cast on stage for the presentation of a large bronze sculpture depicting the head, shoulders, and trademark mandolin of the Father of Bluegrass. Monroe appeared, spryly dancing onto the stage with Emmylou Harris.

Revered by several generations of country music artists, now a Nashville icon, there seemed to be little more Emmylou Harris could accomplish in her career. Various labels put together career retrospectives, the best being the 3-CD Warner/Reprise boxed set PORTRAITS, which includes *Love Hurts* and *In My Hour Of Darkness* with Gram Parsons as well as Emmylou's *Boulder To Birmingham*. The Rhino Records two-disc set EMMYLOU HARRIS: ANTHOLOGY and the Warner Brothers SONGS OF THE WEST are less comprehensive.

But Emmylou remained restless now that the Nash Ramblers and her AT THE RYMAN and COWGIRL'S PRAYER albums had ended their run. When she folded the Hot Band, Emmylou had gone back to country's roots, to bluegrass. This time she was thinking ahead, to what country could be if it were not so narrowly defined by Top 40 radio formats and market research studies. "I wish that radio were a little more open," she told Roman Mitz in *Music Express*, "or that there were some alternative formats. I'd like to see a station that could play Steve Earle and other artists that are slightly left of center but obviously come from that great country base. I would like to see my dream radio format beside Top 40."

"Everyone was encouraging me to go in a radical direction," Emmylou explains. 'Everybody,' she would reveal, included her label boss John Condon and Kyle Lehning, director of A&R at Asylum. Since the release of her debut PIECES OF THE SKY onward, Emmylou had become known for her eclectic taste and the daring mix of songs on her albums. Songs like Leonard Cohen's *Ballad Of A Runaway Horse* and her own *Prayer In Open D* from COWGIRL'S PRAYER hinted that she was headed in a new direction. WRECKING BALL, her next album, defined that direction and led to her 'discovery' by the fans of the emerging Triple A (AAA) and Americana radio formats — and the young forces in the alternative country rebellion.

Wrecking **B**all

"I had all these strange songs that were harder to categorize," Emmylou Harris notes while explaining the genesis of WRECK- ING BALL. "They asked me who I wanted to work with if I could have any producer in the whole world. I said Daniel Lanois, because his work moves me so much." She noted wryly that she was surprised that her label agreed because Lanois "did not exactly have a parking space on Music Row."

At first glance, the pairing of country rock queen Emmylou with the creator of atmospheric soundscapes for U2 and Peter Gabriel was puzzling. However, the pairing of Lanois with Bob Dylan had not been predictable, either. Critics had declared that Lanois had breathed new life into Dylan's recording career, and their album, OH MERCY, had been his best in years. Perhaps, yet another Canadian-born producer could do the same for Emmy- lou Harris.

Daniel Lanois' links to Emmylou Harris were not without a touch of the occult. Lanois' breakthrough production had come in 1987 with U2's Grammy Award-winning album, THE JOSHUA TREE, an album title with connections to Emmylou's first record- ing partner, Gram Parsons, who died in Joshua Tree National Monument Park in California. Emmylou was especially attracted to some of the songs on Daniel's own 1991 album, ACADIE, and his production of Dylan's OH MERCY. "His work is very melodic," Harris told the *Toronto Sun*, "but it's also very rhythmic. I think he finds unusual angles to achieve emotional impact, and I think there's a very haunting quality to his work." She could have been speaking of her former mentor, Gram Parsons, whose presence seems to hang in the air, hovering over the WRECKING BALL sessions like a guardian angel.

When WRECKING BALL was released, everyone was stunned by Emmylou's new direction. To some critics, it was heresy, music so different that many predicted there was not a single track likely to get any country radio airplay at all. "I'm not really paying attention to country," Emmylou apologized at the time of the album's release. "I thought there were things on COWGIRL'S PRAYER that, while not compromising the left field quality of the album, were suitable for country radio. Country radio has not invited me to their party." Fortunately, the release of WRECKING BALL coincided with the creation of two new radio formats. The AAA and Americana formats reflected the changing tastes of the radio audience and responded to the cry for wider formatting that was being raised by the artists themselves. These radio formats proved to be fertile ground for Emmylou's new alternative country hybrid to take root. When she began to tour her new music, teaming up with alt country hero Buddy Miller, she became a champion of the emerging alt country movement.

The story of the Harris-Lanois recording sessions in Nashville and New Orleans was captured in the documentary *Building the Wrecking Ball*, video-taped by Daniel's brother Bob Lanois as he wandered through the New Orleans sessions and edited with two live performances in a special that aired on PBS in the United States and selected European channels. To showcase their new material, Lanois and Harris put together a little band — with Daniel on lead guitar and mandoguitar, Emmylou on rhythm guitar, and a New Orleans rhythm section of Daryl Johnson on bass and Brian Blade on drums.

Building The Wrecking Ball opens with Harris, Lanois, and

their backing musicians performing Neil Young's title track live at a show in Boulder, Colorado, on the eve of the AAA radio convention. Bryan Taylor remembers that concert well, a pivotal show that enabled Emmylou to crack the new AAA format already playing records by her pals, Kieran Kane and Barry & Holly Tashian. "The AAA or 'triple-A' format was just taking off," Taylor recalls. "I remember her show in Boulder, with the band that she put together with Daniel to promote the album. That was good timing. She hit a promotional homerun and became the darling of AAA radio. In the beginning of the AAA format, it was heavily weighted in favor of quality singer-songwriters — people like Sheryl Crow and Shawn Colvin — and with Emmylou at the helm of it, they had a new champion they could support with their hearts. Triple-A radio gradually absorbed all the rock & roll people who couldn't get played on Top 40 formats: Tom Petty, U2, John Mellancamp . . . The next format that caught fire was 'Americana.' They had 'In The Pines' conventions on the East Coast near the lake where *On Golden Pond* was filmed, and Emmylou was a featured speaker at those conventions. She played those conventions with just her guitar, and took over the Americana air play for a while."

From their first face-to-face meeting, Daniel Lanois and Emmylou Harris had simply been the right producer and the right artist in the right place at the right time. As Emmylou recognized, they both came from far left field. "He's got a lot of great left field ideas. Everything he does is very unorthodox."

Lanois flew into Nashville and visited Harris at her home, where they sat around in her living room swapping songs and getting to know each other. "The invitation," Lanois says in *Building The Wrecking Ball*, "came at a time when I was kinda gettin' tired of workin' on my own music, and was a chance to work with one of the greatest singers. It felt real comfortable. I liked the songs that Emmy played for me, and on the spot I said, 'Yeah, let's do it! Let's start next month.'"

During an interview that I conducted with Monty Hitchcock, he told me that "the same weekend that we contacted Daniel, he flew to Nashville, and they got together. He flew in on a Saturday night, they spent some time together that night, and some more on Sunday. I was going to have dinner with them on Sunday night. I walked in the door, and everybody was 'all smiles'. Daniel said, 'We're going to do this.' I said, 'Great, let's eat.'"

When Emmylou suggested they begin recording in Nashville at Woodland studios so that she could return home after the sessions were wrapped for the day, to be with her mother and two daughters, Lanois made no objection. In fact, he was pleased with the gear that he found when he walked into Woodland studios. "I liked the vibe of Woodland," he told *Mix* magazine's Rick Clark. "They had this wonderful old 8068 Neve console and this big old room. It wasn't overly designed and reeking of technology. Sometimes, when places are just too pristine and thought-out, they're too domineering somehow." Lanois' choice of backing personnel included U2 drummer Larry Mullen Jr., who initially played hand drums before moving to his kit and over-dubbing on some of the numbers. Daniel handled many of the bass and guitar parts himself. Emmylou played her favorite studio guitar, a 1946 Gibson SJ-200.

"The lion's share of the album was performance oriented," Emmylou told Clark. "We would sit really close together with no separation and work up the arrangements and go for a performance, with a live vocal and a minimal amount of overdubs. Bleeding into the microphones was encouraged on this record. With that, I think you get another participant on the track, which is the room, and the energy and the performance. It's an ambience that you can only get going with that live situation. Ultimately, I think all of us were into the simplicity of the emotional impact and not hitting people over the head with 'Oh, this is really virtu-oso playing' or whatever. It was all passion driven. Daniel brings something unusual and moving to the sound of the musical instruments. He also has this wonderful rhythmic sense of creating powerful rhythms that don't tromp on the melody. There is all this space happening around everything. That was quite inspiring to sing to. … Working at Woodlands, sitting around playing music, I don't think anybody was that overwhelmed by the red recording button. You don't worry about 'is this musician gonna work with this musician?' It was just an idea what would it be like if we got these people together. Let's see what we come up with, because we weren't trying to make any specific type of record. We weren't trying to make a country record, or a pop record — whatever that is — we were just trying to make music."

"I had certain songs that gave me sort of a concept," Emmylou continues on the *Building The Wrecking Ball* soundtrack, "but I think that it's important to always leave that open because I think a record becomes what it is going to become. So it was a grand experiment." The songs they would tackle were Emmylou's finest selection in years, plus two that Daniel had in his pocket when he arrived in Nashville. Working with Lanois, who improvised at every opportunity, brought out the best in Harris. "Emmy would sing better and better the later it got," Lanois told *Mix*. "As a result, a lot of the vocals we got were night-time vocals."

From Woodlands they moved to Lanois' Kingsway studio, located in an old three-story house in New Orleans, to complete the album. Working with a new group of musicians, including Malcolm Burn, Richard Bennett, drummer Brian Blade, and Neville Brothers' bassist Tony Hall, they began to add overdubs. "All these people were brought together by Daniel," Emmylou explains. "He's very comfortable working in an eclectic situation. I think he's comfortable in all different musical worlds. Obviously, knowing Daniel's work, I was just excited about what he was going to bring to the songs that we both liked, and then whatever songs kinda came our way. I really saw it as a real collaboration. He would have a lot to do with what the record ended up being. He played on every track on WRECKING BALL, and brought something really special and unique — a little fire and a passion to the songs. He also had a really good song sense about the songs we recorded. He brought some of his own tunes to the album. He was involved in every single aspect of the making of this album."

Years before this, Emmylou and Brian Ahern had adopted a similar home-style approach to recording in the living room of their home in Coldwater Canyon, California, where Ahern had the recording gear in his Enactron Truck Studio parked in the driveway. "Kingsway in New Orleans was the perfect spot," Bryan Taylor notes, "because everybody lived at this studio. So, it was an environment where they could roll tape for 18 hours a day, if they wanted. And there were all those wonderful musicians and artists on the record. It was almost as if they went back to the situation of the Enactron Truck Studio, that approach. ... So, a lot of magic happened because everybody stayed at one place. They didn't pack up their stuff and go back to their hotels at the end of the day. They were living and creating together."

On WRECKING BALL, Emmylou's choice of songs is inspired. She selected Steve Earle's *Goodbye* after recording with him on his TRAIN 'A COMIN' album. However, as she revealed to Wes Phillips in the *Schwann Spectrum Guide to Music*, she did not discover the song's potential until she was sent a pre-release final mix of Steve's album. "I just kept listening to that song and pressing rewind," she told Phillips, "and listening over and over and over again. ... I thought, 'God, how on earth did I miss that one? I thought I was pretty familiar with his material.' I think that mystical, magical process that happens in the studio, where a song blossoms into something, occurred when we did *Goodbye*." In a recent on-line poll of what Steve Earle songs are most favored among his fans, *Goodbye* recorded by Emmylou Harris topped the list. As Daniel Lanois comments on the recording of *Goodbye*, "there's a technique that you can use to hang on to the original feel of a track. That's by doing such a good rough mix that you don't better it. And you end up using the rough mix. Which was the case with the song *Goodbye*. We invited the writers to come in and fit in on the session. So *Goodbye* was cut with Steve Earle playin' the guitar." For Steve Earle, "having Emmy record the song was such a compliment," he said. "Emmy is such a connoisseur of songs. It was a great session. Daniel had candles burning in the studio and everything."

"Collaboration always drives me to music," Emmylou confided to journalist Todd Denton while discussing the creation of

WRECKING BALL. "There was this great energy in the room. We were pretty close and leaking into each other's mics. I could hear everything really well, and that created another level to the music. It was like a performance. There was a real sense of abandon to it." As Emmylou continues, "Daniel saw that we needed to create a very intimate group, sort of circling around Steve. … He had the bass player play a shaker instead of a bass. He had one of the world's best rock drummers play a hand drum. And there was just very simple keyboard, and Daniel on mandolin. And yet, when we played it back in the studio, the piano and the mandolin had created this other sound that was very Phil Spector-esque. Which led us to adding the drum kit overdubs. There was a certain fog inhabiting that song that we managed to capture . . . that Daniel managed to capture in the studio."

Working with Steve Earle, Neil Young, Lucinda Williams, Julie Miller, and the McGarrigle Sisters during the 1995 Wrecking Ball sessions, Emmylou benefited from similar collaborations — where vocal harmonies often resulted in transcendent spiritual moments. The arrival of Montreal singer-songwriters Kate and Anna McGarrigle put a smile on Emmylou's face. "They were there for several days, so we were able to hang out," she recalls on the *Building The Wrecking Ball* soundtrack. "Kate would play the piano, we would do a little singing, and it was lovely for me to be able to visit with them because they are two of my favorite people." Emmylou had first heard Anna McGarrigle's *Going Back To Harlan* in Toronto during a McGarrigle's concert she had attended. She requested a demo and waited. A full-year later, as she was preparing for her sessions with Daniel Lanois, that demo tape arrived in the mail. Performed in the friendly atmosphere that had been established in New Orleans, the song became one of the album's highlights. "That's a good part of recording," Emmylou notes, "being able to get together with friends, make new friends, and sometimes bring in old friends on new projects and to enjoy their talents and also their company."

Kingsway is "a wonderful place," Anna McGarrigle observes. "Like something out of Tennessee Williams. It's a big old southern style mansion on Esplanade and Chartres. Inside, instead of having a living room, you have this huge foyer. And you walk in and it's a studio. You just sit around very comfortably and make music." Lanois' composition *Where Will I Be* was tracked and overdubbed at Kingsway, a last minute addition with Anna and her sister Kate adding harmony. This "was on my back burner, half-baked," Lanois says on the soundtrack to *Building The Wrecking Ball*. "I was still wrestling with some of the words, but the track that I had was great. It had a real sound to it. I played it for Emmy and she liked the sort of unusual rhythm of it, and we decided to go after it."

One of the warmest moments in *Building The Wrecking Ball* comes when Neil Young and his wife arrive for the sessions. "Neil Young's name came up pretty early on," Emmylou explains, "because we were doin' a song of his. But even if he hadn't written *Wrecking Ball*, his voice was the voice that should be there doing harmony. We called him and asked him if, perhaps, he would also sing harmony on a song by Lucinda Williams called *Sweet Old World*, and play harmonica on it. He and his wife, Peggy, flew down from San Francisco, came to the house in New Orleans, arrived that evening, and set up a microphone in the middle of the living room where the console was. Didn't use headphones. He knew exactly the sound he was looking for."

On Lucinda Williams' *Sweet Old World*, Lanois took the guitar out of Emmylou's hands, suggesting they let Lucinda play it as she had on her own record. "I think it was a really smart move for Daniel to take the guitar away from me on that particular track," Harris admits. "Because Lucinda plays it in a completely different way than I do, a lot slower, and it forced me to sing it in a completely different way, with a lot more tenderness."

Innovative harmonies and improvised vocals indeed distinguish this album. "We got Emmy singing in Johnny Cash's range" on *Deeper Well*, Lanois remarks. "We built it on top of a rejected rack." As Emmylou recalls, "Daniel stuck a microphone in front of me … 'Now this is in a completely different key, but when we point at you just start singing *Deeper Well*. We'll do the rest.'"

This approach worked. "I really love it," says Lanois. "I love it, too," chimes Harris. "It was almost, like, we got all these tracks that sort of effortlessly came, and now we've got to work." Reminiscent of Buffy Sainte-Marie's rebel bellow on *Bury My Heart At Wounded Knee*, this energetic track is a self-exploration, the very territory that Emmylou Harris must have explored during the troubling period when she was ignored by radio and chastised by critics. The raw lyrics chronicle Emmylou's quest for a musical rebirth.

> I rocked with the cradle and rolled with the rage
> I shook those walls and I rattled that cage
> I took my trouble down a dead end trail
> Reachin' out a hand for a holier grail
>
> — *Deeper Well* (Daniel Lanois, Emmylou Harris, David Olney)

As the documentary *Building The Wrecking Ball* begins to wind down, Emmylou continues to probe and question. "I think that people have eclectic tastes, but radio doesn't really reflect it. Most people, if you go in their living room you won't just find just one type of music. It seems odd that there isn't a station where you can hear all the great stuff. It used to be that way, I remember." She submits her case to the jury. "People can't just say that everything that I do is considered a country record because, at one point, I made a big deal about doing country music. But that was when nobody from my peer group was doing country music. You see, the way I always hoped and envisioned that country music would grow and expand would be to really explore all the subtle possibilities within the musical genre. You have so much that comprises country music. You've got blues, bluegrass, mountain music . . . you got Tex Mex, honky tonk, Cajun. You got folk music. Country music is really a blend of so many different kinds of music. Ultimately, you have got to like the music, and I really like the music we have been doing here."

On WRECKING BALL, Emmylou Harris dug deep and found

water from a deeper well, a new source of energy that she drew upon to refuel her career. And with WRECKING BALL, she found a new audience, not governed by the politics and economics of record labels and broadcasting corporations. "It was very difficult at radio in the beginning," Monty Hitchcock explains. "There were a lot of people who understood exactly what Emmylou Harris was about. Then there were those who had a lot of difficulty listening to WRECKING BALL. And there were those who just didn't know, who were very young, and got caught up in WRECKING BALL right away." This next generation of fans embraced Emmylou Harris's music *because* they first discovered her through WRECKING BALL, which led them to her past efforts, especially the tracks she had made with Gram Parsons.

In October 1995, Emmylou Harris and Daniel Lanois met with the media in the lobby of the Chateau Marmont, Emmylou's favorite West Coast hotel, to launch WRECKING BALL. Emmylou recalled the time she had lived there with her daughter "in a big room on the ground floor with a kitchen" when she first came to L.A. to record with Gram Parsons. Some journalists noted the similarity between Brian Ahern's Hollywood home studio and Daniel Lanois' New Orleans home studio. Lanois' Kingsway Studios was located in a French Quarter mansion that had at one time been a New Orleans brothel. No one pointed out that Gram Parsons' bones and ashes were buried in a cemetery there. This was music that seemed to pick up where GRIEVOUS ANGEL had left off.

For Emmylou, WRECKING BALL was "the logical next step," she told *Dirty Linen*. "I think that definitely there are elements in COWGIRL'S PRAYER that could have led me to several different paths. ... One of them being going more into left field, and exploring more the atmospheric side of the music that I do, sort of like a direct jump from *The Ballad Of A Runaway Horse* into the work with Daniel." The direction taken on WRECKING BALL had a cosmic American country music aura, to use the term Gram Parsons had coined when describing his music. "You just want to shake people up," Emmylou told *The Atlanta Journal Constitution*.

"You want them to ask questions and you want people to be in touch with their real life — whatever that may be. And I don't have any answers, but when I'm singing and when I'm doing music, I feel like I'm in touch with something. I'm closer to something that is more important than maybe anything else. We're all just trying to inch forward — aren't we? Toward something, I mean, we know that we have to do that. And I think music is a way that opens people up to that."

WRECKING BALL was as radical departure from the Top 40 country and traditional bluegrass that Emmylou was known for. As Robert K. Oermann wrote in *The Tennessean*, Emmylou Harris's "new collection breaks with tradition — again." From Music Row to New York City, from Los Angeles to New Orleans, he added, "they're calling it a 'whole new chapter', saying she's 'started all over'. David Letterman has showcased the new music. So has VH1. Rave reviews are pouring in from the nation's music critics."

This music was a peculiar blend of the various musical traditions that had shaped Emmylou Harris's career since her days as a young folk artist who idolized Woody Guthrie, as I noted at the time in my review of WRECKING BALL in *West Coast Music Review*. "*Blackhawk*, the story of two lovers who struggle to keep the romance in their life despite living within the hell-furnace environment of a small milltown, mixes the essence of Woody Guthrie, Ramblin' Jack Elliott, and Pete Seeger, distilling the form, picturing the pathos of people and the system, without editorializing. The album heralds a rebirth of feeling, full of emotionally charged material like Steve Earle's *Goodbye*, Neil Young's title song, Dylan's *Every Grain Of Sand*, and Lucinda Williams' *Sweet Old World*. There is not an air-brushed 'formula' Nashville 'country' tune on the package, and about as close as you get to 'western' is the wonderful set-closer *Waltz Across Texas Tonight*, written by Emmylou and Rodney Crowell."

In keeping with the serendipity that graces her career, Emmylou's promotional tour with Daniel Lanois coincided with the publication of the first issue of the radical music magazine *No*

Depression (An Introduction To Alternative Country Music — What-ever That Is). The founders named the publication after a song by A.P. Carter, a collector and writer of songs who had been one of the first of the musicians from the hills and hollers of east Tennessee to record with RCA Victor field employee Ralph Peer in the late 1920s. *No Depression* magazine's staff championed the alt country movement, citing Gram Parsons as their cult hero, and groups such as Son Volt, Wilco, the Jayhawks, Waco Brothers, Whiskeytown, BR5-49, and Jason & the Scorchers as a next generation of Burrito aficionados. Son Volt was featured on the cover of that first November 1995 issue. Novice record reviewers Grant Alden, Peter Blackstock, Chris Gaffney, and Charles R. Cross were still feeling out the playing field. Cross reviewed WRECKING BALL, introducing readers to the legend of Emmylou Harris. "Overall," he wrote, "the album is as slow and as haunting as the *Twin Peaks* soundtrack or the best work of the Cowboy Junkies. ... Country radio, I predict, will run with hands over ears, as if this album is heresy. Like Johnny Cash's AMERICAN RECORDINGS, this is haunting stuff and not likely to help sell boots and hats. Even AAA radio will be hard-pressed to find anything cheery enough to make the morning drive time. Nonetheless, this is a brilliant experiment that succeeds on every level, the kind of album that grows and grows on you the more you let go and succumb to Dr. Lanois' swinging hypo-watch."

Emmylou Harris had once again become the talisman of a new movement in country music, succeeding herself as the keeper of the country rock flame and founder of the new traditional movement to become the grand dame of alt country. She had found a new audience for her new and for her old music. "I'm very fortunate," she told *New York Times* reporter Peter Applebome, "in that for me there's life beyond radio. I stick my head in the sand and get to do the kind of music that I want to." Emmylou was soon heard again on the radio, on the new AAA and Americana stations, along with her alternative friends. Steve Earle formed his own E-Squared Records in response to the new interest in his music. Keiran Kane, Kevin Welch, Tammy Rogers, Mike Henderson, and Harry Stinson banded together to form Dead Reckoning Records and toured as the Dead Reckoners. Buddy and Julie Miller moved into a house not far from the Exit / In, which was becoming a focus for the alt country scene with Billy Block's weekly "Western Beat Roots Revival" nights. Block's underground shows became a CMT production at the newly restored club that derived its name from the days when there had been no front entrance. Located near Vanderbilt University, amid the bustling club activity on the Elliston Place Strip, the Exit / In was ideally situated, not too far from Music Row, and not too close.

Now seen as the queen of alt country, Emmylou Harris was no longer bound by the narrow dictates that confine a Top 40 country artist. She let herself fly. She took a political stance against landmines and toured her album relentlessly. At the same time, she made guest appearances on so many albums that statisticians would soon declare that the only country artist to have appeared on more albums than Emmylou Harris was Willie Nelson.

Spyboy

During her time recording in New Orleans, Emmylou Harris stumbled across a name for her new band that captured the rebellious spirit of WRECKING BALL. The band would be called Spyboy. "Spyboy is a term that comes out of the Mardi Gras celebration," Emmylou explains. "The spy boy is a person who goes in front of the Mardi Gras parade and acts as a sort of jester or a scout, a kind of troublemaker but in a good way." As she had shown in assembling the Hot Band and the Nash Ramblers, Emmylou proved again she had a keen eye and a fine-tuned ear for talent. "Emmylou Harris is known for assembling extraordinary bands," Nashville critic Michael McCall noted, "but Spyboy may the best she's ever fronted."

Among the fellow "troublemakers" she assembled for her new Spyboy band was Brady Blade, a drummer whose career needed reviving. Because he had not played drums for four years, Blade was surprised to be selected for the band. Brady's brother Brian had played on some cuts on the WRECKING BALL album, but Brian wasn't available to tour. As Brady recalls, "One night I get this phone call, it's Emmylou Harris on the other end, and she's asking me to play some gigs with her. I said, 'I think you've got the wrong guy, I don't even have a drum set!' But she just laughed and said she had the right guy. So, I had to borrow a drum set from my brother to play those gigs." Brady proved to be an inspired choice. After the first Spyboy tour, he found work with Jewel and the Indigo Girls. He attributes his success to Emmylou. "Emmylou Harris is the one who got me back into the business," he said recently. "If it hadn't been for Emmylou, I wouldn't be playing with all these people now. Just a few months ago Jewel came to my parents' house in Shreveport. Dad cooked steak and potato pie. Sometimes I still get tripped by it all. I'm playing with these people, talking to them on the phone, hanging out, yet at the same time I am such a fan. Sometimes, I'll just be sitting back, and I'll think, 'Yo, Emmylou Harris is my friend! Weird. It's still weird."

Not yet called Spyboy, the band set out in early November 1995, accompanied by Daniel Lanois, playing warm-up shows in Knoxville, Tennessee and Glenside, Pennsylvania, before taking on the Beacon Theater in New York. That first show in Knoxville surprised the audience. As Peter Kimball, producer of *Building The Wrecking Ball*, recalls, "the last time she played there she had been with Sam Bush and the Ramblers playing acoustic. At first, the audience didn't get it. Monty Hitchcock and Bob Lanois went out into the house and got the cheering section going. It didn't take much encouragement but most of those people had not heard the album yet and they were just getting used to the new sound."

Their set list kicked off with Emmylou performing the highly recognizable *Songbird* and *Prayer In Open D* before launching into *Blackhawk*, *Where Will I Be*, *Orphan Girl*, and *Wrecking Ball* from the new album. Then came *Going Back To Harlan*, *Deeper Well*, *Calling My Children Home*, *One Of These Days*, *Every Grain Of Sand*, *Sweet Old World*, *Goodbye*, and *The Maker*, a Lanois song not included on the album, mixing something old and something new, something Emmylou and something Daniel. After shows in Northampton, Massachusetts and the Count Basie Theater in New Jersey, they flew across the Atlantic to preview the album for audiences in Amsterdam, London, and Oslo, Norway.

In February 1996, Emmylou and Daniel returned to New

York City to play a free concert in the shade of the World Trade
Center twin towers, as Dan Aquilante reported in *The New York
Post*. "Emmylou Harris played a free concert at the World Finan-
cial Center's marble and glass atrium in the Battery Park complex. Harris's voice soared in this majestic public space, making
for an inspired, memorable concert. Pretty Emmylou looked as
stylish as her predominantly Wall Street audience. She wore a
neat black skirt and leopard-print blouse as she fronted her very
casually dressed band. The one-hour show consisted mostly of
tunes from her new disc, WRECKING BALL, and Lanois' *The
Maker*, which they also performed at Monday's Tibet House
benefit at Carnegie Hall."

When the tour resumed, Buddy Miller replaced Daniel Lanois
and the band took on the name Spyboy. Emmylou and Daniel had
chosen to record Buddy Miller's wife Julie's song *All My Tears* on
WRECKING BALL and invited her to the sessions, but Emmylou
was the one to scout Buddy for Spyboy, as she exclaimed during
an interview in *No Depression*: "*I* found Buddy Miller!" Buddy was
keen to join the band. As he told *Mix*, his ears had perked up the
first time he heard WRECKING BALL. "I love that record, and I
think Daniel Lanois did the initial tour with the rhythm section
he picked. Then they needed a replacement because he needed to
go elsewhere. Meanwhile, I would just call Emmylou's manager
every few months to see if there was possibility of getting an audition. I wanted to let them know that I was interested. I was out
opening for Emmylou, playing guitar for Jim Lauderdale, and
I've always been a huge admirer. So, when they had auditions, I
got to participate, and to tell you the truth, I didn't think I had a
chance of getting the gig. It was a big surprise to me when I did."

"I listened to WRECKING BALL," Buddy told Peter Blackstock, "and heard what Daniel was doing on the guitar. I wasn't
going to imitate it, because he's nuts. He's on the edge of the limb,
at all times, and doesn't care if he comes back. I've got a lot of
respect for that kind of player. Richard Thompson does the same
kind of thing with his playing. It's a much different style, but they
just take chances."

Emmylou's genius was to recognize that Buddy would also prove to be a great singing partner, as good at harmonizing with her voice as Rodney Crowell and Barry Tashian had been, perhaps as good as Gram Parsons. Spyboy's ability to showcase the new songs from WRECKING BALL and also render tour de force performances of her classic repertoire won them praise from both critics and fans. "She started pulling out all these songs," Monty Hitchcock told me. "She gave them *Boulder To Birmingham, Pancho & Lefty* and *Wheels*. At first she would just give them the record. Then she got to where she just played them the songs on the guitar. Quite frankly, Daryl Johnson and Brady Blade weren't familiar with some of those tunes. Buddy Miller was. They brought a whole new life to those songs. She is just so amazing. The one thing that has kept her viable and alive is creating new stuff. She could have easily fallen into a groove years ago and stayed there and made lots of money but she couldn't do that."

"Out of all these alt country artists and bands comes Buddy Miller," Brian Taylor notes, citing Miller as the key ingredient in "that great band, Spyboy, Emmy put together with Daryl Johnson on bass, Brady Blade on drums, and Buddy Miller on multitudinous stringed instruments. Buddy sings harmony with her. He does it all. I haven't seen many four-piece bands that can rock like that — those six and seven minute explorations, where Daryl would put down his bass and switch over to djembe and bass foot-pedals, so that they would have two drummers, with Emmylou's guitar carrying the load. That's why musicians worship her!"

The band toured heavily throughout the year, swinging up through western Canada and down the West Coast. By the time they arrived at the Commodore Ballroom in Vancouver on April 4, 1996, music critic for *The Province*, John McLaughlin, shouted in my ear during the performance, "This is the show of the year!" Everyone was amazed by the performance of Emmylou Harris and Spyboy.

By May they were in Australia for nine shows in 14 days. In Perth, Carlos Santana joined them on stage. Back in Nashville, they played the 2nd Harvest Food Bank Benefit on the lawn of the

Belle Meade Mansion. Even though she was heavily booked on the tour circuit, Emmylou continued to perform regularly at benefits whenever possible. At the request of Roy Huskey Jr.'s widow, Emmylou learned *In My Life* and sang it at Roy's funeral, adding her tribute to her former band-member. When Phil Kaufman was diagnosed with prostate cancer, Emmylou performed at the whimsically named "Concert For Mangler Desh" in October after returning from her third set of dates in Europe. "When I was diagnosed with cancer and said I didn't have any money or insurance," Kaufman said later, "the first thing she said was, 'Right, we'll do a show.'" By the end of the decade, Phil Kaufman was hale and hearty, working again for Emmylou Harris.

For the summer tour season in 1996, rising Canadian artist Sarah McLachlan put together a series of all women shows, initially enlisting her hero Patti Smith and others for a short "Girlie Goddess Tour." In choosing other women artists for these shows, Sarah explained that "everything I've been writing lately seems to sound like old Hank Williams. I don't know where it's coming from. I think I'm channeling some old-country soul or something. I've been listening to Emmylou a lot — maybe she's been inspiring me and bringing up some old ghosts." Emmylou Harris and Crash Vegas's Michelle McAdorey joined Sarah McLachlan, Patti Smith, Paula Cole, Aimee Mann, and Lisa Loeb for concerts in Berkeley and Burbank, where the name "Lilith Fair" first bubbled up as a possible name for these shows. On September 14, 1996 at Nat Bailey Stadium in Vancouver the first official "Lilith Fair" show was staged.

"Next summer I want to do a full tour," Sarah announced at the end of the show, "sort of an anti-Lollapalooza-boys' club thing." Emmylou Harris played a total of ten Lilith Fair shows the next summer. "After I did the show with Sarah," Emmylou told Steve Dollar, "and saw what an amazing artist she is and how open-minded her audience was, it never occurred to me not to do it." At age 50, she was the senior member of this brigade of women. As Mary Houlihan-Skilton reported, "With a music career that spans 30 years, Harris has seen it all come and go.

Along the way, she has always marched to the beat of a different drummer, creating a songbook unparalleled in its creativity and integrity. Harris is a perfect fit for Lilith, the all female concert phenomenon that is taking the outdoor sheds by storm."

"Oh, I'm definitely the senior on this tour," Emmylou told Houlihan-Skilton. "I'm happy to be part of it. While I know many of the artists, I look forward to getting turned on to others I'm not familiar with. Lilith is a great chance to see and hear a lot of great music." Most of all she looked forward to Lilith audiences. "I could tell that a lot of those people weren't familiar with my music. Yet there was this sense that they were going to give it a chance. I think the tour attracts people who are very much into music *and* listening to it." One Emmylou fan who attended a Vancouver show was *X-Files* star David Duchovny. As Allison Glock noted, "Backstage at Lilith Fair women's concert in Vancouver, David Duchovny is listening intently as Emmylou Harris sings *Goodbye*. His feet tap a bit, nothing too overt, just enough to keep him from looking stiff. He mouths the words: 'Somewhere in there I'm sure I made you cry / But I can't remember if we said goodbye.' Behind him disgruntled stagehands grouse, 'Who does this guy think he is? Moses?' Duchovny doesn't hear. His heart is breaking." Not only the grand dame of the alt country movement, Emmylou Harris had now become a Lilith to a new generation of strong young women artists.

During Lilith Fair press conferences that summer, Emmylou surprised many people by speaking out in support of the International Campaign To Ban Landmines. Previously, she had refrained from political pronouncements, her only campaign being her effort to champion alternative country artists on the radio. Now she extended her generosity to the Vietnam Veterans of America Foundation in their international campaign to ban landmines and efforts to reforest the decimated hillsides of Vietnam. The associate director of the VVAF was Gail Griffith, a close friend of Emmylou. They had met early in Emmylou's career at Clydes in Georgetown and had kept up their friendship when Emmylou moved to California. During a telephone conversation, the two women learned that they had both read Michael Ondaatje's novel *The English Patient*, which details the difficulties of disarming antipersonnel mines. "I'd just read an article in *The New Yorker*," Emmylou told Rachel Snyder, "and at that time there were 100 million landmines in the ground. You think it's a misprint." In April 1997, Emmylou hosted a reception at her home in Nashville to rally support for the VVAF. Then she spread the word during her Lilith Fair appearances in 1997 and 1998, citing the statistic that "every 22 minutes someone in the world is killed or maimed by a landmine." As Emmylou acknowledged, she was inspired by what Sarah McLachlan "was able to accomplish, not only musically, but with political issues, too, allowing those of us with pet issues on the forum."

On November 11, 1997, Emmylou and Jamie O'Hara were invited to sing at a Veteran's Day observance at the Vietnam Veterans Memorial in Washington to commemorate the 15th anniversary of its erection. For Vietnam War vet Gary Vizioli, Emmylou's appearance held special meaning. "After years of indifference to the past, and stunned with a numbness I couldn't break, I turned to music," he explains. "Emmylou was the touchstone and beacon guiding my musical journey. In time, something reached deep inside my soul. I found a start on the long road to 'coming home'. I then began to move through a difficult healing process that couldn't have happened without the Wall. A short time after my first visit there, I heard Jamie O'Hara's *50,000 Names*, which moved me in many difficult but necessary directions." After a reading of *In Flanders Fields*, Emmylou harmonized with O'Hara as he sang *50,000 Names*. She also performed *America The Beautiful*, *Orphan Girl*, and Floyd Tilman's *Remember Me*, a song that had come to Emmylou as she was thinking about her cousin, Stephen Hamilton Adams, whose name was on the Wall. "Her voice ever so gently filled the air with *Remember Me*," Vizioli recalls, "and it seemed as though our lost ones were calling to us. There were tears, soft smiles, many bowed heads. She never fails to find the right words and song."

VVAF director Bobby Muller invited Gail and Emmylou to

travel with him to Phnom Penh, Cambodia, where the VVAF had opened the Kien Kleang Rehabilitation Center. In support of the cause, on December 11, 1999, Emmylou was featured singing *Calling My Children Home* and *Abraham, Martin, and John* with a string quartet at the Nobel Peace Prize ceremonies where Muller was rewarded for his dedicated humanitarian work. Later that day she shared an Oslo stage with the likes of Harry Connick Jr., Mariah Carey, Boys II Men, Jewel, and Sinead O'Connor. She performed *In My Life* with Kennedy/ Rose before an estimated tv audience of 200 million viewers. "I know I'm just an attention-getting device, I know that," she later told journalists. "But after going to Cambodia and Vietnam … I've been fully committed to this."

Harris and Muller put together a series of three annual 'Concerts for a Landmine Free World' and released benefit albums on Vanguard Records. Staged each December from 1999 to 2001, these shows featured John Prine, Nanci Griffith, Bruce Cockburn, Sheryl Crow, Lucinda Williams, Elvis Costello, Willie Nelson, Guy Clark, Gillian Welch, Mary Chapin Carpenter, Kris Kristofferson, and Steve Earle. "Emmylou played an elegant and gracious hostess," Sue Keogh wrote in her internet review of a show at the Apollo Hammersmith in the UK. "She sat there draped in her silk scarf woven by a Vietnamese women's collective and introduced her colleagues with great pride, leant her tender backing vocals to their songs, and when she took the spotlight herself I got a tingle right down to my toes." Just before the intermission, Emmylou announced that the scarf was up for auction and suggested that the bidding start at 200 pounds sterling. Keogh was astonished when "it raised a massive 8,000 pounds."

During this period when Emmylou wasn't touring with Spyboy or playing benefits, she often sang on sessions for up-and-coming artists. She contributed to two records by new-generation artists, playing rhythm guitar on Meghann Ahern's *There's A Light*, a track that was released locally through Hillsboro High School, and recording a duet with Jason & the Scorchers lead vocalist, Jason Ringenberg. "I'm just a major fan of Emmy," Jason told *The Tennessean*. "I've been listening to her since I was knee high. I had chills the whole time. I kept having to pinch myself."

Emmylou added her voice to a track on her neighbor's next album, CAR WHEELS ON A DIRT ROAD, by Lucinda Williams, who lived two doors down. This album turned out to be one of the best alt country albums of the era. In one of her most generous gestures, Emmylou also helped Buddy Miller record POISON LOVE, his follow-up album to his 1995 debut YOUR LOVE AND OTHER LIES, singing and playing on six of the 13 tracks, bringing her rhythm section along with her. "Playing with Emmylou has been the greatest in every way," Miller comments. "She gives the players in the band all the room they need to stretch out. I know I've grown from my association with her. ... Emmylou set the tone for every song she played on," Buddy says, "either on vocals or on guitar, which she played in modal tuning. All the tracks we did with Emmylou's band contained little overdubbing." Steve Earle has said that Buddy Miller knows every country song ever written. "One of my main barometers for how fucked-up mainstream country is right now," Steve told *No Depression*, "is that Buddy Miller's not automatically on country radio."

When Robert Redford called and asked Emmylou to record *Slow Surprise* for the soundtrack of *The Horse Whisperer*, she agreed because the healing theme of the film and Redford's aim of paying tribute "to the uniquely American sound of traditional western music" were both worthy causes. Brian Ahern produced Emmylou's session.

In early 1997, Emmylou Harris & Spyboy played a concert at the Exit / In that was videotaped for a one-hour tv documentary and home video similar to *Building The Wrecking Ball*. Emmylou's manager Monty Hitchcock sold *Emmylou Harris: Spyboy, Live at the Exit/In* to PBS and later released it in VHS format. "It's doing surprisingly well," he told me in March 1999. "To be perfectly honest — and I'm happy to say this — I got caught with my pants down. I had to go back and re-manufacture because I underestimated how well it would sell. PBS has responded well to it. We have put it on tv in about 50 percent of the U.S. market places.

Emmylou is not touring this year — she's in Tucson recording with Glynn Johns and Linda Ronstadt — but when she does start to tour again we'll do the same thing that we did with *Building The Wrecking Ball*."

"The Exit / In is a great club," Emmylou narrates at the beginning of *Emmylou Harris: Spyboy Live at the Exit/In*. "It's small, and it's smoky, and it gets a bit hot, but it's one of those places that people come just to see who's playing; out of a sense of musical curiosity. The Spyboy Tour started two years earlier, and then went all around the world, several times. For the most part we played in places of varying sizes, some smaller, and some larger than the Exit/In, but we played for and sought out people who loved music, who wanted to be stirred by it, who wanted to be surprised by it — because, really, WRECKING BALL and Spyboy were kind of a musical experiment. I've always been trying to push the envelopes a lot, but I think I kinda broke right through the paper with this one. I've had an incredible time with this band. It's given me a whole new excitement about music. It shows what we are as a musical family, taking it on the road, doing it really because we love it."

This experiment was also captured on the live album EMMYLOU HARRIS: SPYBOY, recorded on the road at various venues. Buddy Miller is credited as co-producer of the album. As he told *Mix*, "I wanted to record the dates just to have proof that I was actually in the band. I'd bring out a few racks of gear, just because I loved the music so much, and I never thought it would turn into anything. … Dean Norman and Doug Dawson would set up the mics before each show," Buddy explains, "and he'd switch the tape and press 'record' when the show was starting. We got into a little routine and took it out for 20 or 30 dates with that little setup."

"Once we got the gear together," Monty Hitchcock explains, "I just made the call to record the whole show. It was just a matter of tape. Let's go ahead and record. It's just for archival purposes. When we began to listen to the tapes in December of 1977 and January of 1998, Emmy decided it was good enough to be a record." The album would be released on Monty's new Eminent

Records label, as Emmylou explains. "Monty came to me and he said, 'What would you think of putting out a live record? You've taken a year off. The tracks are done. You're without a label. You could do a one-off deal with this new label I'm doing.' I knew this record would have a better shot with this label than with any other because Monty is so devoted to the project."

Emmylou was also keen to capture the live magic of one song, Daniel Lanois' *The Maker*. "I started performing it when Daniel and I were on a short tour together," she told Michael McCall. "I performed the song each night with Daniel; I really loved it and I knew I wanted it on record. But there was no way I could compete with his studio version of it, so I thought I would record our shows so I could get a live version of it to put on a studio album."

The 14 songs on the live album simulate a set list from a show, with *My Songbird* leading to *Where Will I Be*, before the pace picks up on Rodney Crowell's *Ain't Livin' Long Like This*. Emmylou and Buddy had brought the houses down with their harmonizing on *Love Hurts* during their tour, and the track on the CD is one of their best efforts. The set moves on through *Green Pastures* and a seven-minute rock out on *Deeper Well*. For those who hadn't yet heard *Prayer In Open D*, the live album was a revelation. A show-stopper during the tour had been the group's a capella rendition of *Calling My Children Home*, rendered well here before the tempo picks up on *Tulsa Queen, Wheels*, and *Born To Run*. Emmylou's *Boulder To Birmingham*, followed by Julie Miller's *All My Tears*, set the scene for the finale, Daniel Lanois' *The Maker*, an eight and a half minute tour de force performance.

When the album was released in the summer of 1998, *Billboard* declared it to be "a deeply moving, concert-length tale of searching, loss, and redemptive experience." A *Wall Street Journal* reviewer wrote that "Emmylou Harris scaled the peaks of meaningful music long ago, but she never seems to come down the other side." Most glowing of all was *Rolling Stone* magazine's pronouncement: "Right now Harris is making arguably the most daring music of her 30-year career."

Return of the
Grievous Angel

In December 1999, on the eve of the new millennium, Emmylou Harris was named *Billboard* magazine's Artist of the Century, the eighth recipient of this special honor to be awarded during the final decade of the century. "Emmylou Harris has uncompromisingly advanced the cause of roots music in our nation and cultural resonance around the world," *Billboard* editor-in-chief Timothy White declared. "Harris's recordings are the sound of a brave, honest, intelligent heart, digging deeper to help us all grasp music's ability to alter our inner and outer worlds for the better. Anyone who thinks music and those who make it cannot change and even revolutionize the way our culture sees itself should acquaint themselves with her incomparable body of work. Such ongoing achievements are the reason why *Billboard* can think of no artist more deserving of the 1999 Century Award than Emmylou Harris."

Not surprisingly, Emmylou was invited to participate in a number of the 'best of the century' lists, compilations, and tribute albums. For the TAMMY WYNETTE REMEMBERED tribute album, Emmylou collaborated with Linda Ronstadt and the McGarrigle sisters on the George & Tammy classic *Golden Ring*. She also sang harmony vocals on Willie Nelson's TEATRO album, produced by Daniel Lanois in an old theater in L.A. She played the Bluebird with Nanci Griffith, Mary Ann Kennedy, Pam Rose, and Lee Satterfield, performing *Who Knows Where Time Goes*, which she had written for her grandmother with Paul Kennerly, and joined a group effort finale of Kate Wolf's *The Great Divide*. Emmylou performed during Lilith Fair shows, at the "A Lotta Love" tribute to Nicolette Larsen in Santa Monica along with Linda Ronstadt, Crosby, Stills & Nash, Carole King, Bonnie Raitt, Jimmie Buffet, and Neil Young, and a "Save the Rainforest" gala with Elton John, Billy Joel, and James Taylor in New York City. On December 20, she sang harmony with Meghann Ahern at the Subtler club in Nashville, where they performed Townes Van Zandt's *If I Needed You* and a rousing *Hippy Hippy Shake* finale.

While in a collaborative frame of mind, Emmylou Harris had reunited with Linda Ronstadt and Dolly Parton to record TRIO II. They first considered recording another album together back in 1995, but some misunderstanding and conflicting schedules had disrupted the plan. Emmylou had misgivings, as Linda explains. "Emmy, who's more practical than me, was remembering how difficult it had been to get our schedules together, and how difficult it had been to schedule time to promote the record, which we'd felt was really crucial." But the project seemed destined to be. "What the Trio had done was so stunning," Linda explains, "so I fought for that. I would love to repeat that, so I fought for that. I asked Dolly if she would sing on a couple of tracks, and Dolly said no, she wanted it to be a full-on Trio or nothing. Emmy said, 'I really would rather not do that. Don't let her talk you back into a Trio record.' And Dolly talked me back into a Trio record."

Despite opposition from Peter Asher and Ira Kozlow, Linda's management team, and from Bob Krasnow, head of Elektra, sessions were scheduled. Things did not go smoothly. As Linda recalls, "I showed up, Emmy showed up, and the night before we started, Dolly sent us a fax saying there was something wrong with her infommercial and she had go back for 10 days. I had booked all these triple-scale players from Tennessee, and it was going to be very expensive to put them up. Emmy stayed at my house, so that we could save money."

When the album was eventually released in 1999, Dolly, Linda, and Emmylou joined forces to promote their work, with Dolly making light of their tiffs. "We apologized," Dolly explained, "then we all got together in a room and they kicked the shit out of me. They beat me up and I begged for forgiveness. Actually, we just talked that out. You know, we're like family." As Emmylou admitted, "It was great when the opportunity came to finally get the record out, but it was even better to talk to each other again." Their rendition of Neil Young's '70s anthem *After the Goldrush* won Trio their second Grammy Award.

While discussing the dynamic among the trio, Linda notes that Dolly "can sing that Appalachian stuff with complete authenticity because that's where she grew up. When we're working together I stand back and let her do it, because that's what she does well, and I try to sing harmonies, which is what I'm good at." With Emmylou, the collaboration is different. "It's more of a duet," Linda explains. "When we talk on the phone, Emmy and I, you know she'll say, did you hear this latest song by Kate? And she'll start singing it over the phone, and I'll sing harmony, and we'll sing over the phone."

Linda Ronstadt's wish to form the Everly Sisters duo with Emmylou Harris, made that night they first met in Houston back in 1973, was delayed for 25 years by their ongoing Trio project. As a duo, Linda and Emmylou recorded WESTERN WALL: THE TUCSON SESSIONS. During their promotional tour, they exchanged accolades. "There's just nobody that sings like Emmy," Linda noted. "Her voice is like cracked crystal. It's just this beautiful light airy translucent thing that all of a sudden has grit in it. We have a great time. We completely see eye-to-eye. We can finish each other's sentences. Our sensibilities are very matched. And that makes it easy for us to record together."

"We've talked about making this record ever since we first met in 1973," Emmylou noted in return, explaining how Linda had supported her after Gram Parsons' death. "She was there to console me, and bring me out to sing at her shows at the Roxy, and talk to me about record companies and people in the business, and really, it gave me a leg up."

"We've known each other so long that we couldn't get apart," Linda told CNN. "We sing over the phone to each other. This is just the culmination of a long-term musical relationship."

"This is the anti-diva record," Emmylou told *Toronto Sun* music critic Errol Nazareth. "I was speaking to someone who told me that the German edition of *Rolling Stone* didn't like it 'cause it was too beautiful. I said, 'How can you fault something for being too beautiful?' They obviously haven't lived long enough."

The title for the album derived from their rendition of Rosanne Cash's title track: "I don't know if God was ever a man / But if She was I think I understand / Why he found a place to break his fall / Near the Western Wall." Kate and Anna McGarrigle sang harmonies on David Olney's *1917*, Leonard Cohen's *Sisters Of Mercy*, and on their composition *All I Left Behind*, co-written with Emmylou. Producer Glyn John's son, Ethan Johns, played guitars, drums, and percussion. Bernie Leadon showed up, too. Paul Kennerly played electric guitar on his own *He Was Mine*. Neil Young sang and played harmonica on Jackson Browne's *For A Dancer*.

Emmylou's next major project was serving as an executive producer for RETURN OF THE GRIEVOUS ANGEL, the Gram Parsons tribute album. Emmylou Harris and Almo Sounds GM Paul Kremen worked together, defining the territory and rounding up the talent. Kremen had first become inspired to go ahead with the project during an Emmylou Harris show at the Fillmore West in San Francisco and then, during the break, hearing Wilco's debut album played over the house system. "Because she just played a bunch of Gram's songs in the first set," Paul explains, "and he was such a massive influence — so clearly delineated in this new Wilco record. 'Wouldn't a tribute be a great idea?'" When Kremem realized that Almo Sounds founders, Jerry Moss and Herb Alpert, had put out Parsons' Burrito Brothers albums, a light flashed. "Half of Gram's publishing lived at the Rondor Publishing affiliate that

Jerry and Herb owned. It just made it so much more sense for Almo to do this project that I slowly started approaching Emmylou. I didn't want to do it without Emmylou."

While initially cool to the "tribute" idea, Emmylou warmed to the project when she saw it as an introduction of Gram's achievement to yet another generation. "I thought in the case of Gram it wasn't so much a tribute as an introduction," she said later. "Because a lot of people don't know who he is. They've heard his name; they haven't really heard his music. Let's face it, Gram has not exactly torn up the charts." It wasn't difficult to enlist volunteers. Gillian Welch was one of the first to come on board. "His music really played a part in my finding of old-time country," she says. "Through him I got back into Buck Owens and Merle Haggard, and then after that I got into Lefty Frizzell. You put a certain kind of band together, and you play with a certain attitude, and you kind of sound like the Flying Burrito Brothers."

Gillian and Dave Rawlings recorded *Hickory Wind*. Sheryl Crow, Margo Timmins, the Mavericks, Steve Earle and Chris Hillman, Lucinda Williams, Whiskeytown, and Wilco also contributed. Joshua Tree National Park residents Victoria Williams and Mark Olson got together with Jim Lauderdale and Buddy & Julie Miller for the challenging *In My Hour Of Darkness*, leaving the playing field clear for Emmylou in a duet with Beck on *Sin City* and Chrissy Hynde on *She*. The charity benefiting from the album was Bobby Muller's VVAF. The album release was heralded by a "Sessions at West 54th" special and a simulcast radio broadcast by "World Cafe."

When Mary Martin, now a Mercury Records executive, got together with Luke Lewis and Bonnie Garner in 2001 to produce TIMELESS: A TRIBUTE TO HANK WILLIAMS, Emmylou contributed Hank Sr.'s *Lost On The River*, with Mark Knopfler's band accompanying her. One of the most interesting compilations issued in 2001 was CONCERT FOR A LANDMINE FREE WORLD, the first in the promised Vanguard series that will chronicle Emmylou and Bobby Muller's traveling songwriters circle. The album begins with Emmylou singing *The Pearl,* followed by John Prine performing *Big Ol' Goofy World.* Also participating were Guy Clark, Mary Chapin Carpenter, Bruce Cockburn, Nanci Griffith, Gillian Welch and David Rawlings, Patty Griffin, Kris Kristofferson, Terry Allen, and Steve Earle. Both Emmylou Harris and Gram Parsons got boxed set releases that year courtesy of Rhino records, four-and-a-half hours of the best cosmic American music ever put to record.

While contributing to these various tributes and compilations, Emmylou had begun to write new songs for the album she would call RED DIRT GIRL, released on her new label, Nonesuch Records, with Malcolm Burn producing. In order to make a fresh start, Emmylou signed a management deal with Ken Levitan, former head of Rising Tide Records, who had begun signing artists to his newly formed Vector Management team. Levitan was working with a stable of artists that included .38 Special, Dolly Parton, Jack Ingram, John Hiatt, Jonny Lang, Lyle Lovett, Lynyrd Skynyrd, Michael McDonald, Patty Griffin, Patty Loveless, Sixpence None The Richer, Van Zant, and the Warren Brothers. He helped Emmylou secure a contract with Nonesuch Records, an affiliate of Warner Brothers.

Songwriting was still a somewhat daunting task for Emmylou, as she confessed in *Newsweek.* "I spent my career as an interpreter. The idea of writing a bad song horrified me. But I knew if I was going to do another studio record, I just had to write it myself, and either sink or swim."

Daniel Lanois encouraged Emmylou to write more songs from her heart like her sorrowful *Prayer In Open D. Bang The Drum Slowly* is just such a song. "*Bang The Drum Slowly* is an elegy for my father, who died in 1993," Emmylou explains. "A couple of years afterward, I was talking to Jamie O'Hara and said, 'You know, I just feel the need to write about my dad but I can't even get started. I have so many regrets because there are so many things that I could have learned from him that I didn't.' Jamie said, 'Just write that.' I took the song to Guy Clark and he really helped with the lyrics and inspired me to write more."

"My father was a man of enormous compassion and humanity," she told *New York Times* feature writer Daniel Menaker. "And he could do anything. I always felt phoney around him, as if what I was doing weren't real work. He told me he didn't feel that way, but I was always afraid that he did."

> I meant to ask you how to fix that car
> I meant to ask you about the war
> And what you saw across a bridge so far
> Did it leave a scar?
>
> Or how you navigated wings of fire and steel
> Up where heaven had no more secrets to conceal
> And still you found the ground beneath your wheels
> How did it feel?
>
> Bang the drum slowly, play the pipe lowly
> To dust be returning, from dust we begin
> Bang the drum slowly, I'll speak of things holy
> Above and below me, world without end
>
> — *Bang The Drum Slowly* (Emmylou Harris, Guy Clark)

Throughout her career, Emmylou Harris has maintained an unusual reserve in discussing her private life. She has been even more reluctant to reveal details about her parents, especially her father. A press release issued by The Retired Officer's Association (TROA) in 2002 revealed a motive for Emmylou's reticence. Not only had her father, Major Walter "Bucky" Rutland Harris, been awarded the Medal of Honor following his release from a North Korean POW camp in 1953 — his "exceptional leadership and many positive actions while a prisoner are also cited in the 'Code of Conduct' section of the *Marine Handbook*" — but more relevant to his daughter's public life, he had also "served as a Presidential Command Pilot in helicopters for every president from Eisenhower through Carter." Major Harris's "day job" with the

Secret Service would not be a subject of discussion outside the immediate family. Seven years after Emmylou's father's death in 1993, a scholarship was named in his memory. The ceremony was held at TROA Headquarters in Alexandria, Virginia, and attended by Egenia Harris, Emmylou Harris, Rutland Harris, and Rutland's wife, Mrs. Gail Harris.

In her Nonesuch Records press release, Emmylou offers insights into other songs on RED DIRT GIRL. *Michelangelo* had come to her in a dream, but she confessed to cribbing a bit from one of America's signature poets. "I read a lot," she explains, "and I find myself very moved by language. There's almost a direct steal from Carl Sandburg. I just kinda re-wrote it." *I Don't Want To Talk About It Now* is a turbulent, churning track reminiscent of the Beatles *I Am The Walrus*. "Jill Conniff of Luscious Jackson was my co-writer on this," Emmylou notes. "When were cutting this song Jill and Daryl thought, 'This song needs a bridge' and they came up with all those chord changes that really lifted it. She took it to another level. Malcolm Burn added that telephone sound. I brought Julie Miller down to do some singing. I needed something different and she nailed it down with those 'answering' vocals."

Rodney Crowell receives a co-writing credit on the melodic *Tragedy* because Emmylou had unconsciously cribbed one of his old melodies. It wasn't his active co-writing, but she felt she owed him. "Those harmony vocals are Patti Scialfa and Bruce Springsteen," Emmylou explained. "They were in New Orleans performing. I loved Patti's album RUMBLE DOLL and I thought it was terribly overlooked. So I wanted to get her on my record. It turned out that they had the next day off after the concert so they came over."

Red Dirt Girl had come to her while driving from Nashville to Louisiana. "I think this was hovering over the highway, and I drove over it," she suggested. "I am very inspired by the sound of words, and name places are so melodic and beautiful. And I was passing through Meridian on my way down to record in New Orleans, and that's what started it."

Me and my best friend Lillian
And her blue tick hound dog Gideon,
Sittin' on the front porch cooling in the shade
Singin' every song the radio played
Waitin' for the Alabama sun to go down
Two red dirt girls in a red dirt town
Me and Lillian
Just across the line and a little southeast of Meridian ...

— *Red Dirt Girl* (Emmylou Harris)

For upbeat material she continued to turn to other writer's material like Patty Griffin's *One Big Love*, a tune that Malcolm Burn had wanted included because he felt that they needed at least one "groove" number.

Malcolm Burn, like Brian Ahern and Daniel Lanois, is a Canadian. Burn had engineered and mixed WRECKING BALL. On RED DIRT GIRL he used many of the same production techniques. Both Lanois and Burn prefer to record on analog tape at 15 inches per second rather than the current Nashville craze of using digital Pro Tools software — the idea being that if you could come up with a moving performance, you didn't need 48 tracks or pitch-correction software. Lanois and Burn are also fond of printing "loads of low-end information onto tape," as Burn told *Mix*. "Depending on how you hit the tape, EQ, and what not. I tend to add 60 cycles, where most people will take it off. I find that if you hit the tape in the right way, the tape acts as a natural compressor. That's why reggae records and Rap records sound so great. They're pushing that frequency that most rock people are trying to get away from. I tend to go for as much bottom as possible."

"The whole process was magical," Emmylou said at the time of the release. "I didn't want to abandon the steps I'd taken with WRECKING BALL. I wanted to stay in that same general direction because I loved the sound of that record. During those sessions I had been so impressed by Malcolm Burn. It seemed like there was nothing he couldn't do. So we got together last November. It was just me and Malcolm with Daryl Johnson and Ethan Johns. We did the whole record in Malcolm's house in New Orleans, in his living room. Then for the second leg, in March, I came down and spent a week with just Malcolm and myself, working on a new batch of songs I'd finished. Later we started adding other people to the tracks."

On her return trip from Malcolm Burn's New Orleans studio, Emmylou was in a serious automobile accident. Her hard-top jeep skidded from the paved surface through two lanes of opposing rush hour traffic, rolled over, and struck a tree. Napoleon, her big black "standard" poodle road dog, was thrown free. Emmylou had buckled up and survived, too. "I hydro-planed and rolled over twice and hit a tree," she told Jane Stevenson. "I broke three ribs and got banged up pretty bad. But it was actually nothing compared to what it could have been. My dog was okay. My car was totalled. There was this moment when you realize how fragile life is. But I have a feeling that I'm going to be around for a long time."

The incident had also provoked some philosophical assessment. "I'm at peace with a lot of things," she told *The London Daily Telegraph*. "Certainly, I've had an extraordinary life. I'm still here doing the work I love. I've met extraordinary people who have inspired me. I have excellent health, two wonderful daughters, and friends I love dearly, so, I try to be thankful."

When Emmylou set out on tour to support her Nonesuch Records debut, Buddy Miller was still the leader of her band. "It's me, Brady Blade, and Tony Hall on bass," he said at the time. "It's just been three pieces and her for seven years. ... I'll never quit doing Emmylou tours, unless they fire me," Buddy says. "It's almost comical, what a really nice person she is. She never shows up at our house without food or flowers, or something. She's very considerate, very thoughtful. When it's time to get on the bus, she gets in the very back. She has no star trip whatsoever."

Cup of **K**indness

In January 2002, Gibson Guitar Corp issued an Emmylou Harris model guitar, the Gibson L-200. "I love the size of this guitar," Emmylou says. "It's a great guitar to have in your bedroom or down in your music room. It's great to grab when you have an idea and want to work something out." Smaller and thinner than a SJ-200, the L-200 is "braced to produce a powerful natural sound and equipped with a Schertler Bluestick transducer pickup system for concert performances. Classic features from the SJ-200 included flamed maple back and sides, mother-of-pearl 'crest' fingerboard inlays, pearl-inlaid 'moustache' bridge and engraved pick guard."

"Emmylou Harris is one of the most important artists of our time," Henry Juszkiewicz, chairman and CEO of the Gibson said. "We're proud of the role Gibsons have played in her music, and we're excited to be her partner as she continues to make great music in the years to come." With this joint venture, Emmylou Harris became a member of an exclusive guitar club that includes Les Paul, Chet Atkins, and James Burton, who have also had special model guitars named after them.

With each new accolade and award Emmylou was being recognized for her unique contributions to our musical heritage. But she was not done writing and recording new songs yet; in fact, some of her current projects had a momentum all their own. All she had to do was show up and sing. By July 2002, for example, the soundtrack album for Joel and Ethan Coen's *O Brother Where Art Thou* had sold six million records, and the tour, which had begun tentatively at the Ryman with a celebration of the music that the Coen brothers had commissioned for their film, was still going strong.

A sold-out concert at Carnegie Hall had convinced promoters to take the show on the road under the banner "Down from the Mountain." "The artists control the tour," producer Kevin Lyman told *The Tennessean*. "You never know who's going to show up to play with anyone. The show evolves each day." As Emmylou told Craig Havighurst, "It's like being part of a repertory company. The show manages to be Down From The Mountain no matter how many people move in and out of it. It's greater than the sum of its parts." Ralph Stanley regularly performed *O Death*. Allison Krauss performed *Didn't Leave Nobody But The Baby*. Dan Tyminski's delivery of Stanley's classic *Man Of Constant Sorrow* was the highlight of both the album and the show. With Rodney Crowell as master of ceremonies and Del McCoury, Ricky Skaggs, Norman and Nancy Blake, the Fairfield Four, the Whites, and the Nashville Bluegrass Band regularly taking the stage, along with high profile drop-ins like Patty Loveless and Bob Dylan, audiences had swelled from the 2,200 that fit into the refurbished Ryman to more than 18,000 at arena shows along the route.

"Even if this were to end tomorrow," Emmylou noted, "the music would go on, and these people would go on still making the music. Nothing would change. And I think that's the beauty of it. There are people out there who have had their lives changed and their musical tastes broadened and deepened. That's going to stay with them. Because if you 'get it' and it touches you, it will stay with you." T Bone Burnett, producer of the 'O Brother' movie soundtrack, notes that "as we become more technological, people are looking more for authenticity in life. We are in a constant search for identity. This music is so much a part of who we are — really, one of the best parts of who we are."

Emmylou's return to bluegrass roots inspired a collaboration with her ex-husband and former producer Brian Ahern, as Brian explains. "I was discussing the 'Producer's Cut' DVD project with Emmy — she was in Washington D.C.," he told *Mix*. "'You know,' she said, 'we just played for 18,000 people last night and it was all bluegrass. There is a hunger out there for it.' 'Wait a minute,' I said, "why don't we reissue ROSES IN THE SNOW?'" Emmylou readily agreed.

Rhino Records took on the project, but requested two bonus tracks, ideally songs that Emmylou and Brian had recorded but never released. In his extensive tape vault, Brian found a couple of session tapes he thought would work. One was Emmylou's rendition of Hank Williams' *You're Gonna Change (Or I'm Gonna Leave)*, with Ricky Skaggs singing and playing fiddle. As Brian recalls the genesis of this song, "I came up with a bass track, for *You're Gonna Change (Or I'm Gonna Leave)*, which Emmylou had been singing around the house. I took it into the studio, and I got Emory Gordy to write it out and play it on my Ernie Ball bass in unison with me. We threw in a couple of 6/4 bars to make the dancers fall down." To the Rhino Records Deluxe reissue, the traditional song *Root Like A Rose* was also added as a bonus, which Brian had to edit using "computer technology" in order to prepare a track for Emmylou to re-sing her vocal. She had "messed up" on the archive tape.

Emmylou was pleased with the result. "When I put ROSES IN THE SNOW on, she told Rick Clark, "I was pulled in by the beauty and emotional impact of the songs and what everybody played. There were a lot of live vocals and playing on there. I think that Brian did an extraordinary job."

In November 2002, Emmylou joined forces with Bruce Cockburn, Patty Griffin, and Garrison Starr for the third annual Concert for a Landmine Free World. She opened the Birmingham, Alabama show with *Red Dirt Girl* and finished up with *Boulder To Birmingham*. All four songwriters returned for an encore version of Cockburn's *Wondering Where The Lions Are*. The following night, Emmylou was the recipient of the Senator Patrick J. Leahy

Humanitarian Award at a similar show at the Birchmere Center, just outside of Washington. Emmylou hosted this show, introducing each performer and then sitting in a comfortable stuffed chair at the side of the stage, the best seat in the house. She was elegantly dressed in a black evening gown. "They told me this was my night," Emmylou said, "and asked me what I wanted. I told them I just wanted my friends to come sing for me." Gathered for the occasion were Steve Earle, Buddy and Julie Miller, Patty Griffin, Nanci Griffith, Guy Clark, Rodney Crowell, John Prine, and Jamie O'Hara. Mary Chapin Carpenter sent a truckload of flowers that adorned the stage.

One of the show highlights was John Prine's *Hello In There*, his emotionally moving song about parents who lost a son in the Korean War. Jamie O'Hara sang *50,000 Names*. Buddy and Julie Miller performed both Julie's *All My Tears* and Emmylou's *Prayer In Open D*, although Buddy introduced it as *"Prayer In D*, because I can't play in Open D." Emmylou joined a cowgirl chorus of Nanci Griffith, Patty Griffin, and Julie Miller accompanying Rodney Crowell as he performed *Even Cowgirls Get The Blues*.

Senator Leahy was there in person to present the award. "There are thousands upon thousands of people in Southeast Asia, in Africa, in Central America, around the world, who are going to be helped by what you have done," he told Emmylou. "They will never know you, they'll never hear your songs, they'll never know of your fame. They'll never be able to help you, but because you've helped them, their lives are immeasurably better, and how many people in life can say that?"

Backstage, Emmylou's characteristic humility shone through the praise. "Really what I have done has been given the opportunity to reflect, or deflect, some of the light that shines on me because of the nature of my work, and shine it one these people, these causes, these situations. I'm so grateful for the opportunity to be able to do that. Because that's the only way I know to be really thankful for my blessings."

Emmylou's appearances would be limited during the early months of 2003. In January she performed at the Sundance Film

Festival, and in March she performed at a Human Rights Benefit at Vanderbilt University. She was also heard on the sound track of Steven Spielberg's tv series *Taken*, singing *Just Before It Gets Dark*, a song written by one of the tv series producers and produced by Buddy Miller. Meanwhile, many of the contributions that Emmylou had been making to tribute albums and group projects were becoming known to the public as these albums were nominated for prestigious awards. Her name was included on the Grammy Award for Marty Stuart's *Same Old Train* on the TRIBUTE TO TRADITION album. Her contribution to the soundtrack album of the Coen Brothers' film *O Brother Where Art Thou* resulted in her 11th Grammy. Her recording of the Louvin Brothers' *My Baby's Gone*, a duet with Rodney Crowell, was nominated for a Grammy Award in 2004, along with her next album, STUMBLE INTO GRACE, for Best Folk Album.

In what has now become her typical creative rhythm, Emmylou was privately writing songs while making her many public appearances, to be included on her 25th solo album, STUMBLE INTO GRACE. "It's a continuing process," she says in explaining her creative songwriting process. "You just write whenever you get a chance. I try to have time at home when I can clear the slate and not have any touring, and just go into my music room and just spend time there, hoping the muse will visit. Also, I found that interestingly enough last summer — 2002, when I was out on the Down From The Mountain Tour — I found myself in a situation where I had hours and hours when I was at the venue, and was waiting to go on. I spent a lot of time in the dressing room and actually started several songs."

The album eventually included four original solo efforts as well as collaborations with the McGarrigle Sisters, Daniel Lanois, Jill Conniff, Paul Kennerly, and Malcolm Burn. Helping out with harmony vocals and backing tracks were the usual suspects: Kate and Anna McGarrigle, Linda Ronstadt, Julie Miller, Jane Siberry, Gillian Welch, Jill Cunniff, Buddy Miller, Brady Blade, Daryl Johnson, Tony Hall, Bernie Leadon, and producer Malcolm Burn. Also recognized in the liner notes was

Maple Byrne, Emmylou's long-time guitar tech, who had provided her "beautiful instruments" for the sessions.

For the first time in her career, critics focused on the lyrics to these new songs, comparing them to the sparse, introspective, lovelorn, sorrowful poetry of Emily Dickinson. This melancholic tone, this yearning for love, is evoked in the opening song, *Here I Am*:

I am standing by the river
I will be standing here forever
Tho you're on the other side
My face you can still see
Why won't you look at me
Here I am

I am searching through the canyon
It is your name I am calling
Tho you are so far away
I know you hear my plea
Why won't you answer me
Here I am

I am the blood of your heart
The breath of your lung
Why do you run for cover
You are from the dirt of the earth
And the kiss of my mouth
I have always been your lover
Here I am

I am the promise unbroken
My arms are ever open
In this harbor calm and still
I will wait until
Until you come for me
Here I am

— *Here I Am* (Emmylou Harris)

I Will Dream, co-written with Kate and Anna, reiterates this theme: "Even though you say you do not want me / And made no promises to haunt me." The protagonist in *Little Bird* imagines that she might have the strength to lure back her lover by becoming the moon and pulling him back as the moon pulls the tides.

In *Can You Hear Me Now*, she sings, "We make our own Heaven and our own Hell / Tryin' to get across to the other side."

Written in memoriam for June Carter Cash, the lyrics of *Strong Hand* pay tribute both to the love between long-time husband and wife, June and John, but also between Emmylou's brother and his wife. She speaks of "a miracle / How one soul finds another / Just one miracle / Is all it took my brother." The strength of this love is tested when "one must leave the other / And fly up where the voice rings / Out with all the voices that gather." It wasn't long before the Man in Black joined his wife on the "Other Side" and Emmylou found herself singing *The Old Rugged Cross* at his funeral. As Harris told *The Toronto Sun*, "I have told people that it was almost like that song was from June. I have sung it a couple of times since John's death and it seems strange to think that the cycle that I was talking about in the song is complete. I was very grateful for it. I felt I was one of the many millions of people who felt a connection to John and June, and I was lucky enough to know them. They touched so many lives. It's a way of paying homage to one of the great true stories in my lifetime."

Time In Babylon is uncharacteristically political in theme, closer to a folk protest song than the other lyrical songs on the album. Initially written tongue-in-cheek with Jill Conniff several years earlier, the song was overtaken by events of a very serious nature. In *Time In Babylon*, the protagonist comes from a world of "apple pie and mom," becomes an activist for "Civil Rights and Ban the Bomb," survives both "Watergate and Vietnam," and now finds herself dealing with the material world of "Prada, Gucci, and Ferron." She is "doin' time in Babylon."

"Jill and I had actually started it, we actually had some lyric ideas for that quite a few years ago," Emmylou explains, "but both decided, well, it's kind of clever, but it doesn't really have much weight to it. We abandoned it until we could figure out if it was going to have anything important to say. I think a few years maybe had to pass and the world had to shift into another gear before we re-addressed that song. It came at a time when my country was getting ready to go to war and there were more and more reality shows going on in television and sometimes you just think the world has gone absolutely insane. It just came out of the feelings at the time: a general feeling of distress and concern and alarm."

"Everyone is certainly aware that we are in a very precarious situation and the world is a very different place right now," she continues. "The song addresses things even beyond politics. It addresses a kind of sense — if people are aware of it or not — that we have this lack of taking responsibility for one's actions: whether or not it's feeling depressed and thinking that you can solve all of your problems by taking a pill the same way you take a pill for indigestion. My concern that there is a sense of instant gratification and I believe that as a people in my country, that we're better than that. I don't think that's where we came from and certainly not where we should be heading." *Lost Unto This World*, co-written with Daniel Lanois, advances this need for individuals to take responsibility for political atrocities in graphically describing the brutal torture and murder of women and their children during the campaigns of ethnic cleansing that have plagued our planet.

The album closes with an appropriate envoi, Emmylou's own *Cup Of Kindness:*

> You gave yourself up to the mystery
> And sailed the oceans looking for
> The secret of the key
> To unlock a truth that you may never find
> For it was in a cup of kindness all the time
>
> You feel the thirst
> But none can make you drink

The answer's waiting for you here but
It's not what you think
It won't steal your soul or leave you blind
It was just a cup of kindness all the time

And when Mother Mary finally comes to call
She could pass right through your heart
And leave no trace at all
While you were reaching for
The sacred and divine
She was standing right beside you
All the time

And the emptiness
You can't seem to fill
Beauty fades and pleasures cannot
Take away the chill
And the glamor lures you down into a lie
O but the cup of kindness
Never will run dry

You hear the vandals
Howlin' down your walls
And arm yourself against the ones
Who want to see you fall
Till some Holy Grail reveals
The grand design
Well it was in a cup of kindness
All the time

— *Cup Of Kindness* (Emmylou Harris)

The song resonates with sacred and profane allusions, recalling at once the proverbial sayings of Psalms 23:5 ("thou anointest my head with oil; my cup runneth over"), Shakespeares's Lady Macbeth ("the milk of human kindness"), the Arthurian quest for the Holy Grail, and the Beatles' *Let It Be* ("When I find myself in times of trouble, Mother Mary comes to me, Speaking words of wisdom, Let it be"). "Life is a journey on the physical plane we all currently occupy," Emmylou Harris reflects. "And while I'm drawn to the spiritual songs I've written or played because of their uplifting lyrics, I find it difficult to separate the spiritual and the secular." The achievement of STUMBLE INTO GRACE is remarkable. Emmylou Harris completes her growth from a collector of songs, with an impeccable taste, to a creator of songs, with an inspired muse.

During her career, Emmylou Harris has 'brought back' to our lives many classics of traditional country music, first as the torch bearer for Gram Parsons' country rock experiments on albums like PIECES OF THE SKY and BLUE KENTUCKY GIRL, then as the instigator of the new traditional movement with her own bluegrass revival on albums like ROSES IN THE SNOW. "She was really responsible for bringing a lot of that stuff back," Linda Ronstadt observes. "And she was uncompromising and tireless." For this, country music is forever indebted.

Throughout her career, Emmylou Harris has shown heart-felt reverence, not only for her musical ancestors but also for her contemporaries, championing even far 'left field' alternative country artists, who, like her, are not afraid to take a risk. "Another thing I've always loved about Emmy," Linda Ronstadt continues, "is that she has campaigned for other singers and songwriters, very unselfishly. She's been sending me tapes for years. She's got the profound respect of the entire musical community. There isn't anybody who's more revered, in a lot of ways. If you call up Keith Richards and say, 'Emmy needs you to come over and change that cat box, tomorrow morning,' he'll get on a plane and come over and do it. He thinks she hung the moon." For this, her fellow musicians must thank her.

Beyond her reverence for traditional country music and fellow musicians is her abiding sense of awe at the gift of her own angelic voice and the mystery of her melancholic muse, enabling her to sing 'high lonesome' harmonies and write spiritually moving songs like *Boulder to Birmingham, Bang The Drum Slowly, Prayer In Open D*, and *Cup Of Kindness*. "Everything she does is a prayer," Linda Ronstadt notes in paying tribute to her dear friend. We all must thank Emmylou Harris for gracing us with her prayers.

References

Books

Booth, Stanley. *Dance with the Devil: The Rolling Stones & Their Times*. New York, NY: Random House, 1984; as quoted in articles posted at byrdwatcher.com, and elsewhere.

Bowen, Jimmy (with Jim Jerome). *Rough Mix*. New York, NY: Simon & Schuster, 1997.

Brown, Jim. *Country Women in Music*. Kingston, ON: Quarry Music Books, 1999.

Davis, John, T. *Austin City Limits: 25 Years of American Music*. New York, NY: Billboard Books, 2000.

Des Barres, Pamela. *Rock Bottom: Dark Moments in Music Babylon*. New York, NY: St. Martin's Press, 1996.

Einarson, John. *Desperados: The Roots of Country Rock*. New York, NY: Cooper Square Press, 2001.

Fitzgerald, Judith. *Sarah McLachlan: Building a Mystery*. Kingston, ON: Quarry Music Books, 2000.

Garrett, Nick. "A Secret History of Jim Morrison." Posted: geocities.com/jimmozz/endofsixties.htm.

Fong-Torres, Ben. *Hickory Wind: The Life & Times of Gram Parsons*. New York, NY: Pocket Books, 1991; as quoted at byrdwatcher.com, and elsewhere.

Griffin, Sid. *A Musical Biography: Gram Parsons*. Pasadena, CA: Sierra Books, 1977, 1994; as quoted in articles posted at byrdwatcher.com, and elsewhere.

Grills, Barry. *Snowbird: The Story of Anne Murray*. Kingston, ON: Quarry Press, 1996.

Hinton, Brian. *Country Roads: How Country Came to Nashville*. London, UK: Sanctuary House, 2000.

Kaufman, Phil (with Colin White). *Road Mangler Deluxe* (White Boucke); as quoted at philkaufman.com, and elsewhere.

Luftig, Stacy. *The Joni Mitchell Companion: Four Decades of Commentary*. New York, NY: Schirmer Books, 2000.

Marcus, Greil. *Mystery Train: Images of America in Rock 'N' Roll Music*. New York, NY: Plume edition, Penguin Books, 1997.

Nash, Alanna. *Behind Closed Doors: Talking with the Legends of Country Music*. New York, NY: Alfred A. Knopf/Random House, 1988.

Phillips, John, & Jim Jerome. *Papa John*. New York, NY: Dell Publishing Inc., 1987.

Whitburn, Joel. *The Billboard Book of Top 40 Albums*. New York, NY: Billboard Books, 1995.

Whitburn, Joel. *The Billboard Book of Top 40 Country Albums*. New York, NY: Billboard Books, 1996.

Whitburn, Joel. *The Billboard Book of Top 40 Country Hits*. New York, NY: Billboard Books, 1996.

Whitburn, Joel. *The Billboard Book of Top 40 Hits*. New York, NY: Billboard Books, 1995.

Newspaper & Magazine Articles

Adair, Dan. "Country Girl Reaching Country-Rock Peak." *Spokane Spokesman Review*, Mar 3, 1987.

Ali, Lorraine. "Emmy Hits Red Dirt." *Newsweek*, Sept 18, 2000.

Arrington, Carl. "Emmylou: A Little Bit Country, a Little Bit Rock 'n' Roll." *US*, May 2, 1975.

Arrington, Carl. "Emmylou Harris & Brian Ahern Make Beautiful Music Together." *People*, Nov 13, 1982.

Anonymous. "And Then There Were Two: Interview with Linda Ronstadt." *Goldmine*, Aug 1996; as posted at www.crosswinds.net.

Applebome, Peter. "Bending the Borders of Country." *New York Times*, Sept 6, 1998.

Berkowitz, Kenny. "Back in the Saddle." *Acoustic Guitar*, Aug 2001.

Anonymous. "Buddy Miller Interview." *Mix*, Apr 2000; posted at buddyandjulie.com.

Anonymous. "Divas of Credible Country." *Wall Street Journal*, Aug 21, 1998.

Anonymous. "Emmylou Wins Lawsuit." *People*, July 30, 1984.

Anonymous. "Harris Receives Harmony Award." *Tennessean*, Nov 12, 1995.

Anonymous. "Interview with Chris Hillman." *Record Collector*, Oct 1998.

Anonymous. "Prairie & Sky." *Let It Rock, UK*, Dec 1975.

Anonymous. "Review: Cowgirl's Prayer." *Country Song Roundup*, Oct 1993.

Baird, Robert. "Recording of the Month: Red Dirt Girl." *Stereophile*, Oct 2000.

Bakke, Dave. "Emmylou Provides Lively Lead-In to Willie." *Springfield Journal-Register*, Aug 8, 1986.

Barackman, Michael. "Lost in Limbo Between Country & Pop." *Music Gig*, Dec 1976.

Barker, Ric. "Tchaikovsky and Country — It Works!" *Columbus Ledger-Inquirer*, Oct 17, 1989.

Bell, Bill. "Well, Hello, Emmylou." *New York Daily News*, Dec 8, 1989.

Bernhardt, Jack. "Emmylou's 'Bluebird' Country Music Paradise." *Raleigh News & Observer*, Jan 29, 1989.

Bessman, James. "Emmylou Is More than Country." *Music City News*, June 1979.

Blackstock, Peter. "It's Miller Time." *No Depression*. May-June 1997.

Bobb, Ralph P. "Midnight Session a Blast." *Burlington County Times*, June 21, 1973.

Boehm, Mike. "Hard To Complain about Harris." *Orange County Calendar*, Oct 28, 1993.

Boehm, Mike. "The Millers' Tale." *Los Angeles Times*, June 21, 1997.

Bowman, David. "Emmylou Harris: Young Enough to Start Again." *Pulse*, Oct 1995.

Brady, James. "In Step with Emmylou Harris." *Parade*, May 31, 1992.

Bream, Jon. "Emmylou Still Hot with New Band." *Minneapolis Star*, May 14, 1977.

Bream, Jon. "Emmylou Keeps the Faith." *Minneapolis Star*, Aug 20, 1979.

Bream, Jon. "Grammy Doesn't Lead to Gold." *Star Tribune*, July 13, 1997.

Brown, BTG. "Crossing Over Doesn't Rate as Priority." *Denver Post*, Aug 13, 1981.

Calder, Peter. "Emmylou: Singer Songwriter, Survivor." *New Zealand Herald*, Nov 4, 2001.

Cantin, Paul. "Emmylou Landmine Concerts Coming to CD." *Jam!Showbiz*, Sept 14, 2000.

Cantin, Paul. "Q&A with Emmylou Harris." *Jam!Showbiz*, Sept 18, 2000.

Caputo, Salvatore. "Singer Plays with Tradition." *Arizona Republic*, Jan 12, 1992.

Carl, Edith. "Emmylou Harris: Country Madonna." *Stereo Review*, Winter 1975.

Carlton, Bob. "Hometown Girl Takes Center Stage." *Birmingham News*, June 6, 1997.

Cheever, Doug. "A Country Queen in Backstage Court." *Maine Sunday Telegram*, Aug 24, 1986.

Clark, Rick. "The Making of 'Wrecking Ball.'" *Mix*, Feb 1996.

Clark, Rick. "Rare Interview with Brian Ahern." *Mix*, Vol 20, issue 7, 1996.

Clark, Rick. "Emmylou Harris & Brian Ahern." *Mix*, July 1, 2002.

Claypool, Bob. "Emmylou Finds Life on Road Is Not Too Bad." *Houston Post*, Mar 24, 1983.

Clayson, Jane. "Emmylou Harris: Country Songbird." *Associated Press*, Sept 15, 2000.

Cohen, Cactus Mahoney. "Emmylou Arrives on Scene at Right Time." *Las Vegas Review Journal*, March 14, 1976.

Cooper, Daniel. "Out of the Past." *Journal Of Country Music*, 1996.

Cooper, Peter. "Wringing Her Heart Out." *Tennessean*, Sept 17, 2000.

Coppage, Noel. "Transcending both Church & Honky Tonk." *Stereo Review*, June 1975.

Cowan, Peter. "She's a Country Girl Now." *Oakland Tribune*, April 6, 1975.

Cramton, Ken. "Emmylou on Eastern Shore." *Eastern Shore Courier*, July 18, 1990.

Crenshaw, Holly. "Emmylou Steers Clear of Trends." *Atlanta Journal-Constitution*, July 27, 1996.

Cross, Charles R. "Review: Wrecking Ball." *No Depression*, 1, Fall, 1995.

Crowe, Cameron. "Long Hard Road." *Rolling Stone*, May 1975.

Dannelly, Ronnie. "Interview with Barry Tashian." *Bad Trip*, Fall 1997.

Davis, John T. "Life on the Road." *Austin American Statesman*, Oct 2, 1981.

Davis, John, T. "Country's Queen."

Austin American Statesman, June 20, 1996.

DeLuca, Dan. "Emmylou Records at Country's Mother Church." *Applause*, July 1992.

Denton, Todd. "Emmylou Harris." *Country*, Dec 1995.

DeVault, Russ. "Harris Soars on Wings of Bluebird." *Atlanta Journal*, Mar 11, 1989.

DeVault, Russ. "Lilith Fair: Emmylou Harris Speaks." *Atlanta Journal*, Aug 1, 1997.

DeVault, Russ. "Harris: In Total Control." *West Palm Beach Post*, Mar 24, 1989.

DeYoung, Bill. "Things I Wish I'd Said: Interview with Rodney Crowell." *Goldmine*.

DeYoung, Bill. "Rodney Crowell: The Houston Kid." *Goldmine*.

DeYoung, Bill. "Emmylou Harris: Serendipity Singer." *Goldmine*, Aug 2, 1996.

Dillinger, Leigh. "Emmylou's Day Has Come." *St. Paul Dispatch*, Oct 16, 1980.

Dollar, Steve. "Lilith Fair." *Atlanta Constitution*, Aug 1, 1997.

Elson, John T. "Angel of Country Pop." *Time* (Canada), June 16, 1975.

Fahey, Linda. "Ricky Skaggs: Returning to his Roots." *Prairie Home Companion*, Dec 18, 2000.

Farlekas, Charles. "Harris Returns to Mid-Hudson." *Middletown Times Herald Record*, July 27, 1990.

Faurest, Kristin. "Emmylou with the Louisville Orchestra." *Louisville Courier-Journal*, May 2, 1990.

Ferman, Dave. "Folk Artistry Shines." *Fort Worth Star-Telegram*, July 20, 2002.

Fishell, Steve. "James Burton." *Guitar Player*, June 1984.

Flans, Robyn. "Trio Makes More Heavenly Music." *Mix*, May 1, 1999.

Flippo, Chet. "Harris Is Century Nominee." *Billboard*, May 8, 1999.

Fong-Torres, Ben. "Emmylou: Whole Wheat Honky Tonk." *Rolling Stone*, Feb 23, 1978.

Fong-Torres, Ben. "Back with the Old Whammo." Reprinted from *Rolling Stone*, in the *Hayward Daily Review*, May 2, 1978.

Forte, Dan. "The Angel from Alabama Retains Her Modesty and Down-To-Earth Honesty in a Sea of Country Crossovers." *Musician*, Sept 1983.

Frost, Bob. "Interview: Emmylou Harris." *San Jose Mercury News*, April 14, 1994.

Gardella, Kay. "Emmy Winner." *New York Daily News*, January 12, 1992.

Gardner, Elysa. "Emmylou Pens New Album." *USA Today*, Sept 13, 2000.

Gerds, Warren. "Emmylou Delivers Hours of Musical Joy." *Green Bay Press Gazette*, June 6, 1985.

Goldsmith, Thomas. "Joe Talbot to Chair CMF Board." *Tennessean*, May 1, 1986.

George-Warren, Holly. "Gram Parsons." *No Depression*, June 1999.

Giesel, Ellen. "Paul Siebel." *Dirty Linen*, June 1996.

Giesel, Ellen. "Taking Chances, Soothing Souls." *Dirty Linen*, 1996.

Goldsmith, Thomas. "Emmylou Makes Magic on Ryman Stage." *Tennessean*, Jan 12, 1992.

Gordinier, Jeff. "Leaving Normal: Emmylou Goes Eccentric." *Entertainment Weekly*, Oct 1995.

Green, Mick. "Interview: Emmylou

Harris." *Country Music News &
Routes*, June 1994.

Gritten, David. "Another Country."
UK Daily Telegraph, Sept 9, 2000.

Gunderson, Edna. "A 'Trio' in Tune
with One Another." *USA Today*,
March 12, 1999.

Gwilt, Peter. "Emmylou at the
Ryman." *International Country
Music News*, Oct 1991.

Hance, Bill. "Bad Nashville Memories Erased." *Nashville Banner*,
Feb 26, 1977.

Harbrecht, Gary. "Harris Celebrates
Mentor." *Orange County Register*,
Aug 31, 1998.

Harrington, Richard. "Emmylou on
the Verge." *Crawdaddy*, May
1975.

Harrington, Richard. "Return of the
Electric Cowgirl." *Washington
Post*, July 6, 1980.

Harrington, Richard. "Warmly
Acoustic Emmylou." *Washington
Post*, March 15, 1992.

Hauslohner, Amy Worthington.
"Emmylou Harris: Going Back
to Bluegrass School." *Bluegrass
Unlimited*, Sept 1992.

Havighurst, Craig. "Down From
The Mountain Jamboree." *Tennessean*, Aug 21, 2002.

Herbst, Peter. "Country without
Corn." *Rolling Stone*, March 24,
1977.

Hilburn, Robert. "Emmylou: The
Real Country Music Queen."
L.A. Times, Feb 3, 1977.

Hilburn, Robert. "How This
Cowgirl Beat the Blues." *L.A.
Times*, Oct 17, 1993.

Hilburn, Robert. "Emmylou Harris,
Red Dirt Girl." *L.A. Times*, Sept
10, 2000.

Hiltbrand, David. "Review: Wrecking Ball." *People*, Oct 1995.

Hinckley, David. "Emmy Will Take
Her Time." *New York Daily News*,
Feb 14, 1989.

Hope, Maurice. "RETURN OF THE
GRIEVOUS ANGEL: Remember-
ing Gram Parsons, interview
with Tashian, Hillman, Harris."
Rock 'n' Reel, Aug 2000.

Hotaling, Lynn. "Devotion To
Emmylou Brings Unexpected
Rewards." *Sylva Herald*, July 7,
1999.

Houlihan-Skilton, Mary. "Country's
Quiet Rebel." *Chicago Sun-Times*,
Aug 3, 1997.

Howard, Mark. "Emmylou Dazzles
Rapt Opry Crowd." *Nashville
Banner*, Nov 13, 1980.

Hurst, Jack. "Notebook Notations
Helped Emmylou." *Chicago Tribune*, Feb 2, 1977.

Hurst, Jack. "Country Works for
Emmylou." *Orlando Sentinel-
Star*, April 6, 1977.

Hurst, Jack. "Emmylou." *Chicago Tribune Magazine*, Mar 2, 1980.

Hurst, Jack. "New Bluegrass Album
Daring Move." *Virginian Pilot*,
May 25, 1980.

Hurst, Jack. "Thankyou Emmylou:
The Tale of a Big Break." *Chicago
Tribune*, Jan 16, 1983.

Hurst, Jack. "The New Emmylou."
Chicago Tribune, Jan 8, 1984.

Hurst, Jack. "Songwriting Stint
Recharges Emmylou." *Chicago
Tribune*, Feb 26, 1984.

Hurst, Jack. "Hot Acoustic Group
Generates Talk." *Chicago Tribune*,
Mar 7, 1987.

Hurst, Hawkeye. "Emmylou Recording Album with Famous Friends."
Orlando Sentinel, May 11, 1986.

Jarnigan, Bill. "A Country Queen on
the Move." *Truckers/USA*, Feb
1987.

Jim Jerome. "Emmylou Harris."
People, Jan 14, 1991.

Kahn, Joseph P. "Emmylou Enlists in Landmine Campaign." *Boston Globe*, Aug 13, 2000.

Kaplan, Ira. "On the Road with Emmylou." *Soho Weekly News*, July 20, 1978.

Kemp, Kathy. "Emmylou Returns to Three Standing Ovations." *Birmingham Post Herald*, Aug 1, 1983.

Keough, Sue. "Concert for a Landmine Free World." *Guardian*, Jan 2002.

Kot, Greg. "Spyboy Review." *Rolling Stone*, Sept 3, 1998.

Kirby, Kip. "Emmylou." *Country Music Magazine*, Sept 1980.

Lambert, Lane. "Sally Rose Is Show-piece Set." *Huntsville Times*, Feb 11, 1985.

Lambert, Lane. "The Singer & Her Song." *Huntsville Times*, Feb 11, 1985.

Lewis, Randy. "Emmylou's First Special Truly Is." *L.A. Times*, Jan 15, 1992.

Lundy, Ronni. "Risk-taking Emmy-lou Stands by Her Spiritual Songs." *Louisville Courier-Journal*, June 28, 1987.

Mahoney, Elisabeth. "Concert for a Landmine-Free World." *Guardian*, Jan 17, 2002.

Male, Andrew. "*Wish You Were Here*: Rock's Most Decadent House Party; The Evidence." *Mojo*, March 2002.

Mansfield, Brian. "Angel Eyes." *Request*, Oct 1993.

Mansfield, Brian. "Yearning Love." *New Country*, Nov 1995.

Mansfield, Brian. "Emmylou Takes a Break (not that you can tell). *USA Today*, Aug 14, 1998.

Marsh, Rick. "13 Is Lucky for Emmylou." *Ogden Standard-Examiner*, Feb 2, 1986.

McCall, Michael. "Angel Band Sings Gospel for ASCAP." *Nashville Banner* (no date).

McCall, Michael. "A New Stage: Live Album Shows Harris at Her Best." *Nashville Scene*, Sept 1998.

McCall, Michael. "Moving Forward." *Nashville Scene*, Oct 5, 1995.

McCall, Michael. "Emmylou Harris & Spyboy." *Pulse*, Aug 1998.

McCallum, Charlie. "Same Old Song for Emmylou." *Washington Star*, May 25, 1979.

McGraw, Pat. "Country Star Adapts for Symphony." *Denver Post*, March 5, 1987.

McGraw, Pat. "Emmylou's Country but in Her Own Style." *Denver Post*, Aug 16, 1990.

McKenna, Dave. "Emmylou Harris in Her Own Country." *Washington Post*, Sept 20, 2000.

McKenzie, Charlie. "Emmylou Harris: Nashville Diva." *Ottawa Citizen*, Jan 10, 1992.

Menaker, Daniel. "The Romance of Remorse." *New York Times*, Sept 3, 2000.

Millard, Bob. "Review: Wrecking Ball. *Westport Bi-Monthly*, Oct 1995.

Mitchell, Justin. "A First in Country Music." *Rocky Mtn News*, Feb 28, 1985.

Mitz, Roman. "Emmylou: A Dancer Not a Yodeler." *Music Express*, Feb 1992.

Moon, Tom. "New Heights for Mountain Music." *Philadelphia Inquirer*, Jan 30, 2002.

Morris, Chris. "Gram Parsons Tribute Draws Devotees." *Billboard*, June 10, 1999.

Morse, Steve. "Dolly, Linda, Emmy-lou Create 4th Voice." *Boston Globe*, Mar 22, 1987.

Morse, Steve. "Emmylou Stays Busy with Lilith Fair." *Boston Globe*, Aug 5, 1998.

Morse, Steve. "Harris Salutes Parsons with Spyboy." *Boston Globe*, July 31, 1998.

Nash, Alanna. "Emmylou Harris: Spyboy." *Entertainment Weekly*, Aug 21, 1998.

Nash, Alanna. "Emmylou Harris First Concept Album." *Stereo Review*, May 1985.

Norman, Tony. "On Her Own." *Pittsburg Post Gazette*, Aug 22, 1997.

North, Peter. "Emmylou Enchanting." *Edmonton Journal*, Aug 7, 1998.

O'Brien, Lucy. "Road Mangler: How We Met." *The London Independent*, Oct 6, 1996.

Ochs, Meredith. "Gram Parsons' White Soul." *Cups*, Dec 1996.

Oermann, Robert K. "George & Emmylou Tops in Britain." *Tennessean*, April 13, 1983.

Oermann, Robert K. "Emmylou Moving to Music City." *Tennessean*, July 21, 1983.

Oermann, Robert K. "Emmylou Readies for Challenging '85." *Tennessean*, Dec 8, 1984.

Oermann, Robert K. "Emmylou, Kennerly Tie the Knot." *Tennessean*, Nov 16, 1985.

Oermann, Robert K. "Queenston Trio Making Music History." *Tennessean*, Mar 3, 1987.

Oermann, Robert K. "History Making Collaboration." *Tennessean*, Mar 3, 1987.

Oermann, Robert K. "Emmylou: Sing for Yourself." *Muskogee Times Democrat*, July 26, 1987.

Oermann, Robert K. "Emmylou's 'Wrecking Ball.'" *Tennessean*, Oct 28, 1995.

O'Hagan, Sean. "Another Country." *The Guardian*, Sept 12, 1998.

Okamoto, David. "Sally Rose Slows Down Concert." *Tampa Tribune*, May 14, 1985.

Orr, Jay. "Harris, Ryman Mix in Harmony for Live Album." *Nashville Banner*, May 3, 1991.

Orr, Jay. "Emmylou's Last Ramble." *Nashville Banner*, Feb 9, 1995.

Orr, Jay. "Harris Nash Band Ramble on at Ryman." *Nashville Banner*, Feb 13, 1995.

Orr, Jay. "Just a Bunch of Friends Getting Together." *Tennessean*, May 12, 1999.

Ostbo, Stein. "An Evening with a Big Heart." *Guardian*, Jan 17, 2002.

Overall, Rick. "Emmylou: Voice of an Angel." *Country & Western*, March 1999.

Petty, Milt. "Country Livin' with Emmylou." *Van Nuys Valley News*, Mar 20, 1981.

Phillips, Wes. "Emmylou Harris: A Grievous Angel Goes to a Deeper Well." *Schwann Spectrum* interview, Spring 1996.

Pickle, Betsy. "Emmylou Harris' Acoustic Turn Puts Whole Career in Spotlight." *Knoxville News-Sentinel*, Sept 23, 1990.

Pollock, Bruce. "Searching for Identity on Road." *Oregon Statesman*, Aug 19, 1979.

Purvis, Ray. "Emmylou Can't Stay Away." *The West Australian*, Jan 15, 1999.

Ratner, Brett. "Emmylou Harris Band Ramblin' On." *Tennessean*, Feb 2, 1995.

Reggero, John. "Friends of Steve Goodman Pay Tribute." *USA Today*, Oct 23, 1984.

Richardson, Derk. "Harris Takes an Introspective Turn." *Pulse*, Dec 1993.

Richardson, Susan. "Review: Wrecking Ball." *Rolling Stone*, Nov 16, 1995.

Robinson, Ken. "Harris Aims Straight for the Heart on 13." *Fresno Bee*, Mar 21, 1986.

Rowland, Tom. "Emmylou Pursuing New Direction." *Nashville Banner*, Feb 13, 1995.

Ryan, Shawn. "First Show in Hometown in 10 Years." *Birmingham News*, July 5, 1989.

Saltus, Richard. "Harris Steering Rockers to Country." *Houston Chronicle*, Jan 13, 1976.

Santoro, Gene. "Born To Run." *The Nation*, Oct 30, 2000.

Scharpe, Jerry. "Quarter Moon a Rock Disaster." *Pittsburgh Press*, Jan 29, 1978.

Scharpe, Jerry. "Alive & Well in Cimarron." *Pittsburgh Press*, Dec 27, 1981.

Schensul, Jill. "Harris & Band: Sweet & Hot." *Arizona Daily Star*, April 7, 1987.

Schmidhausler, Gretchven. "Emmylou Harris Band Prove They're Troupers." *Ashbury Park Press*, Sept 2, 1986.

Schmitt, Brad. "Emmylou Sings at Nobel Ceremony." *The Tennessean*, Dec 11, 1997.

Schmitt, Brad. "Emmylou Sings Beautifully Scorching Duet." *Tennessean*, June 2, 1996.

Schruers, Fred. "Now Isn't This a Thrill?" *New York Daily News*, May 22, 1977.

Schruers, Fred. "Singer Previews Album at Concert." *Rolling Stone*, June 1978.

Schultz, Barbara. "Buddy Miller Interview." *Mix*, April 1, 2000.

Scoppa, Bud. "Pieces Of The Sky More Country than Nashville." *Rolling Stone*; reprinted in the *Miami Herald*, Mar 14, 1975.

Scully, Alan. "Delicate Wrecker of Categories." *St. Louis Post-Dispatch*, July 17, 1997.

Skanse, Richard. "Something about Three Queens." *Rolling Stone*, Feb 16, 1999.

Skanse, Richard. "Review: Buddy & Julie Miller." *Rolling Stone*, Sept 17, 2001.

Slaven, Wayne. "Trio Seeks Spot in History." *Greenfield Reporter*, March 27, 1988.

Smith, Dan. "Emmylou Goes Deeper to the Soul of Country." *Roanoke Times*, May 16, 1980.

Smith, Dan. "Emmylou's Releases Maintain Versatility." *Roanoke Times*, Mar 2, 1987.

Smith, Russell. "A Sweet Soundin' Rose." *Dallas Morning News*, Feb 2, 1985.

Snyder, Rachel. "Emmylou Harris Gets Serious about the Issue of Landmines." *Chicago Tribune*, Jan 5, 1998.

Sobie, Keith. "Hot Country Music by Harris on Cool Evening at Pavilion." *Lafayette Contra Costa Sun*, Aug 3, 1998.

Soeder, John. "O Ralph Stanley, Where Art Thou?" *Plain Dealer*, Aug 5, 2002.

Stevenson, Jane. "Emmylou Gets Around." *Toronto Sun*, Sept 2000.

Stone, Ted. "Harris Album Lacks Excitement." *Winnipeg Free Press*, May 29, 1983.

Stout, Gene. "Willie & Emmylou." *Seattle Post-Intelligencer*, Feb 4, 1983.

Stout, Gene. "Country Giants Rock Dome." *Seattle Post-Intelligencer*, Feb 9, 1983.

Sylvester, Bruce. "Interview with Chris Hillman." *Goldmine*, April 11, 1997.

Takiff, Jonathan. "From Spectator to Star." *Philadelphia Daily News*, Aug 22, 1997.

Tarradel, Mario. "The Dark Side." *Dallas Morning News*, Sept 28, 1995.

Tarradel, Mario. "Wrecking Ball Most Experimental Album of Emmylou Harris' Career." *Dallas Morning News*, Sept 29, 1995.

Tarradell, Mario. "Emmylou Harris Is Enjoying Single Life." *Dallas Morning News*, Aug 22, 1998.

Tarradell, Mario. "Emmylou Has Split from Her Old Label and Manager to Follow Her Muse." *Dallas Morning News*, Aug 13, 1998.

Thigpen, David E. "Spyboy Review." *Time*, Sept 14, 1998.

Tichi, Cecilia. "Lookin' for Water from A Deeper Well." *No Depression*, Sept 1998.

Tobler, John. "Interview: Emmylou Harris." *Country Music People*, Sept 1989.

Tucker, Ken. "Road Scholar." *Entertainment Weekly*, 1998.

Varias, Chris. "McLachlan, Lilith Acts, Have Power over Girls." *Enquirer*, Aug 10, 1998.

Vizioli, Gary. "Frank Reckard: Interview." *Guitar Player*, 1984.

Webb, Steve. "Footstompin' with Emmylou Harris at the Berkshire Festival." *Albany Knickerbocker News*, July 20, 1984.

Wesley, Joya. "Emmylou Reflects." *Greensboro News & Record*, June 4, 1997.

White, Timothy. "A Journey with Emmylou." *Billboard*, Aug 1998.

White, Timothy. "Spyboy Is a Labor of Love." *Billboard*, June 20, 1998.

Williams, Janet E. "Cowgirl's Prayer Cover Story." *CMA Closeup*, June 1994.

Wilson, Jeff. "Trio Blends Top of Music Crop." *Beckley Register-Herald*, May 23, 1987.

Wilson, Jeff. "Interview w/ Country's Dream Team." *Brunswick News*, April 23, 1987.

Windeler, Robert. "Emmylou Harris: The Lady of Dylan's Desire." *Music Retailer*, March 1976.

Young, John. "McLachlan Leads Lilith Fair into Harmonized Styles." *Post Gazette*, Aug 10, 1998.

Zimmerman, David. "Superstars Cut Hassles and Harmonize." *USA Today*, Feb 6, 1987.

Zimmerman, David. "She's a Torch-Singing Traditionalist." *USA Today*. Mar 7, 1989.

Zimmerman, David. "Live Album Stays True to Her Roots." *USA Today*, Jan 15, 1992.

X. Rea, Steven. "Emmylou Buys Back the Farm." *High Fidelity*, Aug 1980.

X. Rea, Steven. "Emmylou Harris' Latest." *Philadelphia Inquirer*, Nov 13, 1983.

Other Sources

Alexanium, Nubar. "Emmylou Harris." www.northshore.shorenet/nubar.

Anonymous. Artist bios, Warner Brothers, 1977, 1986, 1989.

Anonymous. Artist bio, Asylum, 1993.

Anonymous. BBC Interview with Emmylou Harris. 1976.

Anonymous. "Biographical Notes: Ricky Skaggs." www.bellnet.com/skaggs.

Anonymous. "Cowgirls Angel." Posted: emmylou's Dutch homepage.

Anonymous. "Columbus Discovers Lilith." Posted Aug 10, 1997: www.lilithfair.com.

Anonymous. "Dolly, Linda, Emmylou come together again for Trio II." Posted Feb 14, 1999: Dolly-mania.net

Anonymous. "Father of Singer Emmylou Harris Honored with TROA Scholarship." The Retired Officer's Association Press Release. Posted: June 22, 2000: www.TROA.org

Anonymous. "Gibson, Emmylou Introduce L-200 Guitar." www.Gibson.com.

Anonymous. "Gram Parsons' Room #8." www.joshuatreeinn.com.

Anonymous. "Luxury Liner: Review." From Playboy, May 1977: www.emmylou.net.

Anonymous. "Sid Griffin Interview." www.perfectsoundforever.com.

Anonymous. "Van Tassel & the Ashtar Command." www.survingtheapocalypse.com.

Anonymous. "The Concert for Mangler Desh." Press release, Aug 29, 1996.

Barraclough, Nick. "BBC radio Interview with Albert Lee." April 17, 2002.

Bond, Neville. "Emmylou Harris Extended Discography." www.emmylou.net.

Brown, Jim. "Review: Wrecking Ball." Posted 1995: www.wcmr.com.

Bowman, David. "Red Dirt Girl Is a Masterpiece." Posted Sept 11, 2000: www. Salon.com.

Carter, Walter. "Emmylou Comes Down From The Mountain." www.gibson.com.

Cassell, Chuck. Liner Notes Last Of The Red Hot Burritos, A&M, 1972.

Cimarron. "Last Ramble." EOL posting at aol.com.

Connors, Tim. Byrdwatcher. www.ebni.com/byrds: "The Story of Gram Parsons."

Connors, Tim. Byrdwatcher. www.ebni.com/burritos: "The Story of the Flying Burrito Brothers."

Derr, Kate. Webmaster: emmylou.net: tour dates, links, interviews, articles, discography, awards, etc.

Dexter, Kerry. "Master Interpreter Emmylou Harris Turns To Song." www.VH1.com.

Escott, Colin. Liner Notes, Portraits, Harris, box set, Reprise Archives, 1996.

Fitzgerald, Kara. "Does My Ring Burn Your Finger?" www.Aceweekly.com.

Fowler, Kim. Second Harvest Food Bank Press Release, May 15, 1997.

Fricke, David. Liner Notes, The Byrds, box set, Columbia/ Legacy, 1990.

George-Warren, Holly. Liner Notes. Emmylou Harris Anthology: The Warner/Reprise Years, box set, Rhino, 2001.

George-Warren, Holly & Bud Scoppa. Liner Notes. The Gram Parsons Anthology, box set, Rhino, 2001.

George-Warren, Holly. Liner Notes. Roses In The Snow (reissue), Rhino 2002.

Ginsberg, Allen. Liner Notes. Desire, Dylan, Columbia, 1975.

Glock, Allison. "Duchovny Archives." Posted Jan 1997: www.chimeralpublications.com.

Goldsmith, Tommy. "Emmylou Harris: Guitars." Posted May 1996: www.acousticmusic.com.

Goodman, Frank. "Puremusic Int: Buddy & Julie Miller." www.buddyandjulie.com.

Griffith, Nanci. Liner Notes. *Other Voices, Other Rooms*, Elektra, 1993.

Hammer, Steve. "Emmylou Harris: A Chat with a Legend." www.nuvo.net/hammer.

Harris, Emmylou. "The Songs." Nonesuch Records Press Release: Red Dirt Girl.

Harris, Emmylou, & Daniel Lanois. Narrators: *Building The Wrecking Ball*, 1996. Video documentary produced and scripted by Peter Kimball, directed by Bob Lanois, edited by Craig Culver. Lisa Robertson production assistant. Monty Hitchcock, Paddy Prendergast, and Emmylou Harris executive producers.

Harris, Emmylou. Narrator: *Emmylou Harris: Spyboy*, home video. Executive producers: Monty Hitchcock, Mike Wojciechowski & Paddy Prendergast. Producer Peter Kimball. Music producer Buddy Miller. Director James Burton Yockey. Eminent 1998.

Heylin, Clinton. Author of *Bob Dylan: The Recording Sessions 1960-84*, as quoted in a posting at www.geocities.com/sunsetstrip/performance.

Himes, Geoffrey. "Miller Time." www.Sonicnet.com.

Hobgood, K.D. "Interview with Brady Blade." www.emmylou.net.

Howe, Bob. "Review: Emmylou in Sydney, Australia." www.shownet.com.

Kruger, Debbie. "Linda Ronstadt Interview." Posted June 17 1998: www.Debbiekruger.com.

Marshall, Paul. "Mary Kay Place: The Ahern Sesssions." www.ravenrecords.com.

McLaughlin, Dee. "The Band: With a Little Help from Their Friends, An Interview with Robbie Robertson." www.Virgin.com.

McLeod, Ernest. "Diva of Loss." www.salon.com.

Monkman, Martin. "Review: The Horse Whisperer. www.coastnet.com/backbeat.

Oermann, Robert K. Liner Notes. O Brother, Where Art Thou? Mercury, 2000.

Parsons, Gene. "Stringbender Custom Shop." www.stringbender.com.

Reader, Heather. "Emmylou Harris: This Chick Digs Baseball." Posted Oct 30, 2001:www.MLB.com.

Redford, Robert. Liner Notes. The Horse Whisperer, Soundtrack. MCA,1998.

Scoppa, Bud & Emmylou Harris. Liner Notes. Sleepless Nights: Gram Parsons & the Flying Burrito Brothers, A&M, 1976.

Sydney, Laurin. "Emmylou Harris Review." Posted Aug 21, 1998: www.CNN.com.

Vest, David. "Grammy Ham 'n' Jam." www.rebelangel.com.

Vizioli, Gary. "Emmylou At The Opry — January 27, 1996." www.Emmylou.net.

Vizioli, Gary. "A Gift At The Wall. Nov 11, 1997." www.emmylou.net.

Wall, Jeff. "Interview with Ricky Skaggs." www.steamiron.com/twangin'.

Wyeth, Howie. "The Desire LP & the Rolling Thunder Review." www.geocities.com.

Acknowledgements

For Emmylou Harris, an angel among us.

The author would like to thank Cathy Taylor and Lauren Buford for research at the Country Music Foundation Library and Media Center; Bryan Taylor for the friendship and guidance; John Einarson for setting the country rock record straight; Monty Hitchcock for the hospitality while I was in Nashville; Larry Delaney at *Country Music News* for the archival magazines; my editor Bob Hilderley; Tim Conners, the "Byrdwatcher," for his wonderful archival material on the Byrds, Gram Parsons, and the Burrito Brothers posted at ebni.com/byrds; Kate Derr — your emmylou.net site is a labor of love and devotion to Emmy; Cimmaron at EOL; Peter Kimball for the insights; Phil Kaufman for the road mangling; Ralph Murphy for the camaraderie; Buddy Miller for the awesome pickin' and grinnin'; and everybody who has contributed to Emmylou's legend and legacy.

LYRICS

In My Hour Of Darkness. By Gram Parsons, Emmylou Harris. Tickner Music Co., BMI, 1974.

Boulder To Birmingham. By Emmylou Harris, Bill Danoff. Wait & See Music, BMI/Cherry Lane Music Publishing Co., Inc., ASCAP, 1975.

Sweetheart Of The Rodeo, Rhythm Guitar, Sweet Chariot, White Line. By Emmylou Harris, Paul Kennerly. Emmylou Songs, ASCAP/Irving Music Inc., BMI, 1985.

Prayer In Open D. By Emmylou Harris. Sorghum Music, administered by Almo Music corp., ASCAP, 1993.

Deeper Well. By David Olney, Daniel Lanois, Emmylou Harris. Hayes Court Music, Irving Music Inc., administered by Irving Music Inc., BMI/Almo Music Corp., Hayes Street Music, Daniel Lanois Songs (SOCAN), administered by Almo Music Corp., ASCAP/Almo Music Corp., Hayes Street Music, Poodlebone Music, administered by Almo Music Corp., ASCAP, 1995.

Bang The Drum Slowly. By Emmylou Harris, Guy Clark. Poodlebone Music/EMI April Music, ASCAP, 2000.

Red Dirt Girl. By Emmylou Harris. Poodlebone Music, administered by Almo Music Corp., ASCAP, 2000.

Here I Am, Strong Hand, Cup Of Kindness. By Emmylou Harris. Poodlebone Music, administered by Almo Music Corp., ASCAP, 2003.

I Will Dream. By Emmylou Harris, Kate McGarrigle, Anna McGarrigle. Poodlebone Music, administered by Almo Music Corp./Garden Court Music, ASCAP, 2003.

Can You Hear Me Now. By Emmylou Harris, Malcolm Burn. Poodlebone Music, administered by Almo Music Corp./ Neecha Music, ASCAP, 2003.

Time In Babylon. By Emmylou Harris, Jill Conniff. Poodlebone Music, administered by Almo Music Corp./Songs of Mosaic/ Streetwise Melodies, ASCAP, 2003.

Western Wall. By Rosanne Cash. Chelcait Music, administered by Bug Music, BMI, 1996.

Let It Be. By John Lennon, Paul McCartney. Northern Songs, 1970.

PHOTO CREDITS

Cover	Steve Granitz/WireImage
p. 2	Matthew Barnes/Eminent Records
p. 6	Eminent Records
p. 97	Henry Diltz/Corbis/Magma
p. 98	Henry Diltz/Corbis Magma
p. 99	Roger Ressmeyer/Corbis/Magma
p. 102	Corbis/Magma
p. 103	Tim Mosenfelder/Corbis/Magma
p. 104	Warner/Reprise